Rediscovering Magical Realism in the Americas

REDISCOVERING MAGICAL REALISM IN THE AMERICAS

∼

Shannin Schroeder

PRAEGER

Westport, Connecticut
London

Library of Congress Cataloging-in-Publication Data

Schroeder, Shannin, 1969–
    Rediscovering magical realism in the Americas / Shannin Schroeder.
        p.   cm.
    Includes bibliographical references (p.   ) and index.
    ISBN 0–275–98049–9 (alk. paper)
        1. Magic realism (Literature).   2. America—Literatures—History and criticism.   3.
    Literature, Comparative—American and Latin American.   4. Literature, Comparative—Latin
    American and American.   I. Title.
    PN56.M24S37   2004
    809′.915—dc21   2002044956

British Library Cataloguing in Publication Data is available.

Library of Congress Catalog Card Number: 2002044956
ISBN: 0–275–98049–9

First published in 2004

Praeger Publishers, 88 Post Road West, Westport, CT 06881
An imprint of Greenwood Publishing Group, Inc.
www.praeger.com

Printed in the United States of America

The paper used in this book complies with the
Permanent Paper Standard issued by the National
Information Standards Organization (Z39.48–1984).

10 9 8 7 6 5 4 3 2 1

Contents

PREFACE

In *The Usable Past: The Imagination of History in Recent Fiction of the Americas*, Lois Parkinson Zamora notes, "The relative scarcity of comparative studies of literature in the Americas suggests the difficultly of establishing appropriate bases for comparison" (xii). I cannot pretend that her words sent me on this chase, that she founded my desire to rediscover magical realism[1] for the Americas, though it would provide an even more convincing preface to *Rediscovering Magical Realism*. In fact, I read her words more than halfway through my research for this volume. Yet, as I reflected on Zamora's comment, more and more I began to feel that I had been *preparing* to answer her charge; consciously or unconsciously, I was exploring possible ways to account for, and to begin to compensate for, the existence of that comparative dearth. Like Zamora, I was interested in claiming certain immutable historical and literary "facts" about our continents, and I was using magical realism to "establish an appropriate basis" between our literary histories.

As I collected the materials I needed to write this preface, I also realized that long before my work on this text began, I *had* discovered (and then forgotten that I had discovered) the text *Do the Americas Have a Common Literature?*, in which two other scholars comment on the lack of comparative criticism of Pan-American literature. In his introduction to the work, Gustavo Pérez Firmat points to the laxity of those scholars for whom this comparative tradition should be of vital concern:

Even comparativists working on New World literature have shown relatively little interest in inter-American investigations. . . . The Americas' cultural indebtedness to Europe is but one feature that the literatures of the New World have in common. And not enough has been said about this commonality, about the intersections and tangencies among diverse literatures of the New World considered apart from their extrahemispheric antecedents and analogues. ("Cheek to Cheek" 2)

And Enrico Mario Santí argues that the "modern tradition of Latin American essays which contrast the two Americas" is largely missing in North American scholarship. "This comparative tradition is less marked in North American writing because less powerful nations have a vested interest in understanding their more powerful neighbors, whereas the reverse is not generally the case" (264). While Santí offers a sociopolitical reason for the scarcity that Zamora mentions and while Pérez Firmat implicates those scholars he feels are most to blame, my own task has been to locate reasons for the United States and Canada to maintain an interest in inter-American scholarship, to answer Zamora's implied call for what might prove to be a North American foundation for such comparative work. Because, arguably, magical realism recovers a comparative basis for literature of the Americas, I have come to realize that in *Rediscovering Magical Realism* I am in conversation with Zamora, Pérez Firmat, Santí, and other critics who want to rediscover the bridges linking the literatures of the Americas.

Fredric Jameson, in his more general call for increased comparativist scholarship of the third world—though he says "such comparatism need not be restricted to third-world literature" ("Third-World Literature" 87 n.5)—

suggests the possibility of a literary and cultural comparatism of a new type, distantly modelled [*sic*] on the new comparative history of Barrington Moore.... Such a new cultural comparatism would juxtapose the study of the differences and similarities of specific literary and cultural texts with a more typological analysis of the various socio-cultural situations from which they spring, an analysis whose variables would necessarily include such features as the inter-relationship of social classes, the role of intellectuals, the dynamics of language and writing, the configuration of traditional forms, the relationship to western influences, the development of urban experience and money, and so forth. (86–87 n.5)

Rediscovering Magical Realism addresses many of Jameson's variables, engaging specific texts under the rubric of magical realism in its consideration of social class and marginalization, language, writing, the relationship between Latin American (or, more generally, postcolonial) writing and its Western influences, and the commodification of both literature and individuals.

Jameson's use of the phrase "third world" and Santí's commentary on "New World" literature raise issues pertinent to *Rediscovering Magical Realism* as a comparativist endeavor. This text does not survey an actual body of "Latin American" works but rather revolves around those texts familiarized to world readers by their availability in translation and subscribes to a notion of Latin America that is more a comparativist or academic creation than a social, political, or even geographic reality. It is true that most North Atlantic scholarship[2] treats Latin American literature as one body of work, and it is also the case that diversities in language, culture, geography, and national perception go largely missing in such a treatment.[3] The propensity for Western readers to neglect these diversities may very well be one reason that some authors from Latin American nations actively insist on "national" rather than "continental" categorization. Yet among educators at universities from Stanford to North Carolina State University—within the language of critics such as Fredric Jameson, Roberto González Echevarría, and Lois Parkinson Zamora, and among countless authors and their translators (such as the prolific Gregory Rabassa)—the idea persists that "Latin America" can be considered a self-contained entity.

Of course, *Rediscovering Magical Realism* argues that the U.S. and Latin American literatures share a New World, postcolonial status and suggests that, at times, an "American" brand would be more fitting than the division of the United States and Canada from the rest of the Americas. This demarcation, one echoed in Santí's use of the phrase "North American" above, foregrounds yet another semantic debate of Pan-American comparative literary criticism: the use of "North" and "Latin" America conveniently ignores the fact that Mexico is, strictly speaking, located on the North American continent. Yet, it has become both habitual and acceptable in the literary and critical traditions of the "two" Americas to separate them at the Rio Grande. Thus, in this text, for matters of clarity and consistency—and because no better labels are currently available to the comparativist critic of the Americas—"Latin America" will encompass South America, Central America, the Caribbean, and Mexico; while "North America" will denote Canada and the United States, unless specified. Whenever possible and/or useful, I identify individual authors by nationality, with the qualification that in many instances, having taken nationality into account, I feel it more helpful (though perhaps, for some, less appropriate) to designate the work "Latin American."

In *Rediscovering Magical Realism*, I am also careful to use the label "the Americas," with the implicit assumption that many readers who refer to "American literature" consider that appellation the sole property of the United States. Until relatively recently, I, too, used the term "American" as interchangeable with citizenship or production or literature *of* the United States,[4] and my ethnocentrism was hardly exceptional. In fact, though critic José David Saldívar is surprised that "America, for [John Barth], becomes a synonym for the United States" ("Postmodern Realism" 536), Barth's assumption is certainly the norm not only for citizens of the United States but also for a large percentage of the global community. Only within the last few years has the term "American" received much closer critical scrutiny as a limited descriptor. The perception of "American-ness" is slowly undergoing a much-needed revision in even the most mainstream of forums.

Readers who glance at the titles of the chapters in [*The Columbia History of the American Novel*'s late twentieth century] section [—which contains such chapters as "Canada in Fiction," "Caribbean Fiction," and "Latin American Fiction"—] cannot help noticing that, for the authors of these chapters, the idea of "American" literature has undergone significant change in the latter part of this century. The crucial questions surrounding the canon, national and class boundaries, race, personal identity, genre, gender, the scene and nature of writing, and history are reflected in the proliferations of the "American" novel over the last forty years. (O'Donnell 513)

Indeed, these chapters "might be seen as a mosaic in progress, unfinished, . . . conveying a colorful impression of the liveliness and utter heterogeneity of the literature of this period" (513). Debra A. Castillo reminds us that "for us citizens of the United States used to referring to ourselves simply as 'Americans,' . . . [t]he Great American Novels are arriving as an import, in translation, from that other, intermittently forgotten America" (608).[5] The increasing inclusivity of the term "American" literature "forms one of the most attractive features of the contemporary American novel that challenges the 'the,' the 'contemporary,' the 'American,' and the 'novel' as the defining limits of its exfoliations" (O'Donnell 514). In such an increasingly heterogeneous hemisphere, the connotative limitations of "American" and "magical realism" need to be challenged, rethought, and reappropriated by those who are creating and critiquing literature.[6]

While both my changing perceptions of what "American" means and my increased awareness of the lack of comparative studies between the "two" Americas inspired *Rediscovering Magical Realism*, my most important motivation was the need to counteract the critical tendency to label anything and everything unreal or supernatural in literature as "magical realism." Though James H. Maguire perfectly illustrates my point here, he is certainly not alone in his misuse and exceedingly generic application of the mode. Still, his commentary stands as one of the more extreme examples of a North American critic appropriating the magical realist tradition for North American literature to the detriment of its Latin American counterpart. In a chapter for *The Columbia History of the American Novel*, Maguire comments that James Welch's *Fools Crow* "surpasses the achievement of Latin American 'magical realism,' a novelistic form of surrealism" (457). His haphazard commentary is the bane of true scholarship on magical realism for several reasons. First, Maguire seems to have in mind no clear definition of magical realism (though he does imply that it is a genre). Next, he claims Welch's text as a magical realist work without proof; in fact, *Fools Crow*, a revision of indigenous history before European intervention, is *not* a magical realist work, unless Maguire believes that any indigenous tradition is, by merit of its author's ethnicity alone, "magical." Further, his sweeping claim that Welch surpasses all Latin American examples devalues Latin America's own magical realist tradition without justification. Finally, and perhaps most pertinent to my work, he validates a North American version of the mode without providing evidence that magical realism has its own tradition north of the Rio Grande. Unfortunately, Maguire is not the only critic abusing the concept of magical realism in literary criticism, but his comment illustrates well the need for critical consensus on and attention to the definition and application of the mode. Unlike Maguire, I am not interested in "ranking" the North American magical realist works (or the North American version itself) in relation to the Latin American magical realist tradition, but I do intend to validate the North American mode whose existence his comments presuppose.

Any reader who picks up *Rediscovering Magical Realism* either as an introduction to magical realism itself or as an exploration of the magical realism in a particular region of the Americas probably needs only a brief (as opposed to an extensive) history of the term; the extended version of that account would require (and has required for other scholars) considerable devotion to the mode as a Latin American phenomenon. Indeed, even those texts that purport to cover the history of the Latin American literary tradition, such as Jean Franco's *Introduction to Spanish-American Literature*, updated in the 1990s, raise issues directly pertinent to this work—namely, What of Latin American literature *can* be covered? While trying to "give readers some idea of the range and depth of Latin-American culture" (xi), Franco answers this question by deciding that, for reasons of space, she will generally not include writers born after 1945. Indeed, as González Echevarría notes in *The Voices of the Masters: Writing and Authority in Modern Latin American Literature*, "The dazzling richness of Latin American literature would make an enterprise [of comprehensivity], were it desirable, impossible" (7). Thus, in this text I do not presume to cover Latin American literary history, or even Latin American magical realist history. Like González Echevarría and Franco, in considering this group of nations where literary (not to mention political, historical, geographic, and other descriptors implicitly related to the literary) boundaries have been alternately built up and argued against, I realize it is perhaps most important to establish up front my own boundaries for this work. Consequently, I focus only on those Latin American literary particulars that will further our discussion of magical realism—without jeopardizing the symmetry of the rest of the text.

To that end, my discussion relies heavily on the many works available on Latin American literature, outlines the literary evolution of contemporary Latin American fiction, emphasizes its adoption and use of the magical realist mode, and points to the readiness of that mode for assimilation into a North American literary tradition.[7] Although I describe and define the American (in its broader sense) magical realist mode, my emphasis in *Rediscovering Magical Realism* leans toward the North American vision of magical realism. As a necessary preface not only to my Latin American chapter but, more importantly, to the entire text, Chapter 1 introduces the mode of magical realism, including its origins, misuses, and critical pitfalls, and then redefines the term "magical realism" itself, using Amaryll Chanady's carefully articulated criteria.[8] Chapter 2 narrows in on the magical realist roots and traditions of Latin American writers in order to provide a concrete but limited foundation for the more important discussion of the necessity of and means for North America appropriating the mode for itself. Only one of my chapters, the third, moves from such generalizations about Latin American literature to one specific illustration, that is, to an original reading of magical realism in what is undoubtedly recognized as a (if not "the") master text of the mode, *One Hundred Years of Solitude*. I cover the mode's appropriation into northern America in Chapters 4 and 5, where the effects and distinctiveness of North American magical realism are first justified and then traced through a variety of works. Chapter 4 includes authors as diverse as Louise Erdrich, Ron Arias, Robert Kroetsch, and Toni Morrison; in Chapter 5 I take up Morrison again in a critical discussion of *Beloved*'s title character as the physical embodiment of magical realism. Chapter 6 posits the relationship of magical realism to a variety of marginalized characters and authors of the Americas. While I cannot assume the daunting task of surveying all literary works of Latin America that have been (or should be) classified as magical realism, this chapter covers a representative sample[9] of Latin American texts. In Chapter 7, the concluding chapter, I attempt to rescue the term magical realism for critical use. By drawing on the all-encompassing vision of magical realism found throughout *Rediscovering Magical Realism*, I suggest that, while critics of the magical realist mode should distinguish a North American version from the mode as it exists in Latin America, they should also heed Zamora's call for increased inter-American scholarship by making connections between the variations on the magical realism that both continents so effectively employ.

Thus, while the scope of this project (particularly its dual goals of justifying and covering the works of North American magical realism) dictates that I give more attention to U.S. and Canadian applications of the mode—especially given the voluminous scholarship devoted to those Latin American applications and given the relative dearth of criticism directed at North American magical realism—my larger mission is to increase scholarship in inter-American comparative studies. *Rediscovering Magical Realism*, through its reliance on an extensive range of literary works from the Americas, provides a basis by which North American and Latin American literature can be compared and answers the plea of such critics as Gustavo Pérez Firmat and Lois Parkinson Zamora. As a tradition with roots in both continents, magical realism supplies a vital link in our discussions of the literature of the Americas.

NOTES

1. My choice of "magical" rather than "magic realism" is intentional and reflects the literal translation of the Spanish "realismo mágico." My decision not to use the phrases interchangeably is, in part, an attempt to counter the confusion that arises from vague and inappropriate applications of the mode.

2. And even the work of comparativists and intellectuals south of the Rio Grande.

3. Similarly, some marginalized U.S. writers, who might themselves prefer to be considered in largely ethnic, regional, or other marginal terms, are generally categorized in relation to "hyphenated America,"that is, to their position as minorities in the United States.

4. As a graduate student, I took one of my candidacy exams in "American Literature: 1865–present" without ever once considering (or being asked to consider) such American literature within a context larger than the geographical United States.

5. And have been for some time, though perhaps without being classified simply as "American" literature. According to the November 14, 1968 *Times Literary Supplement* (an entire issue dedicated to Latin American literature), "There is no doubt that the most significant contribution to world literature today comes from Latin America" (qtd. in Retamar 252–53). And Roger Caillois claimed in a 1965 edition of *Le Monde* that "Latin American literature will be the great literature of tomorrow, as Russian literature was the great literature at the end of the last century and North American was the great one from 1925 to 1940; now the hour of Latin America has come. This will be the source of the masterpieces we await" (qtd. in Retamar 252).

6. Equally limiting, at least for some scholars, are the terms "third-world," "Latin American," and "North American." I recognize that such narrow or subjective labels pose a poten-

tial threat to postcolonial countries looking to form stronger national identities and literatures. Though I acknowledge that such boundaries are in many ways arbitrary and/or unwarranted, I follow the predominant trends established by other comparativist scholars and by many of the authors themselves in using these terms for the sake of brevity and familiarity and because other options seem no less arbitrary.

7. Of course, doing these, one encounters the opposing dilemma—that "one quickly comes up against the limits of the generalizations that can safely be made about an entire continent" (Payne 4). I have made a concerted effort not to overgeneralize about Latin America, magical realism, or their connections to the United States and Canada.

8. Chanady gives these criteria in her text *Magical Realism and the Fantastic: Resolved Versus Unresolved Antinomy.*

9. One sadly (but necessarily) negligent in its attempt at a brief, fair treatment of the many regions and countries in Latin America.

ACKNOWLEDGMENTS

To Joe Benevento, whom I feel most fortunate to claim as mentor, teacher, therapist, muse, and friend, for sending me on my first journey into magical realism;

To James Mellard, the "meanest [and most *influential*] bastard ever to comment on my writing," who fine-tuned my skills as a writer and who introduced me to new magical realist texts (perhaps without even knowing it); to James Giles, for having more suggestions for my magical realist reading list than I could ever hope to read; and to Ibis Gomez-Vega, for sharing her books, opinions, pictures, food, and dogs with equal candor and enthusiasm;

To all my friends, family, students, and colleagues—especially those who already seem to know more about magical realism than you ever expected (or wanted) to know—for continuing to listen patiently anyway;

To Deborah Whitford, the editorial equivalent of a lighthouse for the writer experiencing choppy seas, whose kindness and humor and patience and basset hound Maggie brought me safely back to shore; to Judy Zwolak, an extraordinary set of "second eyes" and even better friend; and to Suzanne Staszak-Silva and Marcia Goldstein for their guidance through the editing and permission rights processes;

To Donika Ross, Jennifer Jameson, and Rebecca Hughes, who have all taught an only child what sisterhood is (and without whose help I would still be indexing!);

To my parents, Pam and Giffin Simmons, and my grandma, Beulah Walker, for believing that education is our family's inheritance;

And to Tim, Bailey, and Emma, for providing the magic in my own reality:

My sincerest thanks to all of you for the parts you've played in my life and work.

∼

Dedicated to the memory of my grandmother, Alice Mae Simmons, and my grandfather, Clinton Augustus Walker: I miss your stories.

REDISCOVERING MAGICAL REALISM
IN THE AMERICAS

Magical realism, for many, connotes Latin American literature, but the *denotation* of the term—and its potential for application far beyond one continent's literary endeavors—has been greatly neglected. In fact, many scholars would be hard-pressed to define the phrase. Are the terms "magical realism" and the "marvelous real" interchangeable? Is magical realism a genre? an attitude? a literary style? an esthetic? a movement? Does the magically real work subvert reality? rely on fantasy or magic tricks? rework Surrealism? hinge on political agendas? And does (can) magical realism belong to one nation or continent? In the past, critics and theorists have argued that magical realism conforms to any one or more of these possibilities, in addition to countless other spins put on the phrase. The terms "magical realism" and "marvelous realism" and their "positions with respect to either realism or other concepts in the realm of fantasy (such as myth, faerie, the marvelous, or the fantastic) have seldom been clearly elucidated. As a consequence, magical and marvelous realism have remained rather fuzzy notions, the definition of which is usually taken for granted, or alluded to by an implicative nod to works of 'it' " (Scheel 3). Additionally, "[c]ommentators have used that term 'magic realism' to refer to so many different works of art—mostly written in Latin America—that the term has largely lost its value for making distinctions between genres" (Durix 116).

While more recent scholarship seems no less confusing or cacophonous, several critics have attempted to arrive at mutually acceptable answers to the above questions. Predictably, these answers not only put to test many works we have unquestioningly accepted as magical realist texts but also allow the inclusion of new authors from around the globe. Magical realism, as defined by scholars like Amaryll Chanady, proves to be universal, a code that defies limitations of geography, generation, and language.

Since Franz Roh first coined the term "magic realism" in his 1925 article on post-expressionist art, the term "has become a catch-phrase which obscures the many varieties of fiction that have appeared in the last decades" (Franco 308). Massimo Bontempelli was actually the first to apply the term to both art and literature (Menton, "Magic Realism" 130); in 1927, he "made the term known simultaneously in French and Italian in his bilingual journal *900*" (Delbaere 75). Although, in 1948, Venezuelan writer Arturo Uslar Pietri "was the first to refer to Magic Realism in the context of Latin American literature"(Menton, "Magic Realism" 140), it was Alejo Carpentier who first claimed "lo real maravilloso americano" solely for Latin America in the preface[1] to his 1949 novel, *El reino de este mundo* [*The Kingdom of this World*]; as noted below, his term—though frequently used as such—is not a synonym for magical realism. Angel Flores redefined the Latin American phenomenon as "magical realism" at a 1954 MLA meeting, and cited Old World origins and practitioners alongside Jorge Luis Borges of Argentina. But Flores's "definition is very wide in its application and suggests a reference to phenomena more currently described as the 'fantastic'" (Durix 104). Luis Leal, in 1967, would refute Flores's claims in another attempt to petition for magical realism as a solely Latin American event. Moreover, in the 1970s Miguel Angel Asturias would prove the first to define his own Latin American writing as magical realism (Boccia 22). Still, over sixty years after Borges and his apparent "fathering" of Latin American magical realism, only a few texts provided the bulk of the scholarship on the issue. Indeed, until the Latin American "Boom" in the 1960s, the term had been subjected only to limited scrutiny and had few applications.

The "Boom" expanded scholars' and other readers' opinions of both Latin American literature and magical realism. Authors like Colombian Gabriel García Márquez made "magic realism" simultaneously a Latin American and a literary happening. Rosemary Geisdorfer Feal stresses that the Boom "should not be construed merely as a list of names, dates, and titles, for it was very much a cultural and personal phenomenon as well." Rather, it must also "be viewed as a privileging of the mainstream, the masculine, the universal, and the commercial: this [idea] is not to detract at all from the quality of the writers, but to recognize that all literary history is a hierarchical priorization" (118–19). The new fiction of the 1940s and 1950s, symbolized by such authors as Borges and Carpentier, had already begun to project Latin American literature onto the "global stage" (Saldívar, "Dialectics" 80), but the acquisition of the new catch phrase "magical realism" placed Latin American literature more firmly on the map. One way to reclaim magic realism for Latin Americans came, for some, through the differences it embraced. Unfortunately,

in the 1960s this term became fashionable in literary criticism to designate different types of fiction which actually had little in common: "magic realism," or "marvelous realism," a variation of the former, was applied indifferently to the writings of J. L. Borges and García Márquez. To make matters even more confusing, the Cuban Alejo Carpentier introduced the term *lo real maravilloso* to refer to his literary experience of Latin America as opposed to the European tradition. (Durix 102)

Mireya Camurati notes that

[i]n their eagerness to interpret this conglomeration of lands and peoples some writers, such as Alejo Carpentier, speak of the *real-maravilloso americano*, . . . a juxtaposition of circumstances—impossible in other places on the planet—that occur in Latin American time and space, or to an acceptance, based on faith, of that which is magical or miraculous for others. (89)

By claiming sole rights to magical realism, Latin American authors helped to prove that they could, in fact, create a new literature worthy of world attention; after all, who better to master magical realist texts than writers living on the one continent that could produce it? Still, these writers were beginning to find themselves members of "a creative community whose identity went beyond national or regional boundaries" (Schulman 29).

If Latin American writers wanted (or perhaps still want) magical realism for themselves, they nonetheless manage to maintain a startlingly broad definition of what being "Latin American" means. The Mexican novelist Carlos Fuentes identified "that quality so characteristic of cultured Latin Americans" as "the passion to know everything, to read everything. . . . And, above all, to demonstrate to the European that there is no excuse not to know other cultures" (qtd. in Zamora, "The Usable Past" 33–34). Latin American identity is not singular but rather plural; through their works, "Latin American writers are affirming a plurality of cultures within a larger sense of being 'Latin American.' . . . For despite similarities in historical background what defines the Latin American identity is not one but many ways of being rooted in Latin American reality" (Meyer 8–9). In fact, César Fernández Moreno believes even the term *Latin American* to be too narrow, since it neglects such populations as indigenous peoples, African Americans, and Anglo-Saxons who are equally present. Moreno adds,

Some say of a child that he is identical to his father, others say he is just like his mother; they are all right. The same may be said of Latin America: that it is identical to its mother (the land, the cultures before the conquest) and to its father (Spain, Portugal, Africa, and other "fathers" which reached it from outside). But at the same time, and just like that child, America is different from its progenitors and has its own personality. (10)

These "children" who create Latin American fiction are being read "as writers of a same literature" (Retamar 245)—a New World literature described by Octavio Paz as "a literature of foundations"[2]—whether they be Colombians, Mexicans, or Argentineans.

More recent scholarship has shown that, rather than magical realism being the attitude or the fact-is-stranger-than-fiction reality of any one area, it has been appropriated by a variety of authors, many of whom have no connection to Latin

American literature whatsoever. "Citizens of the world, [these new] Magical Realists write a world literature, appealing to readers in many nations with many viewpoints" (Boccia 23). Lois Parkinson Zamora and Wendy B. Faris reveal Latin America's own interest in the area as the catalyst for the "popular perception of magical realism as a largely Latin American event" (1). But, they stress, "Readers know that magical realism is not a Latin American monopoly. . . . It is true that Latin Americanists have been primary movers in developing the critical concept of magical realism and are still primary voices in its discussion, but [works like *Magical Realism: Theory, History, Community* consider] magical realism an international commodity" (2) and "an important presence in contemporary world literature" (4). It is "an international literature that oversteps national boundaries and languages, with roots deep in many literary traditions" (Boccia 21). Some, like Canadian Geoff Hancock, consider themselves cohorts in a New World literary tradition based on similar pasts, legacies replete with indigenous peoples, beliefs, and cohabitation.[3] Others, like German Franz Kafka, were practicing what may very well have been magical realism *before* the advent of the Boom or even before Roh offered the terminology that could be applied to such endeavors. The fact that magic realism existed before it existed, that is, before we knew what to call it, suggests that its definition will not be limited to any particular region or set of experiences.

Latin American literature itself is not immune to debate over whether it can be appropriated by writers outside of South and Central America. "Jean-Paul Borel's appropriately titled '¿Una historia más?' questions not only geographic boundaries by advocating the inclusion of American Hispanic writers [in the Latin American literary history] but also linguistic boundaries" as he points to the Francophones of Canada, the speakers of Dutch in Suriname, and of speakers of the "Amerindian" or African languages that are excluded when only Portuguese and Spanish texts are entered into the Latin American canon.[4] Furthermore, some of Latin America's most famous practioners are no longer *in* Latin America. For example, Chilean author Isabel Allende now lives in San Francisco; however, in spite of her increasingly North American settings and interests, her fiction is still synonymous with Latin America (and specifically Chile). Though the questions raised by and about Latin American literature will be discussed in more detail in Chapter 2, the fact that they have arisen at all seems to call into question our understanding of literature as we know it in a Western sense.

As international writers continue to borrow from (and elaborate on) the Latin American magical realist tradition and to make it their own, critics are forced to revise their perception of magical realism as the sole property of Latin America. Charles Werner Scheel provides an apt analogy for the exportation of magical realism from Latin American literature, in whatever shape it is ultimately defined, into other cultures. Scheel notes that "good sparkling white wine deserves to be labeled champagne" even if is not French wine. "It is the method rather than the mere ingredients, or their origin, which defines that product, and if local soils and climatic conditions add a particular color, texture, and *bouquet*, so let there be French champagne, Russian champagne, or other champagnes" (1). He goes on to apply his comparison directly to magical realism: "Since the cultural conditions affecting a literature are likely to be more specific—by virtue of their complexity—than the factors contributing to the production of grapes and wine, it should go without saying that narratives written in the same magico-realist (or marvelous realist) mode, but in different countries or even continents, are apt to display strongly distinctive flavors" (1). Balancing not only French texts but also Kafka against the magical realist mode, Scheel asserts, "[O]bviously there is no lack of contradicting world views and beliefs within Western culture. That the realities of experience can be seen and expressed in various fictional modes is amply exemplified in the Old World too, and magical realism is only one of [those modes]" (102).

TOWARD A DEFINITION OF MAGICAL REALISM

Describing Magical Realism

Many critics, in an attempt to offer sage advice regarding magical realism, dip into their own realms of contradiction (or into magical realist scholarship, as it were). Words like "juxtaposition" and "antinomy" fight for space beside several variations on the phrase itself: "lo real maravilloso," "realismo mágico," "magic" or "magical realism," "marvelous realism," or "marvelous real," not to mention the variations in languages other than English and Spanish. Lee A. Daniel believes that "the ensuing critical studies treating magical realism have complicated even more an understanding and a definitive definition for the apparently catch-all phrase" (129).[5] At one extreme is an overly simplified version of the debate, an inevitable conclusion if Brian Conniff is right in proclaiming that "the term has always lent itself to certain simplifications" (168). Daniel, for example, argues, "*Realismo mágico* is actually nothing more or less than its name implies" (129). Edwin Williamson claims a similarly "easy" definability for magical realism:

At the level of simple definition there can be little disagreement: magical realism is a narrative style which consistently blurs the traditional realist distinction between fantasy and reality.[6] Beyond this, critical opinion is divided as to whether magical realism is entirely self-referring or whether it establishes a new kind of relationship between fiction and reality. (45)[7]

Beverley Ormerod argues, "Magical realism is a literary technique that introduces unrealistic elements or incredible events, in a matter-of-fact way, into an apparently realistic narrative" (216). Moreover, Jean-Pierre Durix says, "According to our most restrictive definition of the term, the magic realist aims at a basis of mimetic illusion while destroying it regularly with a strange treatment of time, space, characters, or what many people (in the Western world, at least) take as the basic rules of the physical world" (146).

While some "simple" definitions of magical realism border on the "simplistic," most (such as Durix's and Williamson's contributions) undercut their explanations by introducing new terms ("consistently," "blurs," "mimetic illusion," "destroying," "strange") that themselves demand to be defined before scholars can proceed. For example, Keith Spears questions whether the line between reality and the fictitious is blurred ("interwoven") or juxtaposed (6), which is perhaps a critical distinction in determining the purpose and/or intentions of magical realism. Melissa Stewart claims that critics must work through such debates, since, "[i]n order to define magical realism, it seems necessary to identify the nature of the relationship between the magical and the rational, and indeed, several descriptions of this relationship have been offered. Some of these . . . evoke an 'antagonistic struggle': the magical 'collides' with the rational, as David Young and Keith Hollaman state, or 'another world [intrudes] into this one,' according to Brian McHale" (477).

One such semantic debate is over whether magical realism pits reality against fantasy, and whether the term "fantastic" is interchangeable with the supernatural, the irrational, the mythic, or the surreal; others fastidiously avoid the debate altogether or adopt an "already-been-done" attitude, as when José David Saldívar cites Fernando Alegría's, Robert González Echevarría's, and Amaryll Chanady's debates on magical realism as the reason he will not trace the theoretic and historical problems of postmodern magical realism as a concept ("Postmodern Realism" 523). Yet, Saldívar willingly points out that "[a]lthough Gabriel García Márquez's use of magic realism includes Carpentier's familiar tropes of the supernatural—one of the foundation concepts of magic realism—his version differs from Carpentier's and inaugurates the rise of (postmodern) magic realism globally" (526); in doing so, Saldívar narrows in on one of the fundamental challenges of magical realist scholarship: distinguishing it from that of Carpentier's *lo real maravilloso*.

Alejo Carpentier coined his expression *lo real maravilloso* in the preface to *El reino de este mundo* in 1949. In it, he not only privileged *lo real maravilloso* as a Latin American (and, more specifically, Caribbean or perhaps even Cuban) event; he argued that the very concept itself sprang from the marvelous quality of the Latin American soil. Carpentier's "own conception is rooted in America, latent in the native landscape, and therefore symbolized for him the great international revolution which a small country like Cuba can export to the rest of the world" (Durix 107).[8] His geographic association denied European artists access to *lo realismo maravilloso*, though in fact his own arguments rested heavily on European sources (such as French anthropology) and ignored his own partially European heritage. Carpentier's "vision is," as Durix puts it, "a strange combination of revolutionary ideals and European ethnocentrism" (107). For critics who read *lo realismo maravilloso* as synonymous with magical realism, Carpentier gives "magical realism an ideological value, associating it with certain unique features of West Indian culture such as the religions of *voudou* and *santería*" (Ormerod 216). But even "Carpentier stresses that his *real maravilloso* is different from 'magic realism' because the latter is identified with the artificial quality of the surrealist search" (Durix 107). Stephen Hart does an exemplary job of differentiating between *lo realismo maravilloso* and magical realism. First, he says, it is clear that the experience Carpentier is referring to, since it is couched in the language of divine revelation (Carpentier refers to "miracle," "spiritual exaltation," and "faith"), has much in common with the religious experience. This emphasis . . . is totally absent from magical realism. Yet perhaps the single greatest difference between "lo real maravilloso" and magical realism concerns the role that the supernatural plays in each. According to Carpentier's definition of "lo real maravilloso," the experience of the marvelous is unexpected and unusual. . . . Nothing could in fact be further from magical realism. (43)

Carpentier, like Ormerod, Williamson, and other critics, assumes a role for the reader that is primarily *outside* the text; at the same time he provides a mythological or religious explanation for the "marvelous" qualities of *lo real maravilloso.*

As comparisons with Carpentier's term suggest, a popular method for defining magical realism is by contrasting it with other traditions, that is, by arguing what it is *not.* Its closest European relatives, for example, are perhaps surrealism and the fantastic. S. P. Ganguly claims that "hispano-American" magical realism borrowed directly from European surrealism, but that "the surrealistic technique of psychic automatism and transcription of dreams was supposed to reveal deeper realities and inner marvels" that magical realism was not interested in (172). "[André] Breton and the surrealists (if, for the sake of clarity, one may consider the 'movement' as unified, which it was not) were exploring new territories opened by the discoveries of Freud concerning the unconscious" (Durix 109). Though "[b]oth Asturias and Carpentier were, at various moments, in contact with the surrealists," at the same time they "were rebelling against a vision of Latin America entirely conditioned by the European point of view" (109). Leal argued that surrealism intended to damage reality, but Hart believes that Leal was a bit too strict in his separation of surrealism and magical realism; both are traditions, Hart argues, that "join hands in their appreciation of the value of fantasy, and its paradoxical ability to unlock the secrets of the real world" (38). Hart says that though "the interests and subject-matter of these two literary movements were often similar, the presentation of that subject-matter was rarely so. The surrealist formula, as it stood, was unable to adapt itself to expression in the form of a realist novel" (39). Indeed,

magical realism does not turn its back on reality as Breton and his followers were compelled to do. The difference between magical realism and surrealism is, thus, not to be understood in terms of the cultural gap separating Spanish America from Europe [but rather as a different] degree of familiarity with the realist mode—which is non-existent in surrealism but very alive in magical realism. (39)

Durix suggests that this cultural gap is not so large as some would have us believe, since magical realism might owe as much to surrealism and the European-based traditions as to traditional cultures; he believes that magical realism in fact "may pander to the tastes of Westerners eager to read about quaint exotic worlds. But it also . . . constitutes a counter-discourse which uses fantasy in a manner reminiscent of indigenous literature while subverting its premises [of an unproblematic, organic, and positivist magic world]" (187).

The other close cousin to magical realism, the fantastic, has perhaps a similar relationship to reality as did surrealism, in the extent to which it, too, managed to avoid or distance reality altogether. "Historically speaking, the fantastic emerges roughly at the same time as romanticism" but "serves to question the tyranny of the *logos*" in European narratives (Durix 82, 81). Roger Caillois says, "The fantastic comes after the fairy tale and practically replaced it. . . . The fairy tale is set in a world where enchantment is taken for granted. . . . The fantastic presupposes the solidity of the world but only to ruin it more radically" (qtd. in Durix 82). Karla J. Sanders explains that, whereas the "fantastique is a universal way to present unreality without cultural ties, . . . Magic Realism is a distinctly twentieth century genre that developed as a response to cultural diversity, vast immigration, and colonization" (23). For Tzvetan Todorov, the fantastic requires "the reader's hesitation [a hesitation that a particular character may also experience] . . . between a natural and a supernatural explanation of the events described" (Durix 79).

Defining the supernatural and fantastic traditions *against* magical realism has necessitated a revision of the perception of Latin American writers of the Boom. "Largely because of his close ties with the fantastic, the designation of Borges as a magical realist has created critical dissension, although he is credited by some critics as one of the major early influences on the contemporary magic realism movement which has flourished internationally since the early part of this century" (Simpkins 145). For example, when Jeanne Delbaere stretches the definition of magical realism even further to describe "two branches" of the mode, she argues that those branches are composed of

an intellectual one derived from Borges and the surrealists and a popular one derived from Márquez [sic]. In the former the magic generally arises from the confusion of the tangible world with purely verbal constructs similar to it but without their counterparts in extratextual reality: playful, metafictional and experimental it has much in common with the spirit of fabulation. The other brand, closer to the spirit of the marvelous, accommodates the supernatural, relies heavily on superstition and primitive faith and has its source in popular myths, legends and folklore as well as in the oral tradition; despite the challenge it offers to traditional realism it continues to adhere in its form to the realistic conventions of fiction. (76–77)

For Delbaere, the former (and, therefore, Borges) has an affinity with Old World magic realism, while the other is influenced "by the 'real maravilloso' of the Latin American writers" (99). Though Delbaere attempts to reconcile many of the contentions among critics by making magical realism an Old World *and* a New World mode, her arguments do not convincingly distinguish Borges's work from surrealism, fabulism, or the fantastic. At the same time, her emphasis on "superstition and primitive faith," "popular myths, legends and folklore" privilege Old World myths as "reality" and indigenous ones as "supernatural" in both of her branches; in fact, the magical realists surveyed in this volume invert not only traditional Western mythology but Delbaere's "primitive" myths as well. Later attempts by Delbaere (who had since become Delbaere-Garant) coined "additional concepts—psychic, mythic, and grotesque realism" in an attempt to make her discussion of magical realism widely inclusive (250). Delbaere is not alone in her attempt to claim Borges as a magical realist,[9] but the assertion has, surprisingly, engendered only limited counter-criticism.

In his essay "The Metamorphoses of Fictional Space: Magical Realism," Rawdon Wilson not only provides concrete evidence against the classification of Borges as magical realist but also walks his reader through a comparative example of the fantastic. According to Wilson, "What occurs in fantasy is memorably exemplified in Borges's narrative 'Tlön, Uqbar, Orbis Tertius.' Tlön is a fictional world created within the literature of the people of Uqbar (itself quite fictional)," a world that

obeys, as its chief and consistent axiom, the epistemological principle of Berkeley that nothing can exist (that is, have a place in space) unless it has been perceived. For the inhabitants of Tlön the problem of what happens to certain copper coins when they are not being observed is considered a paradox equivalent, the narrator observes, to those created by the Eleatic philosophers. (219)

Similarly, Wilson adds, "The Garden of Forking Paths" posits that "time bifurcates, that time is labyrinthine, not directly linear, and that fictional space mirrors what is true of time" (219). For Borges, then, space is plastic, unpredictable, deformed, and he uses the fantastic to expand on this notion and "to comment upon the nature of narrative" (219).

The traditions against which magical realism is tried by critics of the mode begin to form, if not an explicit example of what magical realism *is*, then at least a clear illustration of what it is *not*. Stephen Slemon's comment that "[i]n none of its applications to literature has the concept of magic realism ever successfully differentiated between itself and neighboring genres such as fabulation, metafiction, the baroque, the fantastic, the uncanny, or the marvelous" (407) is obviously hyperbolic. Thus, Leal *can* summarize that, "[u]nlike superrealism, magical realism does not use dream motifs; neither does it distort reality or create imagined worlds, as writers of fantastic literature or science fiction do; nor does it emphasize psychological analysis of characters, since it doesn't try to find reasons for their actions or their inability to express themselves" (121).

Much has also been made of magical realism's close association or even synonymity with "post" traditions. Durix implies that only postcolonial writers use magical realism, and that they use it for specific political commentary on their (and their nations') postcolonial status. Postmodernism is alternately a sister tradition and synonymous with the magical realist mode. Faris argues that "the category of magical realism can be profitably extended to characterize a significant body of contemporary narrative in the West, to constitute . . . a strong current in the stream of postmodernism" ("Scheherazade's Children" 165), and that such features as metafictional dimensions, linguistic or verbal magic, primitivism, repetition, and metamorphoses all situate magical realism in the postmodern (175–77). Theo D'haen says "the cutting edge of postmodernism is magic realism" (201); "to talk of magic realism in relation to postmodernism is to contribute to decentering that privileged discourse [of Anglo-American modernism]" (203). Delbaere contends that magical realism "has not superseded the more experimental strain of postmodernism but has merely developed alongside it" (77); similarly, Sanders argues that magical realism is *not* synonymous with the postmodern, which "focuses on technology, media proliferation, and logos, [since] Magic Realism emphasizes a return to cultural knowledge and authority and values pathos" (277). In fact, the North American magical realist mode, as will be discussed in Chapter 3, does focus on both the media and technology. In addition, *One Hundred Years of Solitude*, observed in Chapter 2 through an alchemical lens, in many ways serves as a reaction to technology. Given the similarities between and breadth of scholarship dedicated to the two, some scholars are perhaps too quick in their separation of postmodernism from magical realism. At the same time, the terms cannot be used interchangeably.

While comparing science fiction and magical realism, Kenneth Wishnia suggests that they are "typically classified as 'low' and 'high' culture, respectively" (29) and sees them as "two openings to the same space" (30). But the difference between the two, Wishnia argues, is one of framing; "[i]n magic realism, we have the weird things without the explanatory framing. In [science fiction] (and horror), even the unexplained is explained *by the framing effect of the genre classification:* Weird things happen because it's [science fiction]" (30). Other narrative styles that have previously been described as magical realism are similarly framed. As Ormerod claims, magical realism "relies on the reader's acceptance of the idea that there is an illogical, irrational dimension to the everyday world," an idea she says is also "common to folktales, fairy stories and other forms of narrative throughout the world" (216). Yet in these latter examples, the magical is explained away to the reader who enters the text through the doorway of "once upon a time." Like horror and science fiction, fairy tales are "explained by the framing effect of their genre classifications," while with folktales, cultural mythologies provide the frames. The efforts, not just on the part of critics, but on the part of magical realist writers, to distinguish the magical realist mode from other traditions may in some respects be a by-product of its affiliation with the "New" World literature that itself must work to set itself apart from other, largely European traditions. In addition, such "apparently paradoxical rejection of those whose influence is obvious can be considered a symbolic parricide due to the inevitable anxiety of influence of formerly colonized societies" (Chanady, "Territorialization" 138).

As noted above, magical realist texts do not analyze their characters, but this is not to imply that the mode lacks any correlation with psychology. One frequent assumption about magical realism is that it is a Jungian (as opposed to Freudian) mode. Steven F. Walker advises using "a Jungian psychoanalytic approach to magical realist texts" in order to disengage the *symbolic meaning* that "is the bridging concept that links the study of psychology and literature" (348).

Zamora argues that the psychology of magical realist characters often incorporates a shifting of the relation of the individual to the archetypal (*Usable Past* 81). "[T]he magic may be attributed to a mysterious sense of collective relatedness rather than to individual memories or dreams or visions" (Faris, "Scheherazade's Children" 183). Ganguly says, "The tendency to adopt the epic element [and to rise from the particular to the universal] by these novelists is an expression of a desire to communicate to the world what he sees and understands, that is to say, his vision" (170–71). Indeed, "the effectiveness of magical realist political dissent depends upon its prior (unstated, understood) archetypalizing of the subject and its consequent allegorizing of the human condition" (Zamora, *Usable Past* 83), while its "characteristic instability of strata—individual, community, cosmos—inevitably impels magical realism toward allegory" (87). One aspect of this universal quality is to deny the reader any sense of connection with the characters, a denial sometimes heightened by other literary techniques. For example, as Clive Griffin notes, García Márquez's use of humor in *One Hundred Years of Solitude* denies his readers "any serious involvement with characters or situations which the novel might otherwise have possessed" (92–93).

Its political nature also seems to be a popular definitive aspect of magical realism. It "has typically been seen as the redemption of fiction in the face of a reality that is still becoming progressively more disorderly. Durix's claim that "[m]agic realists usually have a definite idea of their social role and pose political problems, which beset the (post-colonial) country described" (146), presupposes that Europeans either write about postcolonial nations in their works or that they do not create magical realism—erroneous claims no matter which presupposition he intends. Magical realists' social and political "concerns center around legitimizing the Latin American experience to an international intellectual community. Toward this end, magical realists adopt such strategies as retrospective arrangement, inter-authorial solidarity, and a circular model of time—strategies which lend credibility to otherwise incredible narratives" (Spears 8). Some claim that, as "an ideological stratagem," magical realism collapses "many different kinds of writing, and many different political perspectives, into one single, usually escapist, concept" (Martin, "On 'Magical' and Social Realism" 102), but it is nearly impossible to reconcile such a viewpoint with the magical realism of García Márquez, Toni Morrison, and others; their texts refuse to forget the specific histories of the regions in which they are spawned and, instead, prove to be a refutation of the ironically escapist *historical* accounts that have survived.

Thus, some certainties do seem to exist, in that they recur within common descriptions of magical realism—for example, the juxtaposition of the real and the fantastic—although even here there are decisions to be made over what to call the "unreal" in magical realism: the fantastic? the supernatural? the praeternatural? The method and extent of such juxtaposition, as well as the balance struck between them, however, have rarely been discussed or determined. In addition to challenging our ideas about the supernatural, "[m]agical realist texts (also) question the nature of reality *and* the nature of its representation" (Zamora, *Usable*

Past 79), since, "[f]or the Magic Realists, the Magic is real, but the Real is also magic" (Shannon 25). As opposed to the horror and Gothic novels where "the supernatural tends to burst into a world which is otherwise subject to empirical and logical laws" (Hart 40), "[i]n the universe of magical realism, the supernatural plane does not irrupt at certain crucial junctures into the empirical world. Rather, the supernatural is never absent from the magical-realist universe, and, indeed, it is always visible to all. In this particular world, nothing is supernatural or paranormal without being at the same time real, and vice-versa" (41). Moreover, the magical realists "are clearly sophisticated in the use they make of metafiction, intertextual references, an interweaving of the 'realistic' and 'fantastic' modes but also of an implicit questioning of the polarity on which such terms are based" (Durix 146).[10]

If the critics have difficulties determining what magical realism is and how to apply the term, it is perhaps not surprising that writers have similar difficulties. Perhaps the most famous example is García Márquez's claim that he is not a magical realist; but as Delbaere notes, "Writers do not as a rule think of themselves as magic realists or write exclusively magic realist works; if the label fits some of their novels or stories it is usually because what they had to say in them required that particular form of expression. Neither are these works particularly experimental even though they challenge traditional realism" (98). Canadian author Keith Maillard describes the impetus for the writer of magical realism: "Something tremendously important *must* be said, something that doesn't fit easily into traditional structures, so how can I find a way to say it?" (qtd. in Delbaere 98–99).

Hancock, like Maillard and other critics, seems to be searching for a description of what Delbaere calls the "spirit" of magical realism (99). He argues,

A few features [of magic realism] can be identified: exaggerated comic effects; hyperbole treated as fact; a labyrinthine awareness of other books; the use of fantasy to cast doubt on the nature of reality; an absurd recreation of "history"; a meta-fictional awareness of the process of fiction making; a reminder of the mysteriousness of the literary imagination at work; a collective sense of folkloric past. (36)

Elsewhere he states that magic realism "contains some elements of a mythical quest" (40). Hancock's use of the terms "features" and "elements" implies the same variation among texts that Scheel described as "flavor." Hancock's definition, like those of many other critics, seems an amalgamation of characteristics drawn from several texts, the term "feature" implying that the above *may* be included in a magical-realist text, but doing very little to prescribe the qualifying (as opposed to the comparative) formula for magical realism. Still, Hancock's list serves to symbolize the general vagaries that plague magical-realist theory. It is little wonder that magical realism has become a catch phrase. As Durix notes, "Faced with such diversity of implicit definitions, it appears essential to explore and delimit the field" of magical realist criticism (102).

Prescribing Magical Realism

In her work *Magical Realism and the Fantastic: Resolved Versus Unresolved Antinomy*, Amaryll Chanady attempts to rescue magical realism from its beleaguered state. Chanady believes that, "[w]hile some scholars, such as Angel Flores, simply equate magic realism with the fantastic, others see it as a particular attitude towards reality. . . . Because the concepts of the fantastic and magical realism are similar in certain respects, they have frequently been used interchangeably" (viii). The primary difference between the two, according to Chanady, is that the supernatural does not disconcert the reader of the magical-realist work as it is intended to in the fantastic work. "Whereas the simultaneous presence of the natural and the supernatural in the fantastic creates a[n] ambiguous and disturbing fictitious world, it is the essential characteristic of a harmonious and coherent world in magical realism. . . . The supernatural appears as normal as the daily events of ordinary life" (23, 101). Chanady's consideration of the differences between the fantastic and the magically real must also consider the reader, for although "the real reader's response varies according to his cultural background, that of the implied reader is based on the text. . . . The real reader cannot be radically different from the construct of the implied reader if he is to understand the text" (33).

One of Chanady's initial tasks is to refute the idea that magical realism is a genre; instead, she claims it is a literary *mode* that can be found in many types of prose fiction. Were it a genre, she argues, it would be characterized by limitations both historical and geographic (16–17). In his book *The Spirit of Carnival: Magical Realism and the Grotesque*, David Danow defines his topic as "narrative, a mode of human communication and an artistic form for reflecting one world (actual) in another (which is fictional)" (5). Zamora and Faris contend that magical realism is "a mode suited to exploring—and transgressing—boundaries, whether the boundaries are ontological, political, geographical, or generic" and compare it to other modes of fiction, where such spaces or worlds would be irreconcilable (5–6). John Burt Foster, Jr. concludes,

Because magical realism refers to an international cultural tendency, it is broader than any single group of writers and/or painters, such as English Vorticism, Russian Acmeism, or Dutch De Stijl. At the same time, it lacks the all-encompassing cultural scope of categories like modernism, the avant-garde, or postmodernism. Magical realism seems ultimately to belong with such intermediate terms as surrealism, expressionism, and futurism, all of which designate movements with a significant presence in several national cultures but with no pretension to characterize an entire epoch. (267)

Like allegory, or any other narrative mode, magical realism has certainly shown that it will not adhere to boundaries—not even those set by the "masters" of its craft.

Because Chanady's goal is to clear up the confusion between the terms "magical realism" and "fantastic," she creates several straightforward guidelines that ultimately define magical realism extremely well. Phil McCluskey, who also relies on

Chanady's work for his definition of magical realism, says, "The obvious advantage in a purely structural definition of the mode's operation is the ability to identify its presence in various texts. This disturbs the prominent tendency to refer to all Latin American texts of the 60s as 'magic realism,' and similarly calls into question claims for the appearance of the mode outside of Latin America" (89). Over the countless versions of the "definitive" definition of magical realism, Chanady's proves to be not only the most persuasive but also the most easily applicable. Because she has read and commented on critics whose own ideas overlap or frequently, conflict with her opinions, her discussion serves to eliminate certain extremes while still allowing flexibility. Indeed, several of the critics she cites would be able to justify their own beliefs by using Chanady's guidelines.

Chanady offers the three following criteria for magical realism. First, it is characterized "by two conflicting, but autonomously coherent, perspectives, one based on an 'enlightened' and rational view of reality and the other on the acceptance of the supernatural as part of everyday life" (*Magical Realism and the Fantastic* 21).[11] Next is the "resolution of logical antinomy in the description of events and situations" (26). "In magical realism, the supernatural is not presented as problematic[;] . . . it is integrated within the norms of perception of the narrator and characters in the fictitious world" (23). Finally, that resolution is achieved through "authorial reticence, or absence of judgments about the veracity of the events and the authenticity of the world view expressed in the text. . . . If the narrator stressed the exclusive validity of his rational world view, he would relegate the supernatural to a secondary mode of being (the unreliable imagination of a character), and thus the juxtaposition of two mutually exclusive logical codes, which is essential to magical realism, would become a hierarchy" (29–30). Chanady provides an excellent application of these criteria when she discusses Julio Cortázar's "Letter to a Young Lady in Paris": "The protagonist, who is left in charge of a friend's apartment in Buenos Aires, vomits innumerable rabbits that proceed to destroy the carefully kept home of his absent friend." Cortázar "rejects a rational explanation of the events as the product of the protagonist's imagination in what would then be a patently oneiric or hallucinatory account, as well as the treatment of the supernatural in the canonical fantastic, in which the apparently inexplicable events produce disbelief and fear in the observer/narrator" ("Territorialization" 139).

According to Chanady, it is through authorial reticence that authors like Cortázar establish their relationship both with the magical realist text and with their readers. Ultimately, authorial reticence "eliminates the antinomy between the real and the supernatural on the level of the text, and therefore also resolves it on the level of the implied reader" (*Magical Realism and the Fantastic* 36). Authorial reticence relies on narrative innovation:

One way in which such authorial reticence is communicated to the reader is through technique: magical realists are preoccupied with formal presentation of fiction as a work of art. Magic realist fictions always incorporate technical innovations. Levels of language, layers of formal and informal diction, doubles, transformations, stories-within-stories, a blurring of that border between fiction and reality, are all contained within a formally presented and shaped book. The author gets away with such labyrinthine constructions by unifying the narrative with a voice that never questions what it tells. Everything is permitted to the writer as long as he is capable of making it believable, says Gabriel García Márquez. (Hancock 41–42)

These writers also draw upon popular events like weddings, festivals, fairs, and carnivals to insert literary imagination into a community (Hancock 41). What Hancock considers to be a hybrid space, a co-existence of opposite and conflicting properties (70), Joseph Benevento suggests should be termed something else, because "while 'hybrid' often suggests a compromise or mating of two distinct entities, magic realism often seems to be both fully magical and realistic at once" (125). Chanady would surely agree that, in magical realism, neither the natural nor the supernatural is compromised. If the supernatural is not to stand out from realism in a magical realist text, it must be portrayed as normal or ordinary. Zamora and Faris believe "the supernatural is not a simple or obvious matter, but it *is* an ordinary matter, an everyday occurrence—admitted, accepted, and integrated into the rationality and materiality of literary realism. Magic is no longer quixotic madness, but normative and normalizing" (3).

MAGICAL REALISM AS A SCHOLARLY DEVICE

The following exploration of the diverse uses of magical realism as a narrative mode in the literature of the Americas relies on Chanady's general criteria to evaluate a variety of works. Inter-American comparative studies illustrate the extent to which writers in this part of the world have in common an indebtedness to European literature, questions of national identity, and an indigenous heritage, among other issues (Pérez Firmat, "Cheek to Cheek" 2; Zamora, "The Usable Past" 11).[12] Gustavo Pérez Firmat believes that "four approaches to the issue of hemispheric literary communality—generic, genetic, oppositional, and mediative— . . . outline the methodological options available to inter-American comparison," and argues that not enough has been done with such comparison (4). "The relative scarcity of comparative studies of literature in the Americas suggests the difficulty of establishing appropriate bases for comparison" (Zamora, *Usable Past* xii). Like Zamora's *The Usable Past*, this "comparative project is to expand the territory of comparative literary inquiries from its original national parameters in Europe to hemispheric ones in the Americas" (4). Because of the increasing interest in both the literature of the Americas and magic realism, the study of magical realism proves extremely current in American literary studies and creates *more* opportunities for comparative efforts. The primary works (and the majority of the secondary works) included in this text are in translation for two reasons: first, because a study of magical realism *without* translation would require mastery of no less than four languages for the Americas alone; and second, because most students read magical-realist texts—from *One Hundred Years of Solitude* to *The Metamorphosis*—in translation, just as they (and most scholars these days) read any number of other "great" works of literature. González Echevarría more directly implicates the reader in the translation process; as a bilingual reader, he argues, his work is to transfer "a text from one code to another to sift out in that process what holds it together" (*Voices of the Masters* 6). Hancock suggests that magical realism may provide the "glue" in such translations, since it, perhaps more than other narrative modes, is well-suited to being translated: "The experience of magic realism is the vitality of language expressed in images. This quality also lends itself to translation with little loss of meaning" (41). Gregory Rabassa, a well-known translator of Latin-American texts, seems to elaborate on Hancock's judgment, particularly in the case of the best known of all Latin-American magical realists:

The author who knows his language inside out can be either the easiest or the hardest to translate. If he has what might be termed a classical style or use of language, that is, if his sense of words is so pure that as metaphors they approach the object portrayed most closely, the translator is on his mettle to find that same closely approaching word in his language. A writer like Gabriel García Márquez has this gift of language, and he is so exact in his choice of words, getting ever so close to what he wants to say, that indeed, it is difficult to make a botch of a translation of his work as he leads you along to a similar closeness in English of metaphor (word) and object. ("No Two Snowflakes" 8)

When Jorge Luis Borges "told his translator not to write what he said but what he wanted to say" (Rabassa, "No Two Snowflakes" 6), he intimated not only the necessary adjustments that must be made from language to language but, more importantly, his own belief that his words *could* communicate a particular meaning even after translation.

Magical realism, once clearly defined, provides readers entry into hundreds of "new" texts—and perhaps re-entry into texts they have read in the past. Because it delves into the historical, social, mythical, individual, and collective levels of human reality (Hancock 47), magical realism offers new ways of exploring literature. For anyone interested in comparative literature, magical realism supplies structure and variety to countless studies, particularly in the context of the literature of the Americas. Yet, as noted above, this literary mode cannot be confined to one continent, language, or canon. It forces new comparisons even as it challenges former stereotypes and categorizations. For students and professors, scholars and bedtime readers, magical realism creates new worlds of reading, teaching, and analyzing texts.

NOTES

1. According to Seymour Menton, the prologue to this Cuban novel actually first showed up as an essay in *El Nacional* a year earlier (141).

2. Both Bainard Cowan (7) and González Echevarría ("Latin America" 54) cite Paz's phrase, though it is Cowan who describes the foundation specifically as "New World" literature.

3. For example, Canadian writer Steven Guppy, in a letter to Geoff Hancock, wrote:

One of the things we have in common with people in parts of Latin America is our culture, such as it is, is based on a collision between the European intellectual tradition and the "mythic" perspective of a relatively large native Indian population . . . with a rich and quite sophisticated oral literature. This collision between cultures . . . is mirrored in the structure of much magic realist fiction, in which the miraculous events and symbolic characters we associate with the myth or folktale are depicted in the realistic style of a 19th-century European novel. Thus the juxtaposition of realism and fantasy, or myths and logos, if you like, which characterizes magic realist fiction, mirrors the superimposition of European culture on the North and South American landscapes. (qtd. in Hancock 33)

Similar claims could (and probably) have been made by writers from the United States.

4. Amaryll Chanady's analysis of Borel's text appears in her introduction to *Latin American Identity and Constructions of Difference*, xiv–v. Chanady proves an important source for the definition of magical realism put forth later in this chapter.

5. Some of the studies Daniel cites include the works of Flores, Leal, and Carpentier, as well as Juan Barroso's *Realismo mágico y lo real maravilloso en El reino de este mundo y El siglo de las luces*. Menton, who claims that "[i]n order for Magic Realism to have validity as a critical term, it must be placed in its historical context" (126), sets about doing just that in "Magic Realism: An Annotated International Chronology of the Term." Menton also notes that in 1974, "Roberto González Echevarría reviewed critically all previous Latin American literature articles on Magic Realism as an introduction to his erudite analysis of the historical sources of Alejo Carpentier's *El reino de este mundo*. González Echevarría favors the Americanist interpretation of Magic Realism over the international one" (150). González Echevarría, whose analysis is in Spanish, is also cited by Slemon for his critical use of the term "magical realism" in *Alejo Carpentier: The Pilgrim at Home*. Slemon cites a range of texts that critique the term and also notes Fredric Jameson's study "On Magic Realism in Film" (*Critical Inquiry* 12.2 [Winter 1986]: 301–25).

6. In fact, however, such certainty about his "simple definition" seems a bit naïve, given that semantic games alone have already challenged such terms as "narrative style," "consistently," and "fantasy."

7. According to Williamson,

[In] the former view, *One Hundred Years of Solitude* is analogous to the *ficciones* of Borges; its fictional world is autarchic, creating through the act of narrative special conditions of development and meaning which enable the fictive imagination to achieve a free-floating state of pure self-reference akin to the exhilarated innocence of children at play. . . . [S]uch a view . . . cannot explain the political and historical allusion in the novel. . . . The other account would have magical realism expand the categories of the real so as to encompass myth, magic and other extraordinary phenomenon in Nature or experience which European realism has tended to exclude. (45)

This second possibility "endows García Márquez's particular brand of modernism with a unique Latin American character" and reflects García Márquez's own views on magical realism. But "[b]oth accounts regard magical realism as an entirely positive, liberating feature" (Williamson 45–46). In a note, Williamson adds that García Márquez "agrees that the 'rationalism' of European readers tends to prevent them accepting that magical realism is inspired in the fact that 'everyday life in Latin America shows us that reality is full of extraordinary things'" (62–63 n.5).

8. "It sounds as if, through some magic union with the world he was born in, the Latin American writer were gifted with a particular feeling for the mysterious realities of his country" (Durix 110).

9. Similar attempts are made by a wide range of criticism, from the widely cited essay by Angel Flores to Joseph Benevento's pedagogical approach.

10. Durix argues, "This restrictive definition excludes texts such as most of Borges'[s] and Cortázar's works which do not have this broad allegorical framework and [that] concern limited environments and a relatively small number of characters and are best fitted within the category of the fantastic" (146).

11. "[J]ust as James Joyce celebrated Everyman in Bloom's daily peregrinations around Dublin, everyday life is expressed in Magical Realism as both heroic adventure and international multicultural reality" (Boccia 24).

12. These issues are considered in light of the magical realist mode in later chapters, particularly Chapter 4 and Chapter 6.

2

THE BOOMING VOICE OF MAGICAL REALISM IN LATIN AMERICA

The young (and those who are less young) are truly beginning to read Latin America, because Latin America is truly beginning.

—Robert Fernández Retamar

LIBERATING THE LATIN AMERICAN IMAGINATION[1]

Perhaps like most things in the "New World," magical realism has been "discovered" multiple times by vastly different literary explorers.[2] Its evolution as a critical term is disputed, but less controversial are its origins. As Phil McCluskey prefaces an article on magical realism in Australian literature,

Any discussion of magic realism outside of a Latin American context must inevitably begin by using the literature of the Latin American "boom" and its immediate precursors as a site of origin, drawing parallels between the two conditions in order to lend authority to the "translation" of the form. Yet even within Latin America, the term's confusing genesis has meant that critical work on the subject has often been contradictory, thus complicating issues of definition, representation, and culture. (88)

McCluskey's claims regarding problematic definition have already been discussed in detail in Chapter 1, but his comments raise additional concerns regarding magical realism's originary status as an authentic Latin American mode indebted to the splendid and splintered historical, literary, and geographical realities of Latin America. An additional complication for setting down its origins is that "there is implicit in modern Latin American literature an ideology through which both literature and criticism identify what Latin American literature is and how it ought to be read" (González Echevarría, *Voices of the Masters* 6). Luis Rafael Sánchez rightly warns that South America is "a continent that is complex, diverse, and above all, plural," where "there are one thousand ways to write, just as there are one thousand writers who try to portray the faces of our countries in different ways" (qtd. in Winn 416). This "literary diversity, Sánchez argues, makes it 'very simplistic to think that all of this continent writes under the label of magic realism' " (Winn 417).[3] Indeed, the informed critic of Latin American literature presumes no such thing.

Latin America has a literary tradition spanning several centuries, and one that has perhaps been indebted to the European forms since explorers and conquerors first put pen to paper to describe it. Only recently has the continent thrown off the stigma of regurgitating European styles and come into its own as a literary power. This is not to deny "the solidity of Latin American literature's bond to the European tradition," since that denial would, in Roberto González Echevarría's opinion, be "like trying to obscure the sun with one's finger" (*Voices of the Masters* 53). At the same time, as E. Mayz Valenilla says, "American Latinity constitutes itself around a sense of 'forever-not-yet-being,' a sense of permanent disequilibrium intensified by an often defensive inferiority complex toward the cultural productions of the United States and Europe" (qtd. in Debra A. Castillo 608).[4] Because "culture and literature create each other as necessary elements in a process of ideological formation" (González Echevarría 10), one aspect of that ideology focuses on "the populist sentiment of the traditional novel in Latin America [that] saw the writer in the role of an intellectual liberator who would denounce all that was immoral and unjust" (Ganguly 169); thus, the authors who *were* writing have been historically confined by and conforming to this role. This is not to say that original texts of quality do not exist in Latin America; Jean Franco in particular spends considerable time tracing such earlier works. But these works were "discovered," or rather *rediscovered*, by the international literary community only relatively recently; and like the United States's own literary tradition, the literature of Latin American nations, as fodder for criticism and for an international audience, is a relative new-comer. Though Latin American writers cannot turn to a large canon steeped in earlier works, the self-imposed exile of many American authors illustrates the degree to which many writers are willing to embrace even artificial or adopted literary connections. "Nineteenth- and early twentieth-century Latin American writers left for reasons similar to those of U.S. modernists: their sense . . . of America's historical newness and hence its cultural vacuity" (Zamora, *Usable Past* 12).

Yet those writers who stayed often felt the need to turn to Latin America's history itself for inspiration. "The central constitutive idealization of Latin American fiction is that Latin American discourse emerged with the most significant historical break in the West since the birth of Christ: the Discovery and Conquest of America" (González Echevarría, "Latin America" 55). These authors are not only using their history to create literature; they are also using their literature to create a historic canon. "Latin American literature often addresses the impossibility for Latin Americans of situating themselves in a specific historical moment, and reminds them of the inescapability of living simultaneously and of bridging all historical periods from the Stone Age to the Space Age" (Debra A. Castillo 608). Even critics must situate Latin American literature historically, since "Latin America is concurrently a region of premodern, modern, and postmodern societies" (Williams, *Postmodern Novel* v).[5] Lois Parkinson Zamora explains that her rationale for concentrating on fiction in Spanish rather than in English in the second part of *The Usable Past* is largely "historical," given that

contemporary Latin American writers have tended, to a greater extent than contemporary U.S. writers, to flaunt intertextual narrative strategies because they have felt more urgently the need to create their own precursors and traditions, and literature is widely considered a vehicle for doing so.... Even to make the preceding statement is to pose comparative questions: How do Latin American narrative strategies differ from those of U.S. writers in this regard, and why? (xi–xii)

Zamora later claims that the "relative scarcity of comparative studies of literature in the Americas suggests the difficulty of establishing appropriate bases for comparison" (xii); her argument seems to lend support to projects like *Rediscovering Magical Realism*, particularly given the emphasis on magical realism as a basis for some of those comparisons of which Zamora notices a dearth.

Literature sometimes takes the place of written history in Latin American countries, particularly when the fictional can achieve a verisimilitude disallowed in the non-fiction of the nations. "Indeed, in recent years Latin American literature has often responded when the press has failed to address (or has been prevented from addressing) actual political and social conditions" (Zamora, *Usable Past* 43). At the same time, however, documentary writers explore

hypotheses to the effect that Latin American sociohistorical experience exemplifies the magically real, that the Latin American reality outstrips even the most fevered fictional imagination, and that it is hopeless to attempt to interpret official histories with the techniques of rational investigation touted by professional journalism ... [that] have led Latin American writers to pursue ways of interpreting collective experience that a strict critical constructionism would call non-literary, and a professional journalist blatant fiction. (David William Foster, *Cultural Diversity* 21)

But Gabriel García Márquez's comments on journalism seem to illustrate the degree to which he believes journalism embraces the "blatancy" of such fictive accounts, comparing his journalistic writing to magical realism and, in Zamora's words, "referring to ... 'the tricks you need to transform something which appears fantastic, unbelievable into something plausible, credible, those I learned from journalism. The key is to tell it straight. It is done by reporters and country folk'" (*Usable Past* 43).[6]

Franco herself provides one of the most concise and thorough investigations of the roots and development of Latin American literature, beginning with the conquest. Europe and Latin America have been mutually disappointed in their literary expectations, since Europe has proven fallible and since the "exotic dream of America often turns out to be a distorting mirror in which [Europeans] see their own grotesque reflection" (347). Franco describes the single most important motivator for Latin American writers searching for their own literary identity as a consequence of "metropolitan Europe's cultural hegemony and the constitution of non-European cultures as peripheral or marginal" (347). Unlike Europeans, whose "own literature gave them a vantage point for viewing other cultures," Latin Americans (especially those of the newly independent continent) "found themselves viewing their own culture from the vantage point of Europe. Moreover, literary education [predominantly taught using European texts], while it acquainted them with many aspects of human experience, did not give any sense of what it meant to be a Peruvian or a Chilean or an Argentinian" (348). She argues that, historically, a handful of definitive Latin American events culminated in the newer traditions of literature and that the new novel can be "seen as emergent in the '60s," though she stresses that the date is only an approximation (325).[7]

The Boom as a literary event privileged the masculine and attempted to do the same for the status of the literature of Central and South America and of the Caribbean. Suddenly, big-name writers like García Márquez and Carlos Fuentes belonged "to a creative community whose identity went beyond national or regional boundaries" (Schulman 29). Indeed, "never before had so many Latin American writers commanded so large an international audience and such worldwide acclaim" (Winn 399–400), although, ironically, those writers' New World status initially was responsible for bringing them to international attention. This new placement of Latin American literature in the world spotlight, though, raised issues of its own. Since "[l]iterature as we know it and practice it is a Western concept and pursuit" and "we posit that Latin America has a literature, then it has to be part of Western literature, even if some writers deny it, because denying literature or the West is one of the components of the modern literature of the West" (González Echevarría, "Latin America" 54). But the question still remains: How does Latin American literature fit into the Western tradition of literature?

Another question, one at the core of Latin American identity and thought, is whether Latin America is Latin or American (González Echevarría, *Voices of the Masters* 17). What *is* Latin America? The term sometimes excludes places, like the Caribbean, or people, including indigenous populations, African Americans, and Anglo-Saxons, all of which are important elements of "Latin" America. In fact, one of the ironies of the region is that, while it is often viewed as a single unit, its history, society, and culture are "heterogeneous, hybrid, constantly changing, disseminated in space, and ultimately very difficult to define" (Chanady, "Latin American Imagined Communities" xv). Few countries in Latin America actually fit the classic definition of a "nation." Ironically, although "difference" is frequently held up as the foundation for Latin American identity, only recently has the term "magical realism" been associated with marginalized groups in Latin America. These minority writers are entering a forum where, "[a]s inhabitants of an immense region with all of its racial diversity, all the possible climates, and all the imaginable landscapes, divided into more than twenty nations similar and distinctly different at the same time, the position of the Latin American writer is multiple" (Camurati 89). And yet, such writers as Pablo Neruda, Jorge Luis Borges, and Gabriel García Márquez have transcended their national boundaries to gain international readership.

Even the Boom has been slow to change attitudes toward Latin American literature, which has been and continues to be marginalized on an international scale. "They don't know our literatures for the very same reasons that we know theirs," claims González Echevarría. "Theirs are important, canonical, the core of the core curriculum; ours are marginal, exotic, frilly, not part of anyone's cultural literacy program" ("Latin America" 48).[8]

Unfortunately, Franco's work all but dismisses magical realism, citing it merely as a poorly applied construction of critical studies. "Although some reviewers and critics identify the modern novel with 'magic realism,' in fact this has become a catch phrase which obscures the many varieties of fiction that have appeared over the last decades" (308). Thus, while implying its existence as a literary mode, she chooses to avoid the topic altogether.[9] But Franco's comments regarding Latin America's rejection of other literary traditions do offer some indirect evidence for the success of the magical realist mode there. Styles like realism and naturalism "have produced few good novels in Spanish America," Franco argues, because reality "is too complex and bizarre, society too dispersed, for the Balzacian style to be successful" (311). They were "poor and arid" styles of writing in the Latin American context because

these styles were developed to express the textures and tragedies of middle-class quotidian life at a moment when money and money values were replacing Christian-based morality. Latin-American writers, on the other hand, were constantly faced with the odd, the extraordinary, the monstrous, seldom with anything that matched this European middle-class norm; and it was only by devising and inventing literary forms which could encompass these weird mutations that they could achieve verisimilitude of their own. (351)

Thus, "Latin-American Modernism and Brazilian Modernismo both encouraged fantasy rather than realism" (311), but one could certainly add that magical realism has had similar goals of displacing Eurocentric notions of reality. "[I]n a Latin American context, magic realism is often seen as the fictional manifestation of immediate reality" (McCluskey 94). Furthermore, Latin American magical realists look "to traditions preceding the disasters of modernity that magical realism opposes" (Zamora, *Usable Past* 118). The influence of such traditions as Dada and Surrealism "liberate[d] Latin Americans from the last vestiges of the bonds of Spanish rhetoric" (Franco 350). Franco also notes that literature and politics have been closely linked in the Latin American writer's mind since the nineteenth century (348), and that confusion over the function of literature causes much of the early literature to be weak (349).

Arguably, as political and social atrocities began to pile up as quickly as failed revolutions, Latin American writers began to see possibilities for those Modern fantasies and revisions of European Surrealism to lead to the postmodern and to magical realism. In contrast to European Surrealism, "which had to look below surface reality to find the marvelous, Carpentier discovered in Afro-Cuban popular culture, and later in strange juxtapositions of technology and primitivism, a marvelous and a magical that was ready to hand" (Franco 318). In fact, "Alejo Carpentier preceded [Mexican poet Octavio] Paz in theorizing a New World Baroque. . . . He insisted upon the continuity of indigenous Latin American and baroque traditions, arguing that the Baroque is not merely a European art-historical category but the sign of cultural syncretism, symbiosis, *mestizaje*" (Zamora, *Usable Past* 203). Carpentier also argued "that the widely perceived baroque quality of Latin American fiction reflects not a love of fussy ornament but a necessary response to near-universal incomprehension of the most mundane details" (Debra A. Castillo 611–12). Zamora claims that the baroque should not be absorbed into discussions of either magical realism or "lo real maravilloso americano" because baroque artists reject "the opposition between appearance and reality" and since "the essential Baroque trope" is that "life is a dream" (203–4).

What Carpentier sees as a culturally necessary neobaroque style distinguishes the Latin American effort from the more aesthetically motivated formal games of the seventeenth-century European tradition. Rather than a superabundance, the baroque style that typifies these novels is reflected in, and derivative of, an order of experience that represents the near opposite of that excess traditionally associated with the baroque, by a need to assign names to each animal and plant, establishing its reality for a translocal audience. (612–13)

Yet the creation of the magical realist mode relied on more than revision of the versions of reality already accepted. For Paz, "Latin American literature not only is an expression of our reality, or the invention of another reality. It is also a question about the reality of those realities. A question and at times a judgment" (qtd. in González Echevarría, *Voices of the Masters* xii). Stephen Hart explains that the "crucial concern with the real as well as the magical which is the hallmark of magical realism . . . has been successful in Spanish America above all because the mixture proved, paradoxically, more able to express the social reality of the Sub-Continent than any one of the constituents working in isolation" (39–40). Yet "[i]n criticism of the Latin American novel, 'magical realism' has typically been described as an impulse to create a fictive world that can somehow compete with the 'insatiable fount of creation' that is Latin America's actual history" (Conniff 167). Although "the historical and political have been constantly present in the entire tradition of the Latin American novel" (Williams, *Postmodern Novel* 17), Franco says that for authors such as Carpentier, Guatemalan Miguel Angel Asturias, and Peruvian José María Arguedas, "Magic, dream and myth became instruments for exploring the political unconscious of authoritarianism" (318). In addition, the universal myths of Mexican writer Juan Rulfo's *Pedro Páramo* and "the play of imagination governed by intellectual yearnings in discovering reality as expressed in Jorge Luis Borges['s] *Ficciones* and Alejo Carpentier's *los reinos de este mundo* . . . set the tone for a new narrative whereby the mythic imagination was kindled to probe the reality of human ambiguities" (Ganguly 171). As Johnny Payne notes, by the mid 1960s, many Latin American fiction writers

were struggling through a repressive silencing of the social sphere as a whole, where the legal possibilities of speech were almost nil, at the very moment [Susan] Sontag, [John] Barth, and many of their U.S. and European contemporaries felt their own ordeal of silence to be located at the nether limits of verbal profusion. . . . [T]here appears here a historical disjunction—not in the neo-colonial sense of so-called emerging literatures, of playing literary catch-up, but rather in the sense of two sets of writers with different (albeit related) and differently formulated sets of historical concerns and thus a different relationship to the question of the aesthetics of silence and speech. (15)

The concerns of this emerging group of authors creating the new novel in Latin America "had valences somewhat other than the U.S.-European trope of a vacuum of aesthetic silence brought on by too many writers with too little to say" (Payne 15).

[T]he Latin American literary production of recent decades . . . suggest[s] that there has been an epochal break in Latin America that took place in the late 1960s. From the late 1960s . . . a change in attitudes toward fiction and a change in novelistic production is evident[, and these changes] correspond in many ways to what is currently being identified as *postmodern* in First World or North Atlantic academia. (Williams, *Postmodern Novel* viii)

These writers of postmodern fiction "had one aim in common, to challenge their readers and make them re-examine the stereotypes of earlier literature" (Franco 326). These authorial challenges began at the level of the author, who was critiquing his or her own creation of narrative. "Doris Sommer notes that most of the structural innovations of the 'boom,' characterised by the 'demotion, or diffusion, of authorial control and tireless formal experimentation,' were 'directed towards demolishing the straight line of traditional narrative' " (McCluskey 88). Moreover, Donald L. Shaw, who argues that "what above all characterizes the Boom writers is their radical questioning of a. reality and b. the writer's task" (5), hints that the traditions at risk during the Boom were internationally held beliefs. Yet, as Payne points out, "[i]n their aggregate, experimental fiction writers of recent decades, however cosmopolitan and ripe for becoming international commodities, have demonstrated in their writing a concern with the political topography of their respective native cosmopolises at a particular point in time, rather than with the creation of a mythic enchanted, unified continent" (35). Zamora agrees, noting that coexisting "discrete, contradictory, and equally necessary semiotic systems . . . are placed in narrative structures that foreground (rather than undermine) the antinomies of Latin America's multiple histories and traditions" (*Usable Past* 9). As Zamora's terminology suggests, Latin Americans were looking to the paradoxical nature of existence on the margins of Western society. "For Francine Masiello, Latin American writing at its best displays what she calls, following Bahktin, a 'double discourse,' a hybrid language 'that recognizes the structures of power at the same time that it offers an alternative'" (Debra A. Castillo 642). Much scholarship (including Franco's own comments on the Latin American extension of and break with European models, and on the new novel in particular) certainly seems to encompass magical realist possibilities—whether those potentialities are discussed as such or not—but critics seem to warn that these magical realist strains are decidedly political and favor inquiry over aesthetics.

Distinguishing itself from European and North American modes cannot, of course, erase contemporary Latin America's continuing and distinctive bonds with some of those traditions. For example, as "Hispanic Nobel Laureates . . . Gabriel García Márquez, [Spanish author] Camilo José Cela and Octavio Paz" acknowledged their indebtedness to Cervantes, so too they support "the proposition that whatever political or ideological difference may still divide them, Spain and the Spanish-speaking republics have always had, and will continue to have, a very special linguistic bond" (Boland and Harvey 7). The very Boom itself may have roots in Spain,[10] argue Roy C. Boland and Sally Harvey, since its detonations "were to be heard more loudly and more clearly in Spain than anywhere else. Certainly, without Spain and the efforts of the great poet-entrepreneur, Carlos Barral, the 'boom' would not have had the impact nor the reach that it did" (8).[11] Furthermore, although Germán Gullón argues that certain Latin American writers have had considerable influence upon the contemporary Spanish novel, Joaquín Marco believes that "the influence of the 'boom' novelists was not so much upon their Spanish counterparts, as upon the novel-reading public in Spain" by way of literary conditioning (Boland and Harvey 8).

The face of Latin America's twentieth-century history bespeaks the difficulties of a newly emerged postcolonial area, but Latin America still finds itself subject to imperialism, neocolonialism in the name of economics. Post-World War II novelists found "themselves surpassed by the world around them. This is even more serious for the novelists of the third world" where technical progress "is imitative in nature and imposed from outside" (Ganguly 170). The Boom gets its name from North American marketing, Angel Rama contends, and it designates "a sudden jump in sales of a particular product in consumer societies. . . . The surprise was its application to a product (books) which . . . was on the margin of such processes" (qtd. in Payne 30). Debra A. Castillo adds that the narratives of the 1950s and 1960s are Latin America's "most exportable products" and that "boom . . . is an English word hinting at stock market fluctuations and atomic bomb capabilities . . . [and is] for many critics a marker of cultural imperialism at its worst" (613).

The Boom, as a direct result of such cultural imperialism from the United States and other Western "exporters" of the literary products of writers in Latin America, has both commodified and expanded the talents of the continent's writers. The Boom raised the literary world's perception of Latin America, a view that pre-1960s had always cast Latin America "as a cultural backwater" (Winn 400). Though positive world attention and discriminating appreciation resulted from the "dissemination of Latin American fiction in translation, . . . a body of literature, selectively produced and disseminated in conjunction with certain cultural crises and the economic demands of consumer culture, becomes subject to extremely limited possibilities of interpretation within that culture" (Payne 34). Philip Swanson more cynically implicates the artists themselves in the production of Latin American literature as "commodity":

The problem really is one of playing politics with the popular (especially since the relative accessibility of the post-Boom is frequently identified with a tendency towards greater political directness). . . . [I]n *Cien años de soledad* popular culture is not a question of TV, Hollywood or youth cults, but of writing an entertaining book for wide consumption and, more problematically, recreating the popular viewpoint of a Third-World community. (11, 12)

According to Castillo, literary critic Roberto Fernández Retamar sees "the tracks and scars of cultural imperialism throughout Boom writing" (613); Castillo also argues that "writers and critics are themselves 'commodified' by the resources of their respective choices of literary code." For example, though Borges and García Márquez are "the Boom's most typical and enduring products[,] . . . it would be difficult to imagine two writers more different in personality, politics, enduring obsessions, or literary style" (613). Literary codes such as "magical realism" are not the only markers for commodity among Latin American texts. "The marketplace is a key conditioning factor in producing and consolidating marginality," since identities like "blackness" and "third worldism" are marketed (Katrak 666).[12] González Echevarría believes that such commodification "reveals an overseer mentality that is much more that of the colonizer than of the would-be decolonizer" ("Latin America" 50). Ironically, the United States "has replaced Europe as the primary economic and political colonizer of Latin America and yet has itself remained deeply colonized by European cultural traditions and forms of expression" (Zamora, *Usable Past* 10).

Some critics question the validity of not just the international motives behind the Boom but also the works written within its context. The Boom itself, as seen by Swanson, "is merely an exemplification of the sense of 'break with tradition' that has come to be associated with the new novel" (2), rather than an actual break with the traditions of Latin American literature. Although the new novel in Latin America[13] is presumably the progeny of the Cuban Revolution (Payne 20), Swanson seems to argue that the "newness" of the new novel in Latin America, rather than being revolutionary itself, ultimately relies on its packaging, since it derives its newness from the way it looks rather than from its content.[14] This "suggests that its allure may lie at the surface rather than at any truly deeper level," that the new novel is simply "a sophisticated confection for a well-read public" (5, 16). For Swanson, the new Latin American novel replicates what came before; other critics believe it is more original, with possible ties to concurrent traditions in the United States and in Spain, as well as in other parts of the world.

More recently, a reclassification of contemporary Latin American literature has created the expression "post-Boom." In the 1969 of Franco's *An Introduction to*

Spanish-American Literature, "critics could hardly imagine that García Márquez would produce other novels to match *One Hundred Years of Solitude,* nor that such an eclectic variety of writers would emerge in the post-Boom years." In fact, "in the 1990s it is no longer possible to discuss the fiction of the last thirty years in a purely national context. The nation is no longer the community to which the writer necessarily responds and the male intellectual can no longer speak in the name of hitherto excluded minority groups" (Franco x–xi). Franco sees multiple catalysts for post-Boom writers. "Probably more than any other event[s,] the defeat of the Chilean President, Salvador Allende in 1973, the Cuban dependence on the, then, Soviet Union and the contra war in Nicaragua in the late '70s subverted the notion of autonomous national solutions which had allowed writers in the early '60s to conflate narrative space with national space" (309). Shaw argues that the post-Boom seems to symbolize a break with the immediate past, since "the assumptions made by the Boom writers—whether about reality, the human condition, and society or about narrative techniques and the relationship of language to any possible exterior referent—were to be in some cases directly contradicted in the next generation" (10). Post-Boom writers are reacting "not just against foreign models, but against a homegrown movement, and one that brought Spanish-American fiction world attention" (177), that is, the Boom itself. But the two movements share in common a link with the political upheavals of their respective time periods: the 1959 triumph of the Cuban revolution for the Boom,[15] the dictatorial regimes of the 1970s for the post-Boom (11). Though some critics see them as synonymous, Shaw also believes "postmodernism is a far wider ranging concept than is Post-Boom" (39):

The Post Boom [*sic*] does not in general articulate the experience of a disorderly, directionless world in which our awareness of meaning is no more than an unstable and shifting construct with no purposiveness and no ultimate validation. To . . . the extent that some form of collective project survives strongly in it, the [post-Boom] cannot be easily fitted into mainstream postmodernism. Good equivalents are feminism and black culture in the United States. (173)

Because not all Latin Americans (among others) embrace postmodernism in the same way, Shaw urges a decentering of postmodernism itself. By pluralizing postmodernisms, we discover varying contexts "that are not all affected in the same way by political, social and cultural changes" (175–76).[16]

    Raymond Williams responds "to the looseness and vagueness surrounding the term *postmodernism* in the context of Latin American literature" because "several critics have questioned the appropriateness of using the term *postmodern* when speaking of Latin America. On the other hand, others have argued that Latin America, in fact, set the precedent of postmodernity long before the notion appeared in the North Atlantic regions" (*Postmodern Novel* v). Though the First World's tastes for the postmodern are consistent with the maturation of the Boom, its structural innovations, "typified by the 'amalgamation of realism and fantasy' have been hailed as authentic expressions of Latin America" (McCluskey 88–89). Williams himself falls into the second camp and believes,

The argument that Latin American postmodernism precedes the North Atlantic phenomenon can be most convincingly argued in the case of the Caribbean, for the Caribbean is defined by the same heterogeneity that has become a key word for the postmodern. . . . Postmodern culture in the Caribbean region, like that of Mexico, has been considerably impacted by both mass culture and high culture of the United States, and generally more so than is the case in the Andean and Southern Cone regions. (*Postmodern Novel* 95)

In fact, Beverley Ormerod argues that a key issue regarding magical realism in some parts of the Caribbean "would seem to be the importance, or loss of importance, of magical beliefs and rituals in the increasingly urbanized Francophone Caribbean" (225).[17] She states that, although the "device of magical realism is often employed by contemporary French Caribbean novelists" (216), "[o]ne may legitimately ask whether magical realism is relevant or appropriate (other than as a signpost literary game) in the fictional representation of late twentieth-century society in Martinique and Guadeloupe" (225). Karla J. Sanders challenges the notion that magical realism and the postmodern are synonymous; instead, she argues that magical realism "is a brand of contemporary fiction . . . closely associated with the anti-mimetic strain of Postmodernism. . . . While Magic Realism and Postmodernism intersect by deconstructing history, questioning notions of truth, moving toward localized knowledge, and seeking new answers to these questions [of truth], the ways in which these themes develop distinguish these movements from each other" (272, 274).

The distinctions some critics describe between postmodernism and postcolonialism place "the Post-Boom in a wider world perspective, one that foregrounds the ideological differences between a metropolitan movement (which is sometimes alleged to reflect the current late phase of capitalism through a crisis of cultural authority and of epistemological confidence) and a peripheral movement that, being more closely connected with the sociopolitical problems of the Third World, is apt to be more testimonial and militant" (Shaw 176). Since the postcolonial may even resist the postmodern, "accepting ideology and referentiality, and responding to an ongoing need in Third World nations to discover their identity," "the Post-Boom seems closer to postcolonialism than to postmodernism" (176, 177). Yet, as Laura García-Moreno argues, "An either/or perception of postmodernism/postcolonialism problematically assigns the need to produce realist representations of social/historical concerns to certain contexts and limits formal experimentation to advanced societies. It pushes the discussion towards exclusionary directions" (65).

Its postcolonial status has indeed taken a toll on Latin America. David William Foster claims, "Latin American culture is viewed as having been fatally corrupted by the artifacts of a multinational imperialism that is said to exploit Latin American society. Such corruption is foremostly identified with the U.S., as a consequence of the aggressive penetration of the Latin American market during U.S. expansionism after World War II" ("Popular Culture" 11). The implication of Foster's claim is that the role that the United States played in the Boom is that of corruption, rather than one of the globalization of Latin American literature. "Latin American writers thematize the hypotheses of cultural (and behind them, economic and political) dependency," as symbolized by the influence of Madison Avenue, foreign bestsellers and rock bands, and Coca-Cola and Pepsi (12).

In Chapter 4, the extensive exploration of the connections for North American magical realism with popular culture might seem exclusionary in terms of Latin American popular culture. It is certainly true that the popular culture of the United States and its colonizing effects have infiltrated Latin America. But pop culture is frequently rejected in Latin America precisely because of such associations, as a reaction against "the multinational capitalism that imposes a homogenizing mass culture" (David William Foster, "Popular Culture" 4). For example, "Puerto Rican culture is a flotsam and jetsam of fragments of a cultural imperialism that are non-biodegradable: they refuse to go away and they are impossible to assimilate into a healthy life cycle" (13). There are also certain distinctions between the use of the term "popular culture" in Latin American literature in general and its appearance in North American literature. "Popular was originally a legal and political term, from [the Latin] *popularis*—belonging to the people" as opposed to its "transition to the predominant modern meaning of 'widely favoured' or 'well-liked'" (Williams, *Keywords* 236), and "[t]he sense of popular culture as the culture actually made by people for themselves is [still] different" (237). The popular culture "having to do with the populus, the *pueblo* . . . is foremostly associated with folk traditions that . . . embody the specific identity of people viewed in localistic and regionalistic terms as the incarnation of the national genius or spirit. Such a popular or folk culture, whether purely indigenous or a postconquest mestizo amalgam, has continued to survive in Latin America" (David William Foster, "Popular Culture" 5). The Argentine tango is an example of the commercialization of folk culture, as well as an instance of Latin American popular culture having an influence on North American culture and reversing the traditional pattern of influence.

"Folk culture" is sometimes regarded as a less positive national or regional Latin American treasure. Not only is it commodified as an export, but "much of what one finds of folk culture in Latin American cities today is a commercial adaptation" (David William Foster, "Popular Culture" 5). Furthermore, *popular* "in Spanish means ethnic and/or lower-class, unlike the English use of the same word to mean wide acceptance and favor" (Zamora, *Usable Past* 195). Thus, the vernacular in Latin American novels of the early- and mid-twentieth century "signif[ies] (and reinforce[s]) the cultural and social gulf between readers . . . and those characters [speaking in the vernacular]" (195). Though Zamora claims that contemporary fiction in Latin America "aims at achieving the opposite effect of bridging the gulf between the literary and the *popular*/popular" (195), the means for achieving such equality do not draw from pop cultural references as in

North America, perhaps in a direct refutation of the effects of those references on the Latin American culture. And Swanson questions whether or not "the dissolution of the gap between High Culture and Popular Culture undermine[s] the very popular quality of popular culture and generate[s] a new form of elitism" (11).

The cultures of Canada and the United States are perceived as distinct threats to Latin America. As noted earlier, many view the culture of Latin America as corrupted by the exploitive and imperialist societies that both penetrate into and borrow from Latin America (David William Foster, "Popular Culture" 11). "As late as the 1970s, television was viewed by many in the region as a form of U.S. cultural imperialism, projecting North American political ideologies and social values." This changed with the Latin American-produced *telenovelas*, which "were not imitations of U.S. soap operas or movies, but rather adaptations of older forms of Latin American popular culture." In fact, "[i]n Brazil, the roots of the *telenovela* go back still further ... to the oral traditions of storytelling" (Winn 436–37).

Original Latin American popular cultural references have also offered new forums for creativity. Though "[p]opular culture can, without a doubt, be exploited as an agent of oppression, . . . it can also be liberating" (Swanson 166). For example, "[c]onfronted with the evidence that one episode of a popular *telenovela* reached more people than all the copies of all his novels published in Spanish, [García Márquez] decided [to go even further than incorporating pop culture into his novels and] to write a *telenovela* himself" (Winn 441). The increased demand for products like the *telenovela* prove that Latin American popular culture is itself a defense against Northern influences. Peter Winn argues, "Puerto Rican identity [lies] in its popular culture, and . . . its own popular music [is] the best defense against 'the excessive Americanization of culture' on the island" (428). And David William Foster claims that the true popular reading in Latin America is "the *fotonovela*, in which still photographs of actors are accompanied by balloons of text, or the more venerable comic book" ("Popular Culture" 16). Indeed, with the increasingly Spanish-speaking population of the United States and other historically non-Spanish-speaking countries, the influence may slowly be changing directions. "Writers and artists throughout Latin America and the Caribbean are mixing their media and blurring the lines that traditionally separated high and popular culture. In the process, they have produced a rich and vibrant modern culture that has spread not only throughout the region but into the First World as well" (Winn 441).

Ultimately, a variety of factors figure into the evolution of magical realism and the Latin American tradition with which it was originally associated. But magical realism clearly played a part in the reinvention of Latin American literature as an international contender. "Only with the rise of Jorge Luis Borges, then the Boom, the institutionalization of magic realism, and the most recent rise of multiculturalism has it been possible for Latin American writers to be considered a part of the Western canon" (Williams, *Postmodern Novel* 110).

ONE HUNDRED YEARS OF SOLITUDE: THE BOOMINGEST VOICE OF ALL

In the traditions of both the Boom and Latin American magical realism, no single work has had more impact than García Márquez's *One Hundred Years of Solitude*.[18] Futhermore, as Edward A. Shannon suggests in his dictum that "[a]ny study of Magic Realism in American literature must consider its Latin-American roots and its most famous practitioner" (31), the novel's critical impact has been no less important. García Márquez's work created "a literary earthquake," to borrow Mario Vargas Llosa's phrase (qtd. in McMurray, Introduction 1), and positioned "Latin America on the literary map of a world that had generally ignored its existence for far more than a century" (Winn 399). The year of its publication, 1967, "was the first year Latin American literature was finally recognized as one of the world's great contemporary literatures and the publishing 'Boom' in Latin American writing that had begun a few years before with the appearance of Julio Cortázar's dazzling novel *Hopscotch* reached its peak" (Winn 399). The English translation of *One Hundred Years of Solitude* was available by 1970, sparking additional, equally favorable reviews (McMurray 7), and "[w]ithin a decade it had practically come to stand, by way of synecdoche, for all of Latin American literature" (Payne 14). Williams says that "*One Hundred Years of Solitude* represented a culmination . . . of a modernist project that still privileged issues of truth" and that it was "one of the last significant confrontations with truth in Latin American modernist fiction" (*Postmodern Novel* 6–7).

More important, *One Hundred Years of Solitude* maintains integral connections with the world from whence it springs. While Julio Ortega claims that *One Hundred Years of Solitude* "is a lengthy tribute to the reader," from whom it "demands and obtains the best," he also argues that it "demands that a historical parallel be established with its schema, with the century of Latin American events whose vast possibilities of pain and happiness end in death and destruction, that is, in the closing of one period and in the proximity of a different time" (85). *One Hundred Years of Solitude*, Gerald Martin argues, "was born of a nostalgic longing for certain pre-capitalist rural relations in an age of rapid urbanization and the implementation of industrial capitalism" ("On 'Magical' and Social Realism" 98), with the rise of capitalism being symbolized, in Floyd Merrell's opinion, by "Aureliano's fabrication of golden fish for sale and by Úrsula's peddling of her wares" (64). According to Martin, "[s]een in [the light of neocolonialism and the failed line of the Buendías], the novel seems less concerned with any 'magical' reality than with the general effect of a colonial history upon individual relationships," and any "judgment as to whether [individual] traits are inherent or produced by history is as much a political as a philosophical or scientific determination" ("On 'Magical' and Social Realism" 106). Thus, in Martin's reading of the novel, the "apocalypse of the Buendías is not—how could it be?—the end of Latin America but the end of neocolonialism and its conscious or unconscious collaborators" (111). Brian Conniff concurs: "Apocalypse is only the logical consequence of imperialist oppression" (178). Not surprisingly, "*One Hundred Years of Solitude* is required reading in many Latin American history and political science courses in the U.S.," a fact that "goes a long way toward demonstrating the essential truth of García Márquez's novel, its over-all correspondence to a broad social and historical reality" (Bell-Villada 215). Conversely, some critics argue that this "is the novel which, perhaps more than any other, has been taken to confirm the historical demise of social realism in Latin American fiction and to herald the arrival of the linguistic, experimental or post-Modernist novel" (Martin, "On 'Magical' and Social Realism" 101). Ultimately, we must accept that *One Hundred Years of Solitude* can encompass so many possibilities and be read in so many different ways because it presents such "a multidimensional microcosm. The novel can be construed as symbolic of Colombia (the socio-political level), Latin America (the mythico-cultural level), Christianity (the mystico-religious level), the world (the historical/archetypal levels), or the universe (the cyclical/entropic levels)" (Merrell 59).

The greatest proof of *One Hundred Years of Solitude*'s multidimensional status has been its international reception as a masterpiece of magical realism and Latin American literature. The text is an anomaly, a work that "shows every sign of having been manufactured for the home market, Latin America, and yet [one that] has been just as acceptable to European and North American—which is to say, 'universal'—taste. [It] became the first truly international best seller in Latin American publishing history" (Martin, "On 'Magical' and Social Realism" 98). "[T]he novel as text is perfectly aware of its own literary-historical significance, one whose implicit claim is that the *boom* itself is a proof of the end of neocolonialism and the beginning of true liberation" (112). García Márquez was, like his contemporaries, "acutely conscious of the unique experience of Latin America as a region on the edge of 'civilization,' whose history of uneven development belied the West's easy faith in the inevitability of progress." Such "uneven development might be an economic nightmare and a political problem, but they were a cultural resource for writers ready to mine their rich lode of myth, history, and paradox" (Winn 400). Though translating these riches into fiction is a recurrent theme in Latin American literature, "it is García Márquez in *One Hundred Years of Solitude* who has more clearly than anyone before him (even Borges) pointed out translation's key role in the constitution of Latin American literature and culture. The topic of translation in *One Hundred Years of Solitude* is a reminder of Latin American literature's 'impure' and conflictive origins" (González 77). Furthermore, "Gabriel García Márquez's thematization of (postmodern) magic realism and the politics of the possible" inverts, "in a jesting manner, the values of the official Latin American culture" (Saldívar, "Postmodern Realism" 526).

Contrary to Martin's point that *One Hundred Years of Solitude* may be "less concerned with any 'magical' reality" than it is with other considerations is the compelling and extensive amount of magical realism in the text; nearly as convincing is the sheer amount of criticism on the mode as a feature of the text. More than any other technique García Márquez employs in *One Hundred Years of Solitude*, his use of magical realism is responsible for providing those "vast possibilities." As Martin asks, "how magical and how realist is García Márquez?" ("On 'Magical' and Social

Realism" 100) and then chronicles several key opinions on *One Hundred Years of Solitude*:

Julio Ortega insisted that "the play of reality and fantasy is never dual in this novel"; José Miguel Oviedo declared that the novelist had "mixed the real and the fantastic in so perfect and inextricable a fashion that no one can tell where the frontier between them may lie"; and Ernst Völkening commented admiringly that García Márquez was blessed with "the uncommon gift of seeing both sides of the moon at one and the same time." (100–101).

Martin himself agrees that *One Hundred Years of Solitude* "remains the only text of [García Márquez's] in which the mix of real and fantasy elements is both perfectly fused and, analytically . . . perfectly separable" (100); he also argues that if the term "magical realism" "must be used, it is best confined to the . . . kind of writing . . . in which, essentially, there is a dialectic between pre-scientific and scientific visions of reality, seen most clearly in the works which combine the mythological or folk beliefs of the characters with the consciousness of a twentieth century observer" (103).[19] He concludes that *One Hundred Years of Solitude* does indeed establish just such a dialectic. Swanson suggests that, because "Gabriel [a character obviously connected to the author himself] *leaves* the magical world of Macondo," García Márquez seems to privilege realism over magic. Yet Swanson finds his own statement somewhat ridiculous since "the appeal and success of the novel depend more than anything else on its creation of a 'magical' world view stemming from the popular perspective of a rural Latin American community" (13–14). Stephen Hart contends that "García Márquez's fictional world is a water-tight universe where everything obeys its own logic" and that *One Hundred Years of Solitude* "is not only fantastic but also highly detailed in a naturalistic way" (47), with those details not intended to lend padding but rather to invest the fantastic "with a sheen of verisimilitude" (45).[20] "These naturalistic details tend to displace the focus of the narrative away from the fantastic as valuable or noteworthy in itself" and "to make the most magical happenings seem believable" (46). Edwin Williamson believes that the "particular originality of García Márquez's techniques lies . . . in his having followed through to its ultimate consequences the logic of his magical-real discourse" (61).[21] "In the disorderly modern world, magical realism is not merely an expression of hope; it is also a 'resource' that can depict such a 'scientific possibility' " as apocalypse and make it "appear not only credible but inevitable" (Conniff 168).

    One Hundred Years of Solitude is anything but a dull, serious slide into its apocalyptic ending. Even as Macondo's magical realism inverts the traditional authority of religion and economy, it portrays the inversion as a comic one. Clive Griffin cites the "power of the Banana Company to decree that it should rain in Macondo for four years, eleven months, and two days [as] funny because it is an exaggerated and absurdly precise extension of the real power of the multinationals in the Third World," while Fernanda's concern that she loses a sheet when Remedios the Beautiful ascends humors readers with its "inappropriately mundane reaction to a supernatural event with Christian undertones" (86). Griffin argues that interpretations of *One Hundred Years of Solitude* as a work of serious (and pessimistic) intent cannot "account for its remarkable popularity among a heterogeneous readership which has scant knowledge of the history of Columbia or of the recent literary production of Spanish America" (81). But Williamson equates humor with complicity. He says that, by "tipping the wink at his readers" when José Arcadio Buendía "discovers ice," García Márquez makes magical realism transient. He argues that the same "humorous complicity exists" with Remedios's ascent, so that for the reader the phenomenon is de-mystified "because of the underlying assumption (as in the ice scene above) that the reader's world-view is at odds with that of the characters" (47). Yet Williamson's argument does not allow for the fact that García Márquez transforms *all* science that falls outside the realm of Macondo as " unaccountable," nor does he accept that the implied reader—humorous tone or no—is asked to read the supernatural as commonplace. This feat proves much easier to accomplish when, as Griffin points out, everything that the reader "knows" to be "true" has already been challenged: "Just as he laughs at the reactions of the naive inhabitants of Macondo whose description of the first train to be seen in town is of 'a terrifying object like a kitchen pulling a village,' so the reader is invited to laugh at his own reaction when his expectations of the narrative are challenged and he has to suspend his normal judgment about what is possible in reality and fiction and what is not" (Griffin 84).

Though he recognizes that the distinguishing feature of the "civilization" that exists outside the fictional world of Macondo is scientific knowledge, Williamson is unable or unwilling to accept the internal magical realist world of *One Hundred Years of Solitude*. Williamson says, "García Márquez sets up an ironic interplay between the *identity* of opposites promoted by the magical-real discourse and the inescapable sense of *difference* retained by the reader. The novel is, then, predicated upon a dialectic that opposes the experiences of the world *inside* the fiction to that which lies *outside* it" (47). This is, in fact, the same dialectic Martin sees between "pre-scientific and scientific visions of reality" ("On 'Magical' and Social Realism" 103). What seems *outside* the text for Williamson, though, is not necessarily what the implied reader of *One Hundred Years of Solitude* would find to be outside the text. As Martin notes, "to know what reality is" is to accept a U.S. and European metropolitan definition of the idea (103). Williamson, through his inability to accept the world-view expressed not by García Márquez's characters but rather by his narrator, refuses to grant the novel his "willing suspension of disbelief." Perhaps because he reads as one aware that the book is written from a magical realist point of view (a mode he sees predominantly driven by the incestuous themes of the text) Williamson is particularly loathe to let himself *inside* the magical realism of *One Hundred Years of Solitude*.

The fault in Williamson's logic lies in his belief that science and magical realism are diametrically opposed forces in Macondo. He argues that José Arcadio Buendía's "efforts are directed . . . towards undoing the mentality of magical realism within which he is himself imprisoned. He hopes to move out of the world of the novel . . . and into the world of the reader, where 'dreams' such as flying carpets can be successfully distinguished from aeroplanes" (48). Were this the case, García Márquez would be systematically undoing his magical realist novel by creating doubts about the reality of the supernatural events. In fact, as the following chapter demonstrates, José Arcadio Buendía's search for science is actually one for the antiquated and multilevel alchemy, a science much more a part of the internal world of Macondo than of the world outside it.

NOTES

1. Peter Winn uses the phrase "liberation of the imagination" to describe Latin America's break with realism (400). Similarly, Jean Franco uses the expression "decolonizing the Latin-American imagination" in relation to poet César Vallejo.

2. Indeed, historian Edmund O'Gorman's blatantly titled *The Invention of America* argues that America and the idea that it was discovered are both post-Columbus inventions (Debra A. Castillo 607).

3. Various critics stress that magical realism should never be considered to the exclusion of other modes. For example, Johnny Payne, in his discussion of Uruguayan and Argentine writers during the seventies, argues, "magical realism represents only one of the myriad styles and forms these fiction writers explored at the time, in their efforts to counter, or at least to examine, the pseudo-democratic, self-legitimizing expressions set forth by their countries' military governments" (36).

4. Gerald Martin notes that Europeans "have always viewed Latin America, like Africa, through all the twists and turns of a long historical relationship . . . as alternately the earthly paradise or the heart of darkness, their inhabitants as noble or ignoble savages, according to the opportune requirements of the moment" ("On 'Magical' and Social Realism" 96).

5. Williams borrows this notion from "Bolivian social scientist Fernando Calderón[, who] has suggested that Latin America lives in incomplete and mixed times of premodernity, modernity, and postmodernity, and that each of these is linked historically in turn with corresponding cultures that are, or were, epi-centers of power" (*Postmodern Novel* 45).

6. David William Foster seems, implicitly, to agree with García Márquez; he says that documentary writing serves historically to confirm the tenuousness of the separation between high literature and other forms of cultural production: this is so if it is true that categorical definitions of literature are the rather limited but dominant adherence to European classifications. This line of thought also underscores how in contemporary Latin America there is an enormously productive quest after new varieties of writing that both conform to the Latin American experience and reveal it in all its complexity. (*Cultural Diversity* 22)

7. Fredric Jameson even calls the historical move into independence into question for Latin America, since "[t]he fact of nominal national independence, in Latin America in the 19th century . . . puts an end to a movement for which genuine national autonomy was the only conceivable goal" ("Third-World Literature" 81). The effort, a failed one, threatened intellectual and social growth because "to receive independence is not the same as to take it, since it is in the revolutionary struggle itself that new social relationships and a new consciousness is developed. Here again the history of Cuba is instructive: Cuba was the last of the Latin American nations to win its freedom in the 10th century—a freedom which would immediately be taken in charge by another greater colonial power" (81).

8. An increased status of the Latin American text is not enough to combat this attitude in González Echevarría's opinion. "Latin American colonial culture, in many ways medieval, is so distant from that of the United States that gross distortions and misreadings are bound to

occur unless substantial study of it is required in the curriculum" ("Latin America" 51). In fact, he argues, "the very history of Latin America has to be retold, along with the novel, as if scaffolding and building, frame and picture, needed each other to exist as such" (54).

9. Debra A. Castillo's chapter on "Latin American Fiction" in *The Columbia History of the American Novel* similarly gives only fleeting reference to magical realism and uses the term interchangeably with "marvelous realism." As astounding as these critics' neglect of magical realism as a primary mode in Latin American literature is the fact that, when they do use the term, Castillo and Franco further complicate scholarship on magical realism by having no clear definition in mind. In other words, they too refer to it in its "catch phrase" sense.

10. Carlos Fuentes lends credence to this claim in *Terra Nostra*, his 1975 "mythic-philosophical-historical recreation of four hundred years of combined Spanish and Spanish American relations" (Debra A. Castillo 620).

11. Boland and Harvey miss the contradiction of Spain's role as colonizer of much of Latin America; as such, Spain guaranteed not only the "linguistic bonds" between the two regions but also its own ironic role in creating a situation where Latin America would *need* to be "rediscovered" via the Boom.

12. The dialectic between marginality and magical realism will be discussed in more detail in Chapter 6.

13. Boland and Harvey isolate the period between 1975 and 1989 as that "encompassing the so-called 'nueva novela española' or 'la novela de la democracia' and the 'post-boom' novel in Latin America." They also note that, if *One Hundred Years of Solitude* is the classic Boom novel, the classic new novel is *La ciudad de los prodigios* by Eduardo de Mendoza (9).

14. Critics of Fidel Castro could claim that Cuba's "liberation" was itself a product of clever packaging—dictatorship wrapped in the cloak of Communist rhetoric.

15. "It should be remembered that the boom took place on the heels of another momentous event that brought the two Americas, and many of their artists and intellectuals, face to face: the Cuban Revolution" (Payne 20).

16. Shaw's revision of the postmodern to include "local flavors" of that tradition recalls Charles Werner Scheel's champagne analogy for varieties of magical realism, as mentioned in Chapter 1.

17. "[T]he original rhetoric of magical realism in the Caribbean is bound up with a type of nationalism that seeks to revalue the African heritage in popular Caribbean culture, as well as to persuade the reader of the frequent occurrence of astonishing, magical events in this region" (Ormerod 216).

18. It seems García Márquez personally felt that the success of *One Hundred Years of Solitude* was less than deserved; in an interview with Plinio Apuleyo Mendoza, García Márquez marveled at the novel's popularity, given that he had written "more important literary achievements," such as *The Autumn of the Patriarch*. Regarding *One Hundred Years of Solitude*, he says, "[S]ince I knew it was written with all the tricks and artifices under the sun, I knew I could do better even before I wrote it." Mendoza clarifies, "That you could beat it," to which the author replies, "Yes, that I could beat it" (Mendoza and García Marquez 56).

19. Though Martin suggests that magical realism may generally be escapist, a "conspiracy between European or North American critics eager to get away, in their imagination, to the colorful world of Latin America, and certain Latin American writers desperate to take refuge . . . from the injustice and brutality of their continent's unacceptable reality" ("On 'Magical' and Social Realism" 102–3), this is not how he perceives García Márquez's magical realism.

20. Hart gives here as his example of "naturalistic detail" the blood trail of José Arcadio that finds Úrsula in her kitchen. Gregory Rabassa puts an especially "naturalistic" or biolog-

ical spin on this event when he says "the blood of José Arcadio flows backward, reattaching the umbilical cord, a kind of reverse menstrual flow" ("Beyond Magical Realism" 450).

21. As the discussion of *One Hundred Years of Solitude* in the next chapter will argue, the logic of García Márquez's magical realism is itself driven by its relationship to alchemy.

3

"ADVANCING IN THE OPPOSITE DIRECTION FROM REALITY": MAGICAL REALISM, ALCHEMY, AND *ONE HUNDRED YEARS OF SOLITUDE*

> It was as if God had decided to put to the test every capacity for surprise and was keeping the inhabitants of Macondo in a permanent alternation between excitement and disappointment, doubt and revelation, to such an extreme that no one knew for certain where the limits of reality lay.
>
> —*One Hundred Years of Solitude*

Gabriel García Márquez's revision of science in *One Hundred Years of Solitude*, in spite of his radical portrayal of science as both a modern and primal catalyst for the novel's apocalyptic demise, has received only a smattering of critical attention. Some scholars touch on and then dismiss its effects, as when Julio Ortega claims that José Arcadio Buendía's quest for scientific knowledge is "another mythical dream" (87). Yet, as Michael Boccia argues, there is magic in

the simple technology of the inexplicable. So the magic of technology may range from an ice-making machine to a flying carpet. Even a simple magnet may serve to demonstrate the fine line between magic and technology. . . . Magic and science are both explanations of some unknown natural phenomenon. And we should not forget that the history of science is little more than each generation disproving the scientific truths of the past. (29)

Thus, Kenneth Wishnia's treatment of *One Hundred Years of Solitude*, where he revises the book jacket for the science fiction market,[1] is not quite as far-fetched as it might seem.

One Hundred Years of Solitude is a "decodification of the natural order" (Ganguly 176) and of the Western world as well. "This novel is not about 'history-and-myth,' but about the myths of history and their demystification" (Martin, "On 'Magical' and Social Realism" 99); in particular, García Márquez "reveals what is assumed to be natural as praeternatural" and "makes us wonder . . . at the scientific laws of matter and history" (Hart 47). L. Robert Stevens and G. Roland Vela note that "western [sic] man's scientific and technological achievements are in great part due to his ability to separate fact from fiction, myth from science, and illusion from reality. It is a paradox of western culture that it draws its psychological strength from a spiritual-mythical well while its muscle is drawn largely from science and technology" (262). Floyd Merrell believes "that the transmutations in José Arcadio [Buendía]'s conception of reality" are "analogous to the development of scientific thought in the Western World." Although Merrell explores the ways in which the novel creates "parallels between the 'scientific paradigms' postulated and implemented by José Arcadio Buendía . . . and the structural history of scientific philosophy in the Western World" (59), García Márquez erects those structures for the express purpose of undermining their authority. The novel "deliberately subverts [the] trend toward rational objectivity[, for] it presents the laws of the universe, and particularly the laws of science and history, not as if they were objective and self-evident facts, but instead as if they were unnatural and strange productions of man's mind" (Hart 47). Stevens and Vela argue that García Márquez's

view of life, beyond the mythopoeic, is . . . that man is naturally a scientist. The wisdom of the people who live in Macondo is a composite of folk wisdom, hearsay, legend, superstition, and religion—all indiscriminately mixed. And yet [García] Márquez builds into the novel a clear sympathy for a certain quality of knowledge. We might think of this sympathy as an instinct for science. (265)[2]

Yet, though Melquíades and José Arcadio Buendía share with other scientists a "great wonder at the profound mystery of reality" (265), both men's scientific quests are fueled largely by alchemy rather than by modern science.[3] In other words, the worldview of Macondo is arguably one in which scientific facts are external and are the "unnatural and strange productions" for which Stephen Hart argues. Of course, even their quest for ancient scientific "truths" (such as the earth's roundness) *devalues* them in the eyes of the community, since, as Brian Conniff points out, all science seems alternately to mystify and to exploit the other inhabitants of Macondo. Úrsula is convinced that her husband "has lost what was left of his mind" when he dedicates himself to science (172).[4]

One Hundred Years of Solitude also foregrounds the dichotomy that has arisen between science and the humanities and the consequences of the rift between the two (Mosher 89). "José Arcadio Buendía and his neighbors suffer from other numerous failures and disillusions, all of which are linked to science and technology" (90), though "Macondo's ills are not due exclusively to science and technology but rather to a disequilibrium between scientific and humanistic thought" (91). Melquíades, though equally exposed to the sciences, does not illustrate tendencies toward aggression like other characters because he "is an archetype of harmony, one who demonstrates the possibility of reducing, and perhaps even eliminating, the barriers between scientific reasoning and literary artistry" (91).

Melquíades's most meaningful association is with alchemy, a scientific mode that will help (or attempt to help) heal the rift between spirituality and science in *One Hundred Years of Solitude*. R. W. Morrison argues, "The challenge of literature in an age of science and technology is to weave these activities into the tapestry of life as effectively as García Márquez incorporates them into the life of the people of Macondo" (124). García Márquez's "way of seeing things is compatible with both myth and science, but it is neither thing in itself. It has the analytical curiosity of science coupled with the synthetic method of myth" (Stevens and Vela 266). Yet the science García Márquez weaves into *One Hundred Years of Solitude*'s fabric is alchemy, while the "age" of modern or advanced technology stands outside of and is invasive in the magical realist world of the text. Although Melquíades and other characters do attempt to mend the rupture between science and humanity, their attempts rely on the roots (not on the progression) of science, since "[t]he novel's 'apocalyptic closure' is a denial of progress, as conceived by either the scientist or the politician" (Conniff 173). Though Edwin Williamson feels that such pessimistic readings "appear to condemn Latin America to a hopeless condition of historical failure, allowing no scope for change or free human action" (63), García Márquez's own use of literary alchemy redeems, if not this Macondon cycle, then perhaps the next. And García Márquez's own mention of Big Mama's funeral (75) reminds us that there will be a "next time" for Macondo; the experiment will be retried.

ONE HUNDRED YEARS OF SCIENCE

In *One Hundred Years of Solitude*, Gabriel García Márquez creates a world where truth and fiction are equally strange. Macondo is a realm where reality and the supernatural live side by side; from its very inception, the town seems born of paradox. More importantly, the entire balance of Macondo and its inhabitants— particularly the founding Buendía family—hangs upon the fate of magic and its relationship to realism. Magical realism is more than a way of life for Macondons; it *is* the life of the town. Should reality get out of hand, should the outside overwhelm the solitude of the town and the equilibrium between the supernatural and the "real" world, Macondo's inhabitants would not survive the fall. By refiguring science as incomprehensible and magic as comprehensible, García Márquez also sets the stage within *One Hundred Years of Solitude* for a science that is, like magical realism, at once fact and fiction. Alchemy plays a significant role in the novel because García Márquez's own literary alchemy uses the science as a metaphor for the magical realism in the text. More important, it becomes the driving force for *One Hundred Years of Solitude*'s magical realist world; alchemy reconciles the novel's "magical realism as a narrative style with the actual movement of the actions in the novel" (Williamson 46).

Macondo is "advancing in the opposite direction" from almost everything—the town reverts to anarchy from order, to solitude from communality, to the supernatural from the natural, and to alchemy from modern science. By virtue of their roles in that reversion, magical realism and alchemy have much in common within the context of *One Hundred Years of Solitude*. Just as magical realism relies on the juxtaposition of two "realities"—the supernatural and the everyday—so too does alchemy rely on a dichotomy, that is, on its simultaneous physical and spiritual goals. Although alchemy conjures up visions of the ragged scholar locked in his dungeon-like laboratory, doggedly pursuing the transmutation of gold from the base metals—a stereotypical perception that García Márquez intentionally and more than willingly exploits—this typecasting seriously distorts the metaphysical motives behind this ancient science. By referencing alchemy within *One Hundred Years of Solitude*, García Márquez reinforces the two levels of his text, with the ultimate goal of creating a world where Macondo's spiritual and magical demise brings about its physical downfall.[5]

The everyday quality of magical realism can be compared to the physical aspirations of alchemy, as can their respective supernatural and spiritual goals. In other words, both depend on the earthly as well as the "other-worldly." Also, to understand either one, we must accept its duality. Just as alchemy, at its most significant, is at once a spiritual and earthly voyage, magical realism relies on two planes of existence at exactly the same moment. To ignore the "real" in favor of the supernatural or vice versa is to skew magical realism in the direction of such modes as the fantastic or surreal.[6] The magical realist writer, then, is an alchemist of words; he or she metamorphoses both the everyday and the supernatural until they meet on common ground. García Márquez seeks both the real and the supernatural for *One Hundred Years of Solitude*, just as the true alchemist pursues both a spiritual and a physical height. While supernatural occurrences are frequent in *One Hundred Years of Solitude*, they rarely cause heads to turn. On the other hand, the realistic aspects of life in Macondo seem exotic. For example, in the house of the Buendías, the living are as much ghosts as the dead. Úrsula haunts the house far past her prime or her ability to effect any changes in her home. Fernanda ultimately finds herself living with "three living ghosts—Colonel Aureliano Buendía, Úrsula, and Amaranta" (263). Thus, García Márquez makes into the outlandish or strange what his reader generally accepts as "reality." Reality is by comparison so brutal, and the cruelty of the world (as evidenced in part by the Banana Company massacre) so hard to accept, that levitation or flying, ghosts and spirits seem comprehensible and genuine. The "real" atrocities add a new level of verisimilitude to magical realist fiction,[7] and the brutal interruption of reality in the text softens the effect of the magical or supernatural, even when the dead Prudencio Aguilar is attempting murder or when José Arcadio's blood seeks out his mother at his death.[8] Were García Márquez to make the invasion of the outside world, and science in particular, *less* radical for the characters in his novel, he would undermine his own attempt to create a supernatural that looks so very commonplace.

Alchemy reinforces the sense of a magically real world, stressing that what we know as science, Macondons believe to be magic, and vice versa. As resident but worldly alchemist, Melquíades brings the outside (specifically, modern science) to the attention of Macondo *not* in order to clarify things but rather to mystify. But Melquíades is not alone in his "revision" of reality in Macondo. The book begins with the "discovery" of ice and José Arcadio Buendía's willingness to spend his few pesos so that his sons can experience it. The son who will later be unable to see anything but ruin in Melquíades's room, Colonel Aureliano Buendía, feels the ice and declares it to be hot. His misreading of reality seems both fitting—as a translation of the outside world into the magical one of Macondo—and portentous of his own inability to "handle" the supernatural aspects of his world. Similar "magic" includes the magnifying glass, the daguerreotype (an invention that leaves José Arcadio Buendía "mute with stupefaction" [51]), and the magnets, which Melquíades identifies as the "eighth wonder of the learned alchemists of Macedonia" (2). The inhabitants of Macondo attempt to reconfigure the outside world into something magical as it invades the interior of the text and the town. As long as these attempts work, the town will survive the onslaught of reality. When, however, the outside becomes too powerful, when it invades Macondo and cannot be driven or explained away, then Macondo is doomed.

Thus, *One Hundred Years of Solitude* makes no attempts to codify the magical; rather, in Macondo, it is reality that must be rationalized. Furthermore, something about Macondo itself suggests that it alone is home to magical realism. For example, *when* the wise Catalonian—who is himself "linked with alchemy through a mention of Arnaldo of Villanova, the famed medieval Catalan scholar and alchemist" (McNerney and Martin 110), about whom he knows the intimate detail of his impotence from a scorpion bite (405)—refutes magical realism is perhaps more significant than *that* he shuns it. The wise Catalonian does indeed "[condemn] the effects of magical realism: the fascination with the past, the escape from history into memory, the longing to recover a pristine innocence, and the surrender to mindless erotic desire" (Williamson 60). But he does so *only* after he returns to his homeland:

> Upset by two nostalgias facing each other like two mirrors, he lost his *marvelous sense of unreality* and he ended up recommending to all of them that they leave Macondo, that they forget everything he taught them about the world and the human heart, that they shit on Horace, and that wherever they might be they always remember that the past was a lie, that memory has no return, that every spring gone by could never be recovered, and that the wildest and most tenacious love was an ephemeral truth in the end. (408; emphasis added)

Only after he leaves Macondo does he lose "his customary good humor"; we learn that "his memory began to grown sad" and that, "although he himself did not seem to notice it, those letters of recuperation and stimulation [that he sends back to the Buendías] were slowly changing into pastoral letters of disenchantment" (407–8). The official-looking letter that Aureliano refuses to open near the end of the novel seems to bear the news that reality in fact gets the better of the Catalonian once he is outside the confines of Macondo.

Reality and unreality are equally important aspects of García Márquez's vision of *One Hundred Years of Solitude*. For example, when José Arcadio Buendía finds his "immediate reality . . . to be more fantastic than the vast universe of his imagination, he [loses] all interest in the alchemist's laboratory" (39). This is especially significant when we recall that, earlier, José Arcadio Buendía's imagination is described as "unbridled" and as one that "always went beyond the genius of nature and even beyond miracles and magic" (2). Thus, José Arcadio Buendía's immediate reality is neither natural nor magical—it is beyond that, or at least at this point, both at once. Later in the novel, however, he has "lost all contact with reality" (109). Apparently, the balance of the magical and the real is a necessity in Macondo. To do without reality is to go insane, as José Arcadio Buendía proves; Colonel Aureliano Buendía loses touch with that reality during the war ("Little by little, however, and as the war became more intense and widespread, his image was fading away into a universe of unreality" [165]), but pulls himself out of that unreal world by turning his back on the war entirely and, at the same time, by accepting reality with a passionless embrace that distances him from it. In the last of the war's supernatural effects on him, his coldness becomes a physical as well as mental affliction. His final solitude proves that to forego the supernatural is no less dangerous in Macondo than is José Arcadio Buendía's loss of reality. He is, notably, the only family member who sees the decay of Melquíades's room—the singular symbol of the Buendías' immersion in their magical realist world. The reclusive Colonel Aureliano is so out of sympathy with the delicate balance between magic and reality in the Buendía household that he urinates in the courtyard without knowing he is splattering his father's ghost's shoes (269). His faults, at least for his mother, are summed up by her discovery that Aureliano "had never loved anyone" and "was simply a man incapable of love" (254).

The colonel's insensibility illustrates the most significant connection between alchemy and magical realism in *One Hundred Years of Solitude*: the attitude of characters in relation to the two phenomena. Consider the inventions that the townspeople (and José Arcadio Buendía in particular) interpret as magical, or the fact that the cinema angers the inhabitants of Macondo because of the "fraud" of the actors who die in one film and are "resurrected" to star in the next one. Cinema is "a machine of illusion" in Macondo (230). On the other hand, the residents find the notion that they could come to rely on hand-written signs to remember the names of everyday items during an insomnia plague perfectly acceptable. Similarly, José Arcadio Buendía gives up alchemy because Melquíades's "elixir of life" is actually a set of dentures; ice and magnets, on the other hand, are sources of great wonder. Science is magical in José Arcadio Buendía's eyes, while alchemy can be explained away. Not only does such a view of science reinforce the magical realism of this text; it also demonstrates that science, or at least science interpreted through the lens of alchemy, can be equally magical.

Origins of *Al-kimiya*

The fount of science as we know it today, alchemy has been practiced at least since the time of Christ, and quite possibly since prehistoric times (Burckhardt 11). Alchemy's origins trace back to ancient Egypt[9]; indeed, the Arabic term *al-kimiya* originally meant "the art of the land of Khem." Titus Burckhardt explains that the Arabic *kême* or *khem* refers "to the 'black earth,' which was a designation of Egypt and which may also have been a symbol of the alchemists' *materia prima*" (16).[10] *Materia prima* is the underlying fundamental substance of alchemy. Alchemists assume that within this substance lie secret powers capable of working miracles; alchemical texts may also refer to the *materia prima* as the sea, the seed of things, a virgin, "the hidden stone," an ore deposit, or a flowering tree. Carl Jung believed *materia prima* to be a psychological rather than chemical phenomenon (*Alchemical Studies* 205), but whether taken in the physical or the spiritual sense, this "primary matter" symbolizes the starting place, the illusive first material from whence springs the entire alchemical pursuit of the philosopher's stone (Burckhardt 18). *One Hundred Years of Solitude* emphasizes much the same beginning for Macondo, where José Arcadio Buendía raises the first dwellings in the city out of the earth he discovers.

If the *materia prima* serves as the root of the alchemical process, then the philosopher's stone can be considered the end or product. "The philosopher's stone (with which one can turn base metals into gold) grants long life and freedom from disease to the one who possesses it, and in its power brings more gold and silver than all the mightiest conquerors have between them" (Burckhardt 29). In its literal sense, this stone is a physical object that alchemists attempted to synthesize in their labs, using mercury and sulfur. On the other hand, the stone also represented true spiritual transmutation, the act of making the soul "golden." Gold "corresponds to the sound and original condition of the soul which freely and without distortion reflects the Divine Spirit" (72). The stone itself was indicated in the alchemists' texts in many ways. For example, "the stone that the biblical Jacob used as a pillow, and upon which he poured oil, was an accepted symbol for the Philosopher's Stone" (Powell 70). The stone could also be depicted as a peacock, because the colors in a peacock's tail supposedly appeared during the final stage of formation.

Just as the *materia prima* and philosopher's stone can be represented with word or pictures, so too can all the alchemical processes. Because the representations of the process were encoded in this pictorial language, "an additional barrier [to understanding the texts] was erected in the shape of an extensive structure of pictorial symbolism and allegorical expression" (Glidewell 38). A unique example of this is *The Wordless Book*, a collection of 15 engraved plates that gives the alchemical process in its entirety using symbols and drawings of the alchemists at work (Powell 70).

Reading the works of the alchemists is rather like stumbling upon some bizarre recipe.[11] The alchemist steeped his science in poetic language or symbolism not for the sake of the figurative language itself but rather to fool the foolish. "Gold, for example, was represented at one time or another, in more than sixty different ways" (Glidewell 38). Such obscuring of the meaning behind alchemy was an intentional stumbling block to the "puffers," or those who sought out alchemy only to obtain gold (Powell 19). Therefore, the stereotypes by which the alchemists were judged and labeled were actually nurtured by the alchemists themselves. Synesios, who most likely lived in the fourth century A.D., wrote, "[A]re you so simple as to believe that we would clearly and openly teach the greatest and most important of all secrets, with the result that you would take us literally?" (qtd. in Burckhardt 28). Many puffers, of course, did just that; they pursued the physical reality of transmutating gold. Those "who sought only worldly goals failed because alchemical success necessarily requires success within the soul" (Powell 19). The adepts, or authentic alchemists, ranked the microcosm *above* the goals of the macrocosm, that is, they placed greater emphasis on transmutating the soul than they did on personal, worldly gain.[12]

LITERARY ALCHEMY AND *ONE HUNDRED YEARS OF SOLITUDE*

> We, the inventors of tales, who will believe anything, feel entitled to believe that it is not yet too late to engage in the creation of . . . a new and sweeping utopia of life, where no one will be able to decide for others how they die, where love will prove true and happiness be possible, and where the races condemned to one hundred years of solitude, will have, at last and forever, a second opportunity on earth.
>
> —García Márquez[13]

The Alchemists

Alchemy's rich symbolism makes ripe pickings for García Márquez, who explores much of the lore and symbolism to its fullest through his characters. Among the many alchemists García Márquez creates in *One Hundred Years of Solitude*, Melquíades stands out. Melquíades is actually the "father" of alchemy to Macondo, the first to introduce it to the town. He and his alchemy arrive on the first page, on the heels of the Buendía family, so that Macondo exists only for a very short time without alchemy. His indelible mark on Macondo is ensured by what he leaves behind him:

> The rudimentary laboratory—in addition to a profusion of pots, funnels, retorts, filters, and sieves—was made up of a primitive water pipe, a glass beaker with a long, thin neck, a reproduction of the philosopher's egg, and a still the gypsies themselves had built in accordance with modern descriptions of the three-armed alembic of Mary the Jew. Along with those items, Melquíades left samples of the seven metals that corresponded to the seven planets, the formulas of Moses and Zosimus for doubling the quantity of gold, and a set of notes and sketches concerning the processes of the Great Teaching that would permit *those who could interpret them* to undertake the manufacture of the philosopher's stone. (7; emphasis added)

It is no accident that García Márquez places such emphasis on the fact that Melquíades gives José Arcadio Buendía "a gift that was to have a profound influence on the future of the village: the laboratory of an alchemist" (5), since, "[l]ike so many pivotal events in the story, the ending takes place in the laboratory" (McNerney and Martin 111).

The future of Macondo is interconnected with the alchemical experiments of the Buendías in much the same way that it relies on the balance of the magical and the real. The home of alchemy in the text—Melquíades's room—is also residence for, or connected with, many of the magical realist events that occur in the novel. The contents of this room are the tools of alchemy, certainly, but the passage also hints at their importance in the final outcome of the Buendías—many of whom will spend the next hundred years attempting to duplicate Melquíades's apparent successes. But "[t]he Buendías experience the solitude of alchemy without achieving its goals; rather than escaping from the tyranny of time, they become its victims, locked in its inexorable repetitive process, until the deciphering of the parchments brings the family chronicle to an end" (McNerney and Martin 111). In other words, Melquíades leaves not only the rudiments for the study of alchemy but also the foundations for the evolution, decay, and ultimate destruction of the family, since the last Aureliano, "who could interpret" the Great Teachings, also deciphers Melquíades's notes on the family history, albeit too late to change the course of that history.

As if to emphasize Melquíades's paternal role in the alchemy of Macondo, García Márquez associates him with numerous alchemical symbols. For example, the hat continuously perched on Melquíades's head looks "like a raven with widespread wings" (6). According to Kathleen McNerney and John Martin, "In alchemical texts, the raven's wing signifies the purification of the alchemist's soul" (106). Moreover, when lead, the most base of all metals, is blackened, the process is "represented by a raven" (Burckhardt 185). This blackening corresponds to the first stage of the alchemical process, while Melquíades, who is represented by black throughout the text, is responsible for first establishing alchemy in Macondo. García Márquez also refers to the ancient alchemist's hands as sparrow-like. Because the sparrow is often associated with Venus (copper), Melquíades symbolizes both beginning and (near) end of the alchemical procedure. That Melquíades is associated with two such alchemically significant birds within the novel seems to indicate that he himself will be responsible for or active in various stages of the history of alchemy in Macondo. Obviously, Melquíades represents more than the father of alchemy to the town; he becomes a *feature* of alchemy's (and therefore, the town's) settlement.

Melquíades's growth from his "leaden" origins surpasses his association with copper. He enjoys two of the legendary benefits of possessing the philosopher's stone—immortality and the ability to cure diseases.[14] After the insomnia plague strikes Macondo, Melquíades's potion saves the entire town from a life without sleep or memory. At the time of his death, Melquíades tells José Arcadio Buendía to burn mercury for 72 hours after he dies. When José Arcadio Buendía questions him he says only, "I have found immortality" (74). In a novel where ghosts are clearly marked as such—consider, for example, Prudencio Aguilar's haunting of José Arcadio Buendía and Úrsula—Melquíades seems more alive than any of the apparently *living* inhabitants of the Buendía home. If Melquíades has indeed successfully reproduced the stone for himself, he ranks as an adept and functions as a symbol of alchemical success in the novel.

Melquíades's influence over the Buendías produces a long line of alchemists; the patriarch of the family, José Arcadio Buendía, is Melquíades's first student. Initially, José Arcadio Buendía seems to have great potential as an alchemist. He certainly begins with a sincere desire to learn the secrets of the science. He willingly devotes hours to working with Melquíades in the lab, where "with shouts [they] interpreted the predications of Nostradamus amidst a noise of flasks and trays and the disaster of spilled acids and silver bromide" (51)—to the point that he ignores and excludes his family. But José Arcadio Buendía does not dedicate himself to alchemy *or* to his spiritual transformation above all else; instead, he realizes that his family is more important to him, as is monetary gain. When Úrsula returns from her search for José Arcadio, José Arcadio Buendía and the reader both discover his true passion,

for during his prolonged imprisonment [in the laboratory] as he manipulated the material, he begged in the depth of his heart that the longed-for miracle should not be the discovery of the philosopher's stone, or the freeing of the breath that makes metals live, or the faculty to convert the hinges and the locks of the house into gold, but what had just happened: Úrsula's return. (36)

His neglect of those miracles he supposedly seeks in his lab condemns his entire family, while at the same time it implicates them in his ultimate failure. José Arcadio Buendía's intentions for the magnets Melquíades introduces as alchemical wonders, that is, to extract gold from the bowels of the earth, symbolize the puffer in action. He "seeks practical ends through the methodical exploitation of a nature of which he considers himself no integral part" (Merrell 60). His greed digs up nothing more than a copper locket, perhaps most significant because of copper's close but inferior association with gold, inside "a suit of fifteenth-century armor which had all of its pieces soldered together with rust" (2). Conniff notes, "Searching for gold, José Arcadio finds the remains of Spanish imperialism" (170).[15] Thus, in spite of his potential, José Arcadio Buendía maintains his materialistic world-vision (Merrell 63) and does not credit alchemy's higher purposes, nor does he dedicate himself to his science. Instead, he oscillates between alchemy and his many other pursuits.

José Arcadio Buendía's bout with insanity seems more in keeping with the typical image of an alchemist driven to madness by his search (or, as is medically more likely, by mercury fumes). When he destroys the laboratory, he appears to have reached another plane of thought. His new consciousness (proven to be a remarkably lucid state of mind, once Father Nicanor discovers he is speaking Latin) cannot be confused with mastery of alchemy, though, because, in his attempts to destroy the alchemy lab, he denies himself the success of the adept. José Arcadio Buendía—as if to contradict his own potential—intends to destroy the physical tools of alchemy. Without the physical means for the pursuit of alchemy, he can never achieve the science's spiritual end.

Perhaps José Arcadio Buendía's lost sense of time offers the most telling bit of evidence that he has failed as an alchemist. "Today is Monday, too," he says, because his days refuse to look distinct from their predecessors (80). The seven metals of alchemy each correspond to a day of the week. Monday corresponds to silver, the "little work" of alchemy when compared to the "great work," that is, the progression from silver to gold (Glidewell 28). José Arcadio Buendía is stuck on "Monday," or in the "little work," and is therefore unable to reach the higher spiritual plane. Silver, the closest to gold of the silver-colored metals, is still one of the lesser works; perhaps this final challenge—the journey back from the depths of his own soul—is beyond José Arcadio Buendía's reach.

While José Arcadio Buendía is distracted from his alchemy by many other interests and desires, his son Aureliano can only be tempted away from the alchemy lab by two things: war and women. When Aureliano is engaged with either, his work in alchemy suffers. Conversely, removed from the temptations of women and warfare, he returns to the one comfort he seems to have. Paradoxically, when Aureliano is a young man, José Arcadio Buendía actually attempts to divert his son's interest away from the laboratory by offering him "money to spend on a woman, but Aureliano spends it on muriatic acid to make aqua regia, a key substance in alchemical research" (McNerney and Martin 107). Thus, even at a young age, Aureliano seems to realize that the laboratory will prove a balm more lasting (if not more healing) than his relationships with women. After Remedios dies, he experiences "a dull feeling of rage that gradually dissolved in a solitary and passive frustration similar to the one he had felt during the time when he was resigned to living without a woman. He plunged into his work again" (98). Aureliano's productive periods in the lab coincide with the times he is not involved with either of his other pursuits. Yet Aureliano does not have his father's passion for the work, even if he has the patience José Arcadio Buendía lacked. The gold fish he fashions, melts down, and then recreates in his old age seem to connect Aureliano symbolically to the quest for the philosopher's stone, since "[t]he fish is a most common symbol for Christ, who is in turn frequently used in alchemical texts as a symbol of the philosopher's stone" (McNerney and Martin 107–8). But the Colonel's intricate trinkets are not products of transmutation, and he realizes none of the benefits of alchemy. His tin pail—and not the golden charms it contains—perhaps best represents his inabilities, for he too is held by the lesser works that seem to have plagued his father. Aureliano's name,[16] in the context of alchemy, is ironic rather than prophetic.

When Aureliano dies, other Buendías reopen Melquíades's lab; most of them quickly lose interest. Aureliano Segundo, for one, becomes too lazy. The work that once required his full attention can no longer hold him. Like his namesake, he is distracted by other things—most notably, by Petra Cotes. The two exploit their sexual alchemy, but their animal husbandry, like their affair, has purely physical goals and ultimately burns out. Only Aureliano Segundo's brother, José Arcadio Segundo, comes as close as their great-grandfather to reaching adeptness.

Of José Arcadio Buendía's descendants, José Arcadio Segundo shows the most promise as an alchemist. He is the only Buendía, in fact, to make Melquíades's lab his permanent residence. The sole survivor of the Banana Company massacre,[17] he seeks solace in his work. When soldiers search for him, one looks directly at him from the doorway of the laboratory and yet declares, "It's obvious that no one has been in that room for at least a hundred years." The lab provide a sanctuary for José Arcadio Segundo: "In Melquíades' room, . . . protected by the supernatural light, by the sound of the rain, by the feeling of being invisible, he found the repose that he had not had for one single instant during his previous life" (318). According to Scott Sands, the "alchemists work in solitude because they need to be away from impurity and corruption" (25). The importance of this statement is not lost on a text entitled *One Hundred Years of Solitude*, in which the Buendías—from José Arcadio Buendía to the last Aureliano—seek out solitude in a town that attempts to shut itself off from the outside (and potentially corrupt) world. Solitude and being an alchemist necessarily go hand in hand in *One Hundred Years of Solitude*.[18] Consider, for example, how Aureliano awakens out of his solitude when he meets Remedios or how Úrsula's disappearance has a similar effect on José Arcadio Buendía; conversely, José Arcadio Segundo loses himself in the solitude of Melquíades's laboratory as a deliberate response to the "impurity and corruption" of the Banana Company.

As he does for Melquíades, García Márquez describes José Arcadio Segundo through a series of alchemical references. For example, Aureliano Segundo and Santa Sofía de la Piedad note that José Arcadio Segundo has "Arab eyes" (317), associating him with the oldest students of alchemy.[19] The assessment that José Arcadio Segundo's eyes are Arab accompanies his family's fear that he is suffering the "irreparable fate of his great-grandfather" (319). José Arcadio Segundo does not suffer from the insanity that seems to plague José Arcadio Buendía, but both are equally lost to the world. García Márquez does not document any actual experiments in alchemy that José Arcadio Segundo performs, but he does inform us that he "dedicated himself to peruse the manuscripts of Melquíades many times" (318). While we never see the exact content of any of those papers, he seems to be studying both the earlier manuscripts, that is, the transcribed works of the alchemists that Melquíades left for José Arcadio Buendía and the parchments that predict the Buendía family's future. José Arcadio Segundo's devotion is less crazy than it is wholehearted. His reality is "as unreachable and solitary as that of his great-grandfather," but he has no other interest or woman to distract him.

Like his great-grandfather, José Arcadio Segundo does not qualify as an adept. When we see him after the three-year period of rain, he is a massive, green tangle of hair. Green, the color associated with copper or lead (Pachter 263), simultaneously ties José Arcadio Segundo both to the metal closest to gold (in color and in its stage's proximity to gold) and to a base metal—repeating the pattern of association linked with Melquíades through the bird symbolism. José Arcadio Segundo has come close in his quest as an alchemist, as did José Arcadio Buendía, but still does not transmutate the base metal lead into gold, perhaps because he is tainted by the base and vile acts to which he is sole witness. Indeed, the corrupt state of the world is what first drives José Arcadio Segundo into the arms not just of solitude but of alchemy as well. Paradoxically, in spite of his apparently addled state of mind, he is "the most lucid inhabitant of the house" as Aureliano Babilonia is growing up (355).

Aureliano Babilonia deserves mention among the Buendía alchemists because he takes to heart the teachings of Melquíades's manuscripts and holes himself up in the lab, at least for a short time. That Aureliano reaches "adolescence without knowing a thing about his own time but with the basic knowledge of a medieval man" (361) suggests that he would also be conversant in and a student of alchemy. Furthermore, he alone translates the parchments that prophesy his translation of them. Aureliano is the one for whom the untranslated materials Melquíades leaves are intended. Finally, like many before him, including José Arcadio Buendía and José Arcadio Segundo, Aureliano becomes a pupil of Melquíades, whose appearances in the lab provide him with conversation and encouragement. Ultimately, though (and like Colonel Aureliano and the patriarch, José Arcadio Buendía), Aureliano's alchemy is undone by his passion for a woman; his desire for Amaranta Úrsula will tempt him away from his work until the very end of the novel. He is the last in a long line of Buendía men who, for one reason or another, never fully experience complete and total immersion in alchemy. Although he is unique among the Buendías before him in that he has the ability to learn the secrets of the adepts, Aureliano Babilonia lacks the time to fulfill his potential. The Buendías' one hundred years are up.

Macondo as Macrocosm

To consider this novel a macrocosmic alchemy in and of itself, we would need to be able to see the methodology of the science at work within the text itself, and, indeed, García Márquez creates a text in which the literal and fictional worlds are coordinated into one such process. Just as characters in *One Hundred Years of Solitude* attempt transmutations on both the physical and the spiritual planes, García Márquez attempts a dual-level alchemy of his own with the town (and the novel) he creates. The relationship among Úrsula and José Arcadio Buendía, their family, and the town itself becomes an alchemical process—an attempt to produce "gold" out of the marriage of Sulfur and Mercury. By intentionally disrupting the balance between reality and the supernatural, García Márquez ensures that the marriage will result in the destruction of everything the Buendía line first promises to yield. No one and nothing—save the town that García Márquez's later literary alchemy will resurrect—survives this experiment.

The creation and destruction of the Buendía line in Macondo can be considered García Márquez's attempt at one "run-through" of the alchemical process. In this macrocosmic vision of *One Hundred Years of Solitude*, the characters must be the ingredients or "elements." When this town reappears later—during the time of Big Mama's funeral "a century later" (75) —we can assume that new characters (materials) are necessary in order for the cycle to begin again. Alchemists relied on similar repetition in their work to remove impurities—just as many modern chemists repeat their experiments for the same reason. Macondo's impurities—perhaps most evident in the blatantly incestuous Buendía strain—are being filtered out.[20]

Within this particular one hundred years, Macondo and its inhabitants share a noticeably symbolic relationship with alchemy, and several of the characters can be associated with the materials that are important to alchemy. Melquíades can be considered the *materia prima* of alchemy in the text; he does, after all, set the cycle into motion within the town and the novel, and, through frequent association with the color black, also represents the first stage of the alchemical process (Glidewell 28). The many Aurelianos, with gold in their names, are perhaps the most obvious. Yet José Arcadio Buendía, Úrsula, and their entire line of descendants provide more interesting, and more significant, connections with the materials.

Before alchemy can be undertaken, production of the *materia prima* is required, and for that process the alchemist needed sulfur and mercury.[21] More to the point, Melquíades actually requires José Arcadio Buendía and Úrsula in order to set into motion both their line of descendants and his work. Without them, Macondo has no need of his miracles, prophecies, or manuscripts. As the parents of the Macondon strain of Buendías, José Arcadio Buendía and Úrsula serve both Macondo and *One Hundred Years of Solitude* as the sulfur and mercury, respectively. Burckhardt explains that "the marriage of Sulphur and Quicksilver, Sun and Moon, King and Queen, is the central symbol of alchemy" (149). This marriage is vital to the process, and José Arcadio Buendía and Úrsula, through their perpetual roles in the text and through their offspring, provide the symbolic representation of mercury and sulfur. As the basis for their branch of the Buendías, they are perhaps also related to lead, the most base of all metals and the origin from which all transmutation must begin. Úrsula and José Arcadio Buendía become one of the most important aspects of the connection between *One Hundred Years of Solitude* and alchemy, and they set into motion the first of the six "stages" or generations of Buendías.

The alchemical process has six stages that rely on the metals important to alchemy;[22] while Úrsula and José Arcadio Buendía coincide with the first stage of the science, other stages provide interesting parallels with the six generations of Buendías in *One Hundred Years of Solitude*. For example, applying these six stages of alchemy to the Buendía family genealogy explains one of the most bizarre and confusing aspects of the novel: Remedios the Beauty's ascension. According to alchemy, the act of changing base lead into gold requires descent before the alchemist can ascend and reach perfection; the alchemist must journey to the deepest part of his or her own soul in order to purify it. Thus, the first three stages represent a movement downward, especially in the spiritual sense. Ironically, Remedios is born into the fourth of six generations of Buendías. In other words, her "stage" in the family history coincides with the stage of alchemy where metals and the soul begin their ascent toward gold. Her ascension, then, mirrors the progression of the macrocosmic journey of the novel toward some potential, ultimate perfection.

Unfortunately, the Buendías will never achieve the spiritual heights that Remedios's ascent anticipates. Although Gabriel García Márquez creates a nearly ideal setting in which more than one of the Macondons (and particularly the Buendías) could excel at alchemy or reach a "golden" state within the larger context of the novel, only Melquíades seems to find adeptness in the ancient science that he introduces to the town. Though the Buendías provide six generations of offspring, they grow multiplicatively rather than spiritually, proving that, in spite of the prowess Melquíades exhibits as an alchemist, he apparently cannot or does not share his philosopher's stone with his friends. From one Aureliano spring seventeen golden sons; on the surface, then, it looks as though Macondo fulfills the cycle of alchemy. Instead, it is a multiplication that goes nowhere, since only one son will even live into his twenties. When, in fact, children are born to the Buendías, they are almost without exception "tainted" by ancestors, as illustrated by the frequent and confusing repetition of common names of the progeny.[23]

Most significantly, the Buendía line ends just as it begins—with an incestuous couple and their "golden" offspring. "Gold" (Colonel Aureliano), then, is the first thing born in Macondo and, when the red ants carry off the newborn corpse, it is the last thing borne out of it. This final Aureliano, who appears to be "predisposed to begin the race again from the beginning" but who has "the tail of a pig" (417), is not the symbol of alchemical or familial success but rather is false gold. The cycle will grind to a halt for the gold-seeking Buendías. *One Hundred Years of Solitude* produces no more gold than it started with; any impurities are passed from generation to generation, culminating at the end of the novel, where the character Amaranta Úrsula carries out the two greatest fears of her namesakes: she has an affair with her nephew and her child is born with a pig's tail. The final line of the novel tells us "races condemned to one hundred years of solitude did not have a second opportunity on earth" (422). As we already know from earlier in the text, Melquíades has predicted a future Macondo *without* Buendías. To the extent that these characters serve as the "soul" of the text, their failure to make the final alchemical leap suggests that the macrocosmic alchemy of *One Hundred Years of Solitude* will fail as well. In Macondo, at least this time around, the alchemical process and all attempts to master it, fail.

The final generations of the Buendía family open a last ironic chapter in the alchemy of *One Hundred Years of Solitude* with Amaranta Úrsula and Aureliano Babilonia, who "commit incest without fully realizing the true nature of their kinship" (Williamson 51) and who signify both the diametric Adam and Eve and the next José Arcadio Buendía and Úrsula. "They saw themselves in the lost paradise of the deluge," "the paradise of misery" (414, 417). They are not the only humans on earth, but their solitude emphasizes that Macondo maintains its faithfulness to García Márquez's title in spite of outside intervention.

In that Macondo forgotten even by the birds, where the dust and the heat had become so strong that it was difficult to breathe, secluded by solitude and love and by the solitude of love in a house where it was almost impossible to sleep because of the noise of the red ants, Aureliano and Amaranta Úrsula were the only happy beings, and the most happy on the face of the earth. (409–10)

In flouting the failures of past generations, this Edenic state suggests that the incestuous couple has the power to reverse the apocalyptic spiral of *One Hundred Years of Solitude.* Amaranta Úrsula and Aureliano continue the sexual alchemy their ancestor, Aureliano Segundo, begins with Petra Cotes. Whereas Western alchemy typically accepts a rather chaste view of the science, the Eastern tradition required a type of sexual mastery of the body that ultimately led to the soul's transmutation into gold.[24] In a sense, then, Aureliano Babilonia and Amaranta Úrsula, (as *materia prima*) have even more promise of kindling the magical realist potential of the family line through the alchemy they practice in the bedroom. Moreover, unlike Aureliano Segundo and Petra Cotes, Amaranta Úrsula and Aureliano are driven by true love rather than by greed.

By treading on the very taboos that force José Arcadio Buendía and Úrsula to flee to Macondo one hundred years earlier, Amaranta Úrsula and Aureliano fall prey to the biological pitfalls of their union and falter as a result. Williamson argues that they fail because,

[l]ike magical realism, incest tends towards the fusion of differential categories, and as such constitutes a threat to social organization, since it weakens the vital distinction that underpins cultural order: the difference between self and other. In this sense, incest can be taken as a symbolic equivalent of the solipsism that underlies magical realism. For, when kinship differences are not properly marked, communication or constructive social intercourse are [*sic*] rendered ineffective. (47)

Though Williamson argues that science is José Arcadio Buendía's defense against the threat of incest, "since its basic concern to discover objective facts about the material world excludes by definition the introverted, solipsistic mental attitudes represented by incest" (48), in fact, "José Arcadio Buendía's search for scientific understanding is soon frustrated, not just because his mentor Melquíades is an alchemist whose knowledge is rooted in occultism and medieval learning, but chiefly and decisively because he chooses to abandon it and give way to Úrsula's priorities" (49). In spite of the fact that it is alchemy and not modern science that Melquíades introduces, the primary reason that the Buendía family line will find science no defense at all is because they consistently abuse it. At the end of the novel, the Buendía line cannot be saved because, like the patriarch, Aureliano Babilonia has chosen Amaranta Úrsula (and therefore, incest) over his scientific pursuits. "In the Buendía family tree, analogies and parallels override particular differences; the experiences of the various generations conform to stock patterns which repeat themselves with such regularity that the linear sequence of historical events appears to be distorted into cycles of time revolving around a still centre of eternity" (Williamson 52). As Úrsula says earlier in the novel, "I know all of this by heart. . . . It's as if time had turned around and we were back at the beginning" (199). Even apocalypse has "a strange air of eternal repetition" in *One Hundred Years of Solitude* (Conniff 168).[25]

Ultimately, though the Buendía family fails, García Márquez succeeds in his literary alchemy. He creates a world where the believable is unbelievable and where the odd barely causes a stir. Yet García Márquez is working a finer alchemy in *One Hundred Years of Solitude* than is first apparent. His characters, setting, and events frequently mimic the alchemical process itself, and his use of magical realism becomes a tool for his alchemical metaphors. Although the magical realist world cannot save Macondo's founding family—which is, in fact, doomed from the start, just as Melquíades's manuscripts predict—it does not destroy them, either. Magical realism suspends the fate of the Macondons by trapping them in a cyclical web from which they cannot escape. Macondo must, like the alchemists' experiments, be redone, tried again, refined. The one hundred years of solitude announce the failure of the Buendía family alone. Ironically, among the many paradoxes surrounding them on a daily basis, the Buendías suffer from their inability to cope with the juxtaposition of their solitude and the outside world that is so at odds with the world of magical realism in which they live. When the even mixture of magic and reality is tainted by too much reality from the outside world, war, death, and capitalism conspire to reduce Macondo's magic to smoke and its reality to ashes.

NOTES

1. Wishnia renames García Márquez's book *Lonely Century*, touting it as the story of the Gooddays, "A Family Trapped in Time!!!" and asking, "Can the Gooddays decipher [Melquíades's code] before it's too late?" (34).

2. Merrell cites the "mythopoeic" as one of the elements that make up García Márquez's poetic vision of things. "The village of Macondo is a microcosm and the one hundred years recounted in the novel is a compression of the whole history of man" (263).

3. Melquíades and José Arcadio Buendía do not, as Brian Conniff argues, "assume that science is essentially democratizing" (170); alchemy is certainly not a science of democratization, given its privileging not only of metals (the physical) but of spiritual states (the metaphysical).

4. "It is easy from the vantage point of a highly developed technological culture, to think of Melquíades and José Arcadio as being naive, having too many gaps in their learning to be true scientists. There are loose ends in their knowledge which make them seem provincial. Should we judge them thus, however, we would betray only our own provinciality, for all science has loose ends" (Stevens and Vela 265–66).

5. If magical realism and alchemy share much in common as tools of the fictional inventiveness of García Márquez's *One Hundred Years of Solitude*, though, they evoke even more comparisons within the fictive domain of the novel itself: Melquíades will be responsible for introducing both to the town; both will fail in Macondo; neither will survive (or save the town from) exterior influences.

6. For more on the distinction between magical realism and other literary modes that deal with the supernatural, see Chapter 1 and its discussion of Amaryll Chanady's *Magical Realism and the Fantastic: Resolved Versus Unresolved Antinomy* (NY: Garland, 1985).

7. And, Brian Conniff argues that because these people are "so improbable, and so real . . . a 'resource' like 'magical realism' is needed to depict them" (178).

8. In this respect, we can compare García Márquez and Toni Morrison (see Chapter 5 for more on Morrison's take on brutal reality).

9. Kathleen McNerney's and John Martin's assertion that "the roots of alchemy can be traced back to ancient India" is a claim not substantiated in their article and one directly refuted by the sources on alchemy cited here, though it would suggest a reason that "the manuscript be set down in that tongue [Sanskrit]" (110). Aníbal González's argument that Spanish has roots of its own in India, since "Sanskrit is, of course, the *Ursprache* [i.e., the origins for the linguistic genealogy] of Spanish" (73), as well as Melquíades's connection to India through his gypsy roots, are perhaps as convincing a reason for Melquíades's use of Sanskrit.

10. In this way, alchemy shares common bonds with the Hebrew term for Adam, which etymologically may be a wordplay on the word for "earth" (*The Interpreter's Dictionary of the Bible* 42). This is not the only bond *One Hundred Years of Solitude* establishes with Adam, since during the insomnia plague, José Arcadio Buendía functions as a modern-day Adam, who, "[i]n giving things names, . . . also gave them reality." García Márquez "seems to tell us that anything which may be forgotten by man may lose its existence and, perhaps, its *reality*" (Stevens and Vela 264)—a seemingly plausible possibility, given the Banana Company massacre's historical "nonexistence."

11. Melquíades's texts pose a similar challenge—although whether merely through encryption or allegory, only Aureliano knows.

12. "The physical transmutation of metals was a sign which manifested outwardly the inward holiness both of gold and of man—of the man, that is, who had completed the inward work" (Burckhardt 204).

13. From "The Solitude of Latin America," as quoted in Winn, 441. Although Richard Cardwell's translation of García Márquez's Nobel address is included in the references, Winn's version of this particular passage is the more striking translation.

14. Paracelsus, the legendary alchemist, was reputed to have been seen several times after his death in 1541 and declared that "only ignoramuses allege that Nature has not provided a remedy against every disease" (qtd. in Pachter 14).

15. Ironically, the Spanish conquerors themselves might be considered puffers, in that their exploration of the New World was actually an attempt to exploit its gold.

16. The Latin word for gold is "aurum"; "oro" in Spanish.

17. Oddly enough, García Márquez describes the placebo given to the Banana Company workers as "the color of copper sulfate" (306), or royal blue. Alchemically, the color suggests the philosopher's stone, but because this is false medicine, it is also symbolic of false alchemy. The Banana Company does not offer a future to its workers; instead, it seals their tragic fates.

18. McNerney and Martin, who cite alchemy as "a prominent leitmotif" in the novel rather than a major force, nonetheless support the connection between solitude and alchemy when they argue that, although the science is "[i]mportant in its own right, alchemy is also inseparable from the two major themes of the narrative: time and solitude."

19. Perhaps García Márquez intends to reveal that José Arcadio Segundo has the soul of an alchemist, as revealed by his "windows" to the soul.

20. For more on incest and magical realism, see Edwin Williamson, "Magical Realism and the Theme of Incest in *One Hundred Years of Solitude*" (In *Gabriel García Márquez: New Readings*. Bernard McGuirk and Richard Cardwell, eds. Cambridge: Cambridge UP, 1987), a portion of which is discussed elsewhere.

21. Though Melquíades functions as Macondo's *materia prima*, García Márquez also associates him with mercury—in that his immortal state relies on it. His role as the master alchemist who introduces the science to Macondo, though, emphasizes his additional importance to the macrocosmic alchemy of *One Hundred Years of Solitude*. In a way, he uses mercury and sulfur, as represented by José Arcadio Buendía and Úrsula, as the origins of the process.

22. That is, lead, tin, iron, mercury, silver, and copper (Burckhardt 185–93). Gold is the end product rather than a means for transmutation and is therefore not associated with a stage of alchemy.

23. So that, for example, José Arcadio Buendía fathers José Arcadio, who begets Arcadio, who begets José Arcadio Segundo, who begets José Arcadio.

24. This fact is borne out by Chinese historians: "When we hear of alchemy, or read books about it we should always keep in mind that many of these books can also be read as books of sex" (Wolfram Eberhard, *A History of China*, qtd. in Jameson, "Third-World Literature" 87 n.8).

25. Conniff later adds, "For García Márquez, such an assertion of history's circularity is not merely a matter of philosophical speculation; it is a calculated attempt to make the outrages of oppression, ancient and recent, visible again; it is an attempt to make Colombian history credible" (177).

4

WHO'LL BUY THESE MAGIC BEANS?
THE NORTH AMERICAN MAGICAL
REALIST EXPERIENCE

To look over [Borges's] shoulder as he reads U.S. literature is to see a tradition of fantastic literature that U.S. readers will scarcely recognize, and to find the makings of magical realism everywhere.

—Lois Parkinson Zamora, *The Usable Past*

Until recently, magical realism has been such a geographically-bound commodity that it was difficult to imagine it in terms of literature outside Latin America, much less to apply the phrase in scholarly criticism of other literatures. While some, like Alejo Carpentier, have claimed "marvelous" or magical realism as a uniquely Latin American property, Borges insisted "upon the fantastic nature of U.S. literature in comparison to the more 'rhetorical' nature of Latin American literature. In the course of his discussion of Nathaniel Hawthorne, Borges reverses our usual sense of U.S. literature as less prone to myth and magic than Latin American literature" (Zamora, *Usable Past* 92). Although "Borges wrote this [1949 essay on Hawthorne] before the flowering of magical realism in Latin America" (93), his words anticipate the first challenges of magical realism's status as the "property" of any one area. In fact, the very features that distinguish magical realism as an historically situated mode—its postcolonial nature, its shared history with postmodernism —also keep it from conforming or from being "owned."

Magical realism, as Borges suggests, may have germinated in, rather than having been imported into, the United States. Lois Parkinson Zamora proposes that "nineteenth-century U.S. Romance is an early and local flowering of twentieth-century magical realism" (*Usable Past* 96). Her argument rests on evidence from Latin American writers. For example, "Borges' references to Emerson's

Transcendentalism [and] Coleridge's . . . Romanticism . . . suggest the confluent sources of his magical realism and tie it to the nineteenth-century U.S. romance tradition" (87). Although Borges may not actually be the magical realist Zamora claims him to be, as Chapter 2 demonstrates, his role as a father to the movement in Latin America can be asserted without dispute. Like Zamora, Wayne Ude argues that magical realism is the "contemporary incarnation" of the romance novel, that is, that "the traditional American romance-novel has developed into what we will call North American Magical Realism" ("Forging an American Style" 63, 50). Ude explains, "Increasingly over the past ten years we have found our models to the south, and very recently we've seen past those models to some of the North American models which South American writers, in turn, had earlier looked to" ("North American Magical Realism" 21). Both Zamora and Ude contend that the United States, by looking "to the south," is actually rediscovering its own influences on the Latin American magical realist tradition. But Ude's statement here is especially pertinent to *Rediscovering Magical Realism* for two reasons: first, because he corroborates Zamora's claims of magical realism's Romantic roots, and second, because he notes the existence of a strain of magical realism peculiar to North America. The second aspect of Ude's claim, as illustrated by the magical realist literature of Canada and the United States, will be discussed in more detail later in the chapter.

Those common influences on these two literary styles manifest themselves similarly in magical realism and the romance novel. According to Ude, Richard Chase's "definition of romance possesses some striking points of resemblance to [George] McMurray's definition of South American magical realism" ("North American Magical Realism" 25). For example, Chase's claim that romance signifies "an assumed freedom from the ordinary novelistic requirements of verisimilitude, development, and continuity" and "a willingness to abandon moral questions or to ignore the spectacle of men in society, or to consider these things only indirectly or abstractly" (qtd. in "North American Magical Realism" 25). As Vernon E. Lattin argues about one of the texts to be considered below, it creates "a new romanticism, with a reverence for the land, a transcendent optimism, and a sense of mythic wholeness" (637–38). In *The Usable Past*, Zamora expands on these similarities. She contends that both American Romanticism and magical realism reject "the rugged Cartesian individual" (87), that both exhibit a tendency to "archetypalize the self, to move away from the specific historical portrayal to historical existence as such" (78), and that "their shared project [is] the expansion and redefinition of our conceptions of subjectivity against the ideological limitations of Cartesian (and Freudian) consciousness, Hegelian historicism, and scientific rationalism" (96); elsewhere she notes that both movements were counterrealist in intent (118). According to Ude, "Romance was able to recognize[—]and techniques learned from romance, the Gothic novel, and the folktale were able to present[—]the possibility that wilderness existed not only as an external set of conditions but within characters as well, and so could not entirely be banished beyond a frontier" ("Forging an American Style" 54–55).[1] Ude thus hints that the frontier myth plays a part in the emergence of the North American strain of magical realism and extends the mode's family tree to include the Gothic and folklore traditions as well.

But if magical realism shares a resemblance to and birthright with early American—and especially American Romantic—traditions, it has even closer familial ties with postmodernism. The term postmodern "stands for a combination of those technically innovative qualities most highly regarded by contemporary critical movements such as poststructuralism" (D'haen 192). Several of these innovative postmodern features, including metafiction, eclecticism, multiplicity, discontinuity, and the erasure of boundaries, are the frequent tools of magical realists. The magical realists, like the postmodernists "[i]n their vision of an American culture in which history and the self are unavoidably mediated, if not produced, by mass culture, . . . treat the history of mass culture as the history of an epistemology" (Simmons 2). Victoria Nelson claims that the magical and fantastic in North America have been relegated to the mass culture and to mass culture forms (particularly movies) because of the conception that they have no place in high art (Spark 15). Indeed, the idea that the "popular" and "high" cultures are mutually exclusive has led to the "problems associated with the definition of the term 'popular' culture," where "such a category is used as a dumping ground for everything academic criticism has rejected or been slow to recognize as a legitimate object of analysis"; in turn, these issues reflect "the definitional limitations imposed by the parameters of elite culture only able to accommodate what official cultural arbiters consider beneficial" (David William Foster, "Popular Culture" 4).[2] Magical realism and postmodernism pose possible solutions to the antinomy between the elite and the popular, their reaction being "an aggressive mixing of 'high' and 'popular' cultural styles" (Simmons 2). Both the postmodern and magical realist texts address these definitional limitations in an attempt to reclaim the popular for high art, as well as to challenge the elitist notion of high culture itself.

In addition to the attributes that define and shape them, the labels "magical realism" and "postmodernism" also share in common a geographical heritage rooted in Latin America. Most scholars tend

to agree that the very term "postmodernism" originated in the 1930s in Latin America, with the critic Federico de Onis, and was reinvented or reused, covering different fields and carrying different meanings, throughout the 1940s and '50s both in Europe and the United States. . . . In the period in which "post-modernism" and "magic realism" gained their present meanings . . . their use was restricted, respectively, to North- and South-American prose developments. (D'haen 193)

While both literary modes developed in the Americas, their expansions into northern America have taken decidedly dissimilar routes.

Postmodernism itself, of course, no longer restricts its influence to the Americas. John Carlos Rowe, who calls postmodernism "a global phenomenon,"[3] says that the term signifies an abandonment of the traditional concerns of the novel to represent social reality, the complex relation between psychological and social experience, and the essential terms governing our "lived" realities. *Reality* and *realism* were attacked by the postmoderns as mystified terms. The moderns had attempted to criticize the conventions of everyday life, proper behavior, and thus the consensually established terms for reality; the postmoderns claimed to go beyond their modernist ancestors by abandoning reality altogether. (181)

Rowe's use of the phrase "everyday life" is particularly revealing in the context of magical realism, because, unlike the variations of postmodernism Rowe cites as examples,[4] magical realism never fully abandons those everyday objects and experiences that Amaryll Chanady claims to be so important to the perpetuation of the mode itself.

Still, Romanticism and postmodernism do share their counterrealism with magical realism. Romanticism created readers who were ready for something new, for authors and texts that would counter scientific reason. Postmodernism discarded our conventional definitions of reality and challenged the literary techniques constrained by that reality. Both paved the way for magical realism's journey north and, in doing so, prepared its readers for the "new" mode.

Magical Realism as a Commodity of "The American Dream"

As if magical realism's bonds with postmodernism and American Romanticism were not enough to ensure that magical realism could hold its own in North America, our shared history with Latin America and the changing face of the American reading public augmented its appeal. The United States shares with Latin America an historical commonality. The "conceptions of history in the U.S. and Latin America are not as radically different as is sometimes supposed."[5] Most of the nations of both American continents share a postcolonial/"New World" status, and native and colonial cultures have collided in both the United States and Latin America. "Difference," a buzz-word in definitions of Latin America, is no less a symbol of identity within the stereotypical melting pot of the United States.[6] Because of this shared postcolonial status, the Americas are reshaping and redefining our past and our present. Zamora argues, "During the course of the 19th century, writers throughout the Americas faced a common task: to recreate or create a national past and to use that past as a means to understand the present" ("Usable Past" 42). We have in common the challenges that historical self-definition poses for what is still, from Europe's perspective, the "New World"—over 500 years after Columbus set foot in the West Indies. Magical realism is a catalyst "for the development of new national and regional literatures" (Zamora and Faris 2), a development perhaps best understood by nations whose national literatures have only been written and studied for a relatively short time. For example, an historically young nation like the United States has an even younger literary tradition—one that was not even studied as such until the twentieth century. The Americas, in sharing a certain cultural indebtedness to the historical and literary traditions of

Europe, also have in common the goal of independence and distinction from those traditions. Writers and their critics use this past to distinguish and investigate what is particularly "American." Authors in the Americas "command Western culture without being dominated by it[, allowing them to] play freely, even irresponsibly, with literary and cultural traditions" (Prieto 318). But our literary revolutions mimic the martial revolutions that preceded them, and no fight comes without a cost.

For the Americas, and particularly for non-whites, the cost of freedom has been (and continues to be) dear. Frequently, civil unrest and political extremes and turmoil have helped to nourish a skepticism strangely at odds with the optimism of the American dream. Much of that unrest has been brought upon our "historical selves" by the arriving white Europeans who attempted to superimpose European culture onto the indigenous races they found in the Americas. To some extent, the subjugation of the natives in northern America was unusual in that it largely excluded indigenous peoples, pushing them ever westward, while Spaniards were greatly concerned with including or "civilizing" the natives. "Thus, unlike modern Mexico, [for example,] which is a mestizo culture resulting from imperial policies that included and assimilated indigenous cultures, modern U.S. culture is the product of a pluralist model that moved indigenous cultures to the margins, and then off the edge" (Zamora, *Usable Past* 111). Of course, some Native Americans, who lived in places such as East Texas and who were as settled as the Mayans or Aztecs, were conquered by Spaniards rather than by the predominantly British invaders of the United States and Canada. Even when most of the North American continent had been explored and conquered by the new arrivals, and even when space was at a premium, the attempt to "incorporate" Native Americans brought about reservations and mock assimilation, ritually presented to the indigenous peoples as their "chosen" course of action.[7] Both options, and particularly the establishment of reservations, proved exclusionary of the native cultures, disallowing the incorporation of the indigenous peoples' beliefs or practices into mainstream America. In fact, "[o]ne of the reasons behind herding North Americans onto reservations was the theory that such containment would make conversion easier" (Sanders 196 n.1).

European rule of the Americas also introduced marginalized groups in addition to creating them out of the people they found here. Slavery, though another extreme from indigenous people being pushed off their own land, initiated a new kind of unrest, one that would fan itself slowly and erupt into a conflict that cost both blacks and whites their lives. Significantly, although the Civil War is a prime example of such conflict, slavery was also practiced throughout the Caribbean and South America—areas that, like the United States, continue to experience the reverberations of internal strife. While the Civil War freed the marginalized African American, it could not revise their status in the eyes of the white South. The Civil War also created new margins in its wake. For example, Carlos Fuentes argues that Faulkner and writers of the U.S. South share "with Latin America the historical experience of colonial exploitation and political failure" (Zamora,

"Usable Past" 14). Zamora explains that the well-known Gabriel García Márquez's own literary

debt to Faulkner and to the writers of the U.S. South . . . is due, in part, to the parallel histories of Hispanic America and the Deep South: colonization and exploitation of land, feudal systems of land tenure with their accompanying aristocracies and enslaved or indentured people of color; the burden of defeat by invading armies from the North (Yankees/yanquis); belated and abrupt modernization that masked (and sometimes exacerbated) long histories of political, racial, and economic inequity; and the similar attitudes of Southern Protestants and Hispanic Catholics. (*Usable Past* 119)

In its role as "colonizer" of an unwilling region, the North assumed the role of the European exploiter, and the poorly carried out Reconstruction not only failed to advance African Americans within the Southern culture but also failed to resurrect the dignity of the defeated South.

The make-up of the New World, largely through the colonizers' own doing, is heterogeneous rather than homogenous. Of course, not all marginalized groups are brought to or made out of nations against their wills, as illustrated by the tremendous influx of Latino/a people into the United States. These new arrivals carry with them their traditions, whether historical, religious, or cultural; in addition, they transport their language and their literary legacies. As individual, marginalized groups, natives and immigrants create only slight tremors in the structure of the nations they call home. Still, together, they challenge ideas of national language and culture; out of their oppression and misfortunes spring the tools of change—multicultural and bilingual education, affirmative action, political correctness. In addition, the features of their literary conscience are slowly being woven together with the traditional strands of the majority.[8]

Just as the Americas are refining questions of "nation," they are also either forming or redefining questions of national identity. Many writers in the United States and Latin America "share the experience that [Fredric] Jameson describes of being torn between incompatible pasts and futures and . . . between contradictory conceptions of subjectivity. Traditional (mythical/archetypal) standards of selfhood based on similarity compete with modernity's standards of difference" (Zamora, *Usable Past* 119). Literary modes like magical realism play an important role in the reviewing and revision of our "selves." Magical realism causes "political and cultural disruption," resulting in cultural corrections and forcing readers to reconsider reality as they know it (Zamora and Faris 2). Such disruption, with its antibureaucratic stance, is beneficial to marginalized groups. Through modes like magical realism, the margins can provide a "biting criticism of the vanity of Western civilization and an understanding of cultural relativity" (Young and Hollaman 3); literature is the means by which assimilation of different influences is reflected. Because assimilation can sometimes mean the loss of culture, narrative modes like magical realism constitute a reaction to such potential loss. Moreover, since magical realism juxtaposes the "reality" of America with other options, it provides an excellent forum for the marginalized voices in the Americas.[9]

Any "new" world inevitably places particular emphasis on the land itself; the land is a powerful element, both symbolically and aesthetically, in the shaping of our fictions. "American literature has traditionally reflected what Annette Kolodny calls America's 'oldest and most cherished fantasy': a dream of harmony between man and nature, a dream repeatedly betrayed as the land is exploited" (Lattin 625). Debra Spark claims that when she tried to write magical realism in the United States, she found herself "hobbled by an inability to get [her] imagination to work in this country," and she asks, "Why is it so hard for me to imagine magical realist fiction on my own soil?" (15). Later, she claims that "the paucity of North American literary models [of magical realism] suggests other North American writers are similarly cowed when it comes to letting their imaginations loose within this country's borders" (15). Although she ultimately attributes her "problem" to the "lack of a collected mythology in the United States and to [her] participation in a Western society which valorizes the empirical" (16), the idea that the geographical location dictates (or disallows) the muse of magical realism threatens to lead us back to Carpentier's claiming of magical realism as a solely Latin American experience. Yet critics like Jean-Paul Borel question "not only geographic boundaries by advocating the inclusion of American Hispanic writers [in the Latin American literary history] but also linguistic boundaries" by referring to the countless Spanish-speaking inhabitants of the United States and those not speaking Spanish or Portuguese in Latin America itself (Chanady, "Latin American Imagined Communities" xiv). Borel manages to blur the lines between definitions of what is "Latin American" and what is "American" from the perspective of the United States.

In essence, Borel and Spark both rely on the same tactic, that is, relegating the magical realist mode largely to the margins. Spark, though, argues that

there *is* a kind of magical realism that requires some cultural reckoning, and the degree to which one is willing or able to do this is the degree to which one is able to free up one's imagination. This explains, in part, why magical realism has flourished in areas where people need to reclaim their cultural identity and why "minority" writers produce much of the States' magical realism. (17)

The battle over creativity that Spark describes is ultimately individualized rather than marginalized. Perhaps most importantly, through the work of critics like Borel, Spark, Zamora, and D'haen, magical realism's status as a Latin American phenomenon becomes blurred. Our proximity to Latin America and our distance from the rest of the "Western world" bring about comparisons and connections that survive only in the Americas. Charles Werner Scheel argues that, like champagne, fine magical realist texts can come from a variety of regions, each steeped with the distinctive flavor of the area from which it emerged. He cites the obvious wealth of contradictory world views and beliefs in the Old World as proof that it, too, can exhibit magical realism (1). Similarly, Zamora and Wendy B. Faris believe that, in spite of its "popular perception . . . as a largely Latin American event," readers still recognize magical realism as a world-wide mode (1). While this volume is concerned with exploring magical realism in the literature of the Americas, rather than with excluding it from the forum of other world literatures, it is still important to note that, since most of Europe does not find itself in the literary predicament of validating its literature and does not share a recent past of colonialization, the inspirations for Europeans using magical realism differ from those shared by writers in the Americas. In addition, critics frequently misrepresent other European literary modes—surrealism, for example—as magical realism. Such errors skew the application of the term magical realism and create criticism that contaminates the magical realist mode.

Though the United States and Canada share with Latin America similar histories, oppressions, and "inspirations," their readily noticeable distinctions ensure that, while they share in common an interest in the mode (one borne out of oppression and postcolonial status in particular), the magical realism north of the Rio Grande nevertheless differs from that of its Latin American applications. If Latin American magical realism is an outgrowth of and reaction against the Latin American political and socioeconomic situation, the magical realism of North America is (necessarily) something quite different. As relatively stable nations, with no major overturning of their *system* of government in the past 200 years, the United States and Canada reflect facades of stability. At the same time, this literary mode is affected by (and may indirectly address) the political rhetoric of capitalism and the consumer culture.[10] "Frederic Jameson . . . sees postmodernism as 'the cultural logic of late capitalism'" (Simmons 19); if we accept the shared backgrounds of magical realism and postmodernism, we might even suggest that they both spring from such a capitalistic perception. Johnny Payne argues,

The U.S. writers from the sixties onward . . . have been experiencing the apparently wholesale capitulation of liberalism and left politics to a consumer society . . . bent on making dissent appear irrelevant by claiming progress and democracy as natural states of affairs and by using the rhetoric of liberalism, tolerance, and the open society as a normative tool. (6)

Such North American magical realist writers as Laurie Foos and Ana Castillo challenge the rhetoric that equates the consumer society with cultural norms by infusing the consumption of goods with "supernatural" qualities. The magical realism of the United States and Canada also frequently manifests itself as an extension of the marginalized, the "other" of Western culture and society, as illustrated by the revision of accepted religious, historical, and even supernatural beliefs by marginalized authors Louise Erdrich, Thomas King, and Toni Morrison. As such, magical realist literature ultimately makes powerful statements about America as both a consumer culture and the "other" in North Atlantic society, but the foundation of its assertions is primarily social or cultural rather than predominantly political. If the Boom privileged the white male center of Latin American culture, the North American counterpart has set out to dethrone the center.[11]

Ironically, even the Boom itself points to the role that consumerism plays in the North American magical realist experience. "The boom gets its name from North American marketing, [says Angel Rama] and designates 'a sudden jump in sales of a particular product in consumer societies. . . . The surprise was its application to a product (books) which . . . was on the margin of such processes'" (Payne 30). The concerns of the American "other" focus around the "haves" and the "have-nots" of North America. In a capitalist, consumer culture, the "have-nots" do not live in remote villages where little interaction between the upper and lower classes takes place. Instead, daily life continuously emphasizes the differences between the two, and the popular culture is largely responsible for highlighting for the less-fortunate the paradox of living in America without living the "American dream." Thus, the North American brand of magical realism dramatizes both the popular culture and the consumer culture in all their manifestations, thereby challenging the authority of those cultures and their effects on the American population.

THE CASE FOR THE MAGICAL REALIST MODE IN NORTH AMERICAN LITERATURE

Some North American texts lend themselves easily to a discussion of the magically real, upholding the precepts for magical realism set forth by Chanady.[12] *Ex Utero, Beloved, The Road to Tamazunchale,* and "The Kugelmass Episode," in spite of drastic differences among their authors, tones, settings, and purposes, provide clearly definable instances of magical realism north of the Rio Grande.[13] Other works, frequently described as magically real, require more extensive justification in order to be considered as such. Some of these may incorporate particular elements of magical realism but may ultimately fail to sustain the supernatural in juxtaposition with the real across the expanse of the text; others provide the acceptable rationale of religious beliefs, counteracting the possibility that the text can be read as magical realism. Before any attempt to address the magically real texts of North America, it is necessary to justify the claims of compliance for magical realist works and to rout out the imposters. On the surface, some choices for this chapter may seem particularly uncommon and perhaps have never been associated with magical realism in any previous scholarship. One such work is Woody Allen's "The Kugelmass Episode," a short story that provides a unique approach to the supernatural. Using a mode that relies on the everyday and its juxtaposition with the supernatural, Allen heightens the paradoxical nature of his short stories by refiguring the everyday as the out-of-the-ordinary.[14] Allen's short story is magically real in spite of its reliance on The Great Persky's magical cabinet, which sends Kugelmass into the text of *Madame Bovary,* where he has an affair with the title character. Rather than explaining away the supernatural events in Kugelmass's life, the "cheesy homemade box" (12) provides an ironic trap for Kugelmass in the world of the supernatural. Indeed, in spite of the fact that both the cabinet and Persky are "magic," the magician is a contradiction of the stereotypes one would associate with his craft. Kugelmass, like the reader, is surprised by the "short, thin, waxy-looking man" who answers the door in the run-down apartment building: "*You're* Persky the Great?" (12). Allen refigures the supernatural as the ordinary by reducing the flash and mystery of magic to an ordinary-looking little man and his cheap wooden cabinet pasted with ugly rhinestones.

A more conventional choice of North American magical realism, given that it has previously been touted as such, is Bernard Malamud's "The Jewbird." Like "The Kugelmass Episode," "The Jewbird" inverts our expectations about its supernatural elements. When the Jewbird, Schwartz, lands on the Cohen's dinner table, his arrival is seemingly met with surprise: " 'It's a talking bird,' said Edie *in astonishment.* 'In Jewish,' said Maurie. 'Wise guy,' muttered Cohen. He gnawed on his chop, then put down the bone. 'So if you can talk, say what's your business. What do you want here?' " (323, emphasis added). The father's ready acceptance and the bird's subsequent requests for food and shelter (without ever truly answering Harry Cohen's questions) both deflect Edie's wonder and circumvent any discussion of the supernatural as irrational. In fact, Cohen sees Schwartz only as "an A-number-one troublemaker" (328) and, stepping into the ironic role of the "Anti-Semeets" whom the Jewbird fears, does away with the bird. The Jewbird refuses the easy answer that he is a devil or "ghost or dybbuk" (i.e., an evil spirit) as easily as he dismisses the suggestion that he is "an old Jew changed into a bird by somebody": "'Who knows?' answered Schwartz. 'Does God tell us everything?'" (324). Thus, most of Cohen's arguments focus on the inconvenience of Schwartz's appearance instead of on that appearance itself. Like Allen, Malamud also draws on humor to enhance his story's magical realist flavor, as when Schwartz interrupts his litany of complaints and requests with "whatever you give me, you won't hear complaints"—a vow he breaks (yet again) when Cohen brings home dried corn in a bird feeder (325). Though the supernatural elements in both stories are mixed blessings that ultimately lead to a "tragic" ending, Schwartz's tragic end provokes more sympathy among readers than Sidney Kugelmass's pathetic—but fitting—demise. That Kugelmass ends up in an eternity where the Spanish verb "tener" continuously chases him is both fitting and bizarre, since his desire "to have" what he does not is what leads to his downfall.

Similar cases can be made for the magical realism of Foos's *Ex Utero*, where the supernatural aspects of the story are no less sensational than any other talk show topic: Ron Arias's *The Road to Tamazunchale*, with its reliance on what Eliud Martínez says is the Kafkaesque "logical development of an absurd premise"(16); Robert Kroetsch's *What the Crow Said*, in which the supernatural heightening of natural events turns a Canadian municipality upside-down; Ana Castillo's *So Far From God*, where the miraculous associations typical of religious faith are revised; and Toni Morrison's *Beloved*, in which the fleshed-out existence of Beloved lives alongside the everyday events of a post-Civil War society. Of the above examples, *What the Crow Said* is perhaps the most inundated with the supernatural, frequently echoing the apocalyptic mood of *One Hundred Years of Solitude*. As with García Márquez's monumental magical realist text, the supernatural and apocalyptic events in Kroetsch's work center on one family—that is, on the lives and tragedies of the Langs—in what Martin Kuester refers to as "Robert Kroetsch's flirt with magic realism" (148). In what is an all-too-familiar response to tragedy and personal misfortune, the women in *So Far From God* (who gravitate toward rebellion) and *Ex Utero* (whose bodies have rebelled against them) become media icons. Castillo's characters experience a very traditional set of supernatural occurrences in extremely unconventional ways. Castillo references resurrection, saints, *curanderas,* and even La Llorona in such original ways that the miracles can no longer be explained away by the religion that supposedly produces them. Foos insists that the reader not only accept that her main characters' sexual organs have "closed up shop," but also that the effects on the male (and, as such, primarily secondary) characters are so drastic. Drawing upon the everyday settings of the television studio and the shopping mall, Foos directly implants the supernatural into the ideological constraints of North America, restrictions that typically guard against the representation of the supernatural as anything other than a ghost story.

The temptation for some readers of magical realist fiction, given these ideological compulsions, is frequently to rely on more traditional or popular claims to explain away the supernatural elements in the texts. One popular attempt at contextualizing Morrison's novel has been to refigure it as a ghost story; in her own discussions of the work, Morrison herself describes it as such. Though Chapter 5 spends considerable time justifying *Beloved* as magical realism, some general claims should be set forth here. *Beloved's* continual presence, along with the other supernatural events in the novel, bump up against but do not consume the natural aspects of the story. Because her reappearance in the novel encompasses many possibilities, her primary effect on both the implied reader and the characters in the story is not horror or suspense. Instead, we must consider what she implies about and for the characters. Similarly, the supernatural effects of *The Road to Tamazunchale* force us to reread the main character, Fausto, a character who seems to offer us a definitive representation of insanity. Though Catherine Bartlett claims that the uniqueness of Cervantian permutations "has worn somewhat thin, . . . [still,] the novel's imitation might be a logical first step for a writer beginning to establish a new Chicano literature" (31); and, as Lattin notes, "unlike his legendary European namesakes, Fausto Tejada escapes disillusionment, death, and damnation" (628). Rather than casting him as the predicable reincarnation of Don Quixote tilting at the windmills of modern-day Los Angeles, Arias—through the reading of Fausto's "insanity" with (and not against) the "realities" of others—repeatedly forces us to believe what elsewhere we might have found unbelievable. Arias's evocation of Quixote also allows the text to refute what Lattin argues are the "beginnings of sacred vision" (626), since Fausto's journey does not appear to be spiritually motivated. Even Lattin's classification of *The Road to Tamazunchale* as sacred vision draws upon startlingly magical realist validation: "After Fausto's death the novel continues for one more chapter without suggestions of distortion or logical violation. Fausto and his friends continue as in the past: there is no funeral or burial; the logic of the world and the dichotomy of life and death have been transcended" (628).

While the case for some texts is more straightforward, several works included in this survey require special consideration; *Dreaming in Cuban* by Cristina Garcia and Thomas King's *Green Grass, Running Water* are two such texts. *Green Grass, Running Water* is situated within the confines of an extremely complicated system of frames, in which an unidentified first-person narrator helps four old Indians[15] teach Coyote the story of creation.[16] King's frames enhance the main narrative; eventually, the progression of the two seems interdependent. Indeed, while relating an alternate version of the creation story, one that usurps traditional white male texts, King begins to introduce characters who participate in the main narrative and who are largely responsible for the magical realism in the novel. Like Castillo's Christian references, the Native American experience King creates in *Green Grass, Running Water* counteracts its own spiritual origins by humorously reframing the traditional myths.

Though King's supernatural frame permeates the text of *Green Grass, Running Water* with magical occurrences, *Dreaming in Cuban*'s questionable magical realist status results from Garcia's almost hesitant use of the supernatural. The magical realism seems compromised by the fact that, generally, only one or two characters experience the supernatural at any one time. Lourdes's and Celia's visits with Jorge del Pino are private, personal moments with no other witnesses.[17] Some events also can be accounted for by religion; Felicia's dependence on the very traditional, Caribbean spiritual medium of Yoruba offers several moments that, though supernatural in tone, cannot be considered magical realism, and ultimately her reliance on the occult fails her. But Garcia also incorporates other indefinable elements into *Dreaming in Cuban*, redeeming the magical realism by interspersing these examples throughout the text. Characters' knowledge of death or danger continually precedes word of mouth or the mail, depending on knowledge "brought" by visions (for Celia) or in conversation with ghosts (as when Lourdes learns from her father's ghost that her sister has died). Celia, who unlike Felicia is a non-believer, matter-of-factly visits a *santera* in order to remove the lump from her son Javier's neck, as well as to rouse him from the misery of losing his family. Significantly, the *santera*'s smoke-laden disappearance and Celia's later discovery of the lump, now in her breast, never cause her alarm. More importantly, these supernatural events do not compromise her atheism—her disbelief in religious explanations for the "miracle." She seems as willing to accept her granddaughter Pilar's readings of the Chinese charts.

Celia and Lourdes are not the only characters in *Dreaming in Cuban* who encounter the supernatural in inexplicable ways. Pilar sees an "image of Abuela Celia underwater, standing on a reef with tiny chrome fish darting by her face like flashes of light. Her hair is waving in the tide and her eyes are wide open. She calls to me but I can't hear her. Is she talking to me from her dreams?" (220). In fact, Pilar's vision references two other "magical" moments in the text: Celia's sighting of Jorge in the water calling to her (in words that she, like her granddaughter, is unable to hear) and Celia's walk into the ocean at the end of the novel. Pilar also receives her grandmother's essence (along with her stories, since Celia believes that her preparations to die require Pilar to carry on her legacy). Like her daughter, most of Lourdes's magical experience (i.e., those events centering around her father's ghost) lead her to a closer relationship with Celia. Lourdes's obsession with food, however, also operates magically in the text; though her overindulgence renders her overweight, she uncovers a new sexual energy and agility incompatible with her otherwise sluggish body.[18]

Magical realism has become such a buzz-word for novels containing *any* aspect of magic that most authors writing in the Americas (including many mainstream authors, as well as marginalized writers not of Latina/o descent) who draw upon the supernatural are inevitably labeled as magical realists. However, unlike those in *Dreaming in Cuban*, the supernatural elements in many other novels are less cohesive and unobtrusive. Catherine Bartlett, who attempts to trace the Latin American influence on three Chicano writers of magical realism, chastises Ron Arias for blatant "borrowing" from magical realist masters like Borges and García Márquez; nonetheless, her arguments still frame his novel as magical realism. Her claims for the postmodern work *Y no se lo tragó la tierra*, on the other hand, provide no such affirmation and inevitably fall short of convincing her reader that Tomás Rivera fulfills the requirements of magical realism. Likewise, in spite of Ude's arguments for the magical realism in Rudolfo Anaya's *Bless Me, Ultima*, Leslie Marmon Silko's *Ceremony*, and *Mumbo Jumbo* by Ishmael Reed, the criteria he sets forth[19] do not provide as convincing (or as easily applied) a model as Chanady's. For Silko's novel in particular, the answer is in the question, that is, the title provides us with evidence that the Silko intentionally depends on established means of spirituality or magic. The works Ude mentions rely on very traditional, sacred systems appropriate to the characters' respective backgrounds: on *curanderas* (*Bless Me, Ultima*), medicine men (*Ceremony*), and voodoo (*Mumbo Jumbo*). Additionally, the first two require a rejection of the "insufficient" Christian values and a return to inherited beliefs, spiritual journeys—or ceremonies or vision quests—that are as traditional to everyday indigenous practices as they are in these texts.

Thus, the evidence against the spiritually explainable *Ceremony* or *Bless Me, Ultima*, or against the disbelieved (though perhaps not disbelievable) ghosts in Paula Martinac's *Out of Time* and the relatively limited magic of Louise Erdrich's *Tracks* and *The Bingo Palace*, exemplifies the difficulty of arguing the case for magical realism as a continuous force in such works. The most damning evidence against *Out of Time* as magical realist is that Martinac's novel and its lesbian hauntings confine themselves to Susan. Martinac, through the first-person narrative, seems to disallow the possibility of other encounters with the supernatural; even Susan's girlfriend, Catherine, refuses to believe her story, much less to experience the magic for herself. For the other works, the myths and folklore of the Native American or Hispanic peoples play significant, and at times even primary, roles in the magical aspects of the novels. *Ceremony*, for example, is *not* magical realism because Tayo's restoration to sanity centers around "native stories and ceremonies" (Maguire 457), an embrace of and adherence to traditional and cultural values similar to that in the Hispanic *Bless Me, Ultima*. On the other hand, Lipsha Morrissey's vision quest is not motivated by a desire to revert to or commune with his heritage but rather by a need to impress both Shawnee Ray and his uncle; the skunk that visits him is a sign of the skewed meaning behind his quest. *Tracks*'s Fleur, contrary to what her Native American ancestry might suggest, seems to have a power born out of her communion with nature and not of any particular connections with her heritage (as opposed, for example, to Nanapush's communion with spirits). We see a similar connection between nature and Vera in *What the Crow Said*; the penetration of the bees literally impregnates her, empowering nature in an extremely sexual manner. Pauline's vengeful, self-serving abilities prove her similarly capable to Fleur, though equally without (perhaps especially without, given her mixed blood and her misguided acquiescence to Christian values) rational explanation for her abilities. Like Morrison, Kroetsch and Erdrich create worlds that are largely unappreciative of ancestors and their powers, realms where those powers, or the living who call on them, abuse the rules of the supernatural. As Karla J. Sanders notes in her work on the magical realism of Louise Erdrich, "*Tracks* discloses a more desperate and violent struggle as its characters attempt to create or hold onto a viable subjectivity in a changing cultural world, while *The Bingo Palace* relates the attempt to recapture what was lost" (12). These two works represent the opposite ends of the United States's project to absorb the Native American culture, a portrayal that requires Erdrich to move beyond the constraints of both the Native American traditions and most contemporary literary devices. As texts on the fringe of the magical realist definition, *Tracks* and *The Bingo Palace* require particular attention.

In *Tracks*, though Erdrich creates two female characters whose powers are apparently not derived from traditional, religious, or mythological sources, for each woman those sources will hold particular importance. Their powers seem to cement some odd relationship between the two characters as well, as is apparent by Pauline's use of her charge, Sophie, not only as a tool for her own voyeuristic sexual gratification but also as a means of revenge against Fleur (whose relationship with and power over Eli seem especially painful for the shy but smitten Pauline). Similarly, Fleur's calling on nature to wipe out the men who rape her follows on the heels of Pauline's inability or unwillingness to attempt to help her during the act itself. Though Pauline frequently seems the direct or indirect cause for the unexplainable supernatural events in the novel, it is Fleur who manipulates nature for her own purposes, rather than as a means of revenge on Pauline. Instead, Fleur turns the forces of nature against the white "invaders" of her body and her land.

Like Nanapush, to whom she owes her life, Fleur symbolizes the end of her family's line, and both of them are associated heavily with the traditions of Native Americans. Nanapush prays to their ancestors to give them peace, but at least in *Tracks*, Erdrich seems to suggest that the old ways cannot save the indigenous people he seeks to protect through prayer. Rather than the past returning to haunt the reservation, Nanapush and Fleur face their greatest threat from the present, in the form of the whites who intend to take their land by any means legally (or quasi-legally) possible. Fleur, whose supernatural elevation of the forest at the end of the novel horrifies the men who have arrived to clear it, also instills fear in her own people on the reservation because of her "near-death" drownings, from which she is apparently spared through her relationship with Misshepeshu, whom Pauline describes as "the water Man, the monster, [who] wanted her for himself. He's a devil, that one. Love hungry with desire and maddened from the touch of young girls, the strong and daring especially, the ones like Fleur" (11). Pauline ironically foreshadows the failure of her own attempted self-sacrifice to Misshepeshu, since she is nothing like Fleur. Instead, we realize that the monster with whom she grapples is really a human form, in this case Napoleon. By that point in the novel, Pauline's own skewed reading of Christianity has transfigured *her* into a monstrous figure.

Like many of the writers included in this chapter, "Erdrich's Magic Realism challenges her readers to accept" multiple systems. In *Tracks* and *The Bingo Palace*, we must allow that Catholic and Native American religious systems are "both valid and flawed. Like her characters, her fiction both accepts and subverts each of these" (Sanders 15). In particular, her creation of Lipsha in *The Bingo Palace* illustrates the degree to which both internal and external forces have played a role in flawing his character. Though he is "caught in a foreign skin, drowned in drugs and sugar and money," Lipsha's original problems stem from his mother, June, who attempts to drown him by putting him in a gunnysack and throwing him in a slough. But when Zelda shares this story with Lipsha, she begins by telling him about his great grandmother Fleur's attempts to kill herself and how she was unable to drown. Just as Fleur's inability seems to represent some terrible, magical connection to the water and to nature, Lipsha shares a similar association with nature when Zelda tells him, "You were in that sack for twenty minutes, though, maybe an hour. . . . Something else has always bothered me though. . . . Lipsha, you were in that slough a long time. . . . *So why weren't you drowned?*" (51). Lipsha's link to the supernatural translates into the "resistless" power of his healing hands, but when he attempts to mix the supernatural with the consumer culture, that is, when he begins to charge for his help, he loses his "medicine."

"Buying Into" Magical Realism

Although the collection and consumption of goods is an everyday aspect of existence, it is frequently the foremost concern in North American culture. People work overtime to make goods and to make the money to buy goods. To paraphrase comedian George Carlin, we buy bigger houses in which to store all our stuff, only to discover that we need more stuff to fill our bigger houses. Thus, the consumer culture is cyclical and self-perpetuating. "By growing accustomed to each new level of need satisfaction, the consumer abandoned himself to the 'soft pressure' that entangles him in ever-changing needs."[20] Shopping, the consumption of goods, and consumers themselves all play important roles in the creation and perpetuation of the consumer cycle. Yet the consumer culture has proven to be "the solvent of modern subjectivity" (Livingston 416). William Leach explains why: "[O]nce glass separated shoppers from goods on display, the relation between subjects and objects was obviously attenuated—glass walls 'closed off' smell and touch, diminishing the consumer's relationship with the goods" (62–63). Thus, while "glass democratized desire . . . it dedemocratized access to goods" (63); the separation of customer from goods contributed to the increasingly obscured "difference between the real and the unreal" (189).[21] As Jürgen Habermas says, "Consumer culture designates the unity of two incompatible elements; incompatible, among other reasons, because culture is critical and consumption is not" (qtd. in Wyrwa 447). Because even the language used to describe the consumer culture is rich with the same rhetoric of magical realism (where "the difference between the real and the unreal" is blurred and "two incompatible elements" are united), it stands to reason that the narrative mode is appropriated as an effective means for discussing North America's socioeconomic condition. Magical realism, as a mode dedicated to obliterating the "difference between the real and the unreal," resolves the antinomy between these incompatible elements and refigures the consumption of goods into an experience beyond most everyday realities.

What little consumption, beyond alcohol, that Kroetsch features in *What the Crow Said* seems to have only a minimal effect on the magical realism of the novel. Occasionally, though, the meaningless ambitions of the men Kroetsch creates perpetuate a dangerous cycle of consumption and destruction. For example, Tiddy initially supports the card players who inhabit her dining room, believing that the men need a break from the difficulties of physical labor. Later, when the schmier game—a reaction to "the inadequacy of truth" (76) to determine the father of Gladys's baby—degenerates into an almost supernatural marathon of card playing, Tiddy attempts to rescue the men from their lengthy, self-destructive behavior with the lure of food, that is, to revive them by reconnecting them with the consumption of goods. John Skandl's scheme to turn the endless winter into a useful money-making ice-cutting business begins with his statement, "Every snowflake is a penny" (48), and ends with the ice break-up and destruction of the ice-block lighthouse he creates. And when Vera's Boy's predictions bring prosperity to the municipality, "Father Basil finally preached his famous sermon on greed, for four hours and twenty minutes, to a completely deserted church" (140)—deserted because the congregation is harvesting or cooking the rewards of their efforts. Perhaps Liebhaber, at least, needed to hear Father Basil's message; instead, he learns from Isador Heck's successful parlay of the schmier game's pot into a tour of the continent that "[i]t was obvious, the lesson: money would buy happiness" (143). Ironically, though Vera's Boy's and Liebhaber's prophesies rarely miss, their failures generally hurt Vera's brothers-in-law, as when Mick O'Holleran puts his life savings into an oil drilling venture at Liebhaber's persuading. Money and happiness, at least for Tiddy Lang's family, are not necessarily by-products of magical realism.

When he calls upon the consumer culture in *Green Grass, Running Water,* Thomas King emphasizes the distinctions between the Native American characters who scrape by and the more well-to-do whites like Bursum, who seems to come to much the same conclusion as Liebhaber. "Everything sa[ys] money" to Bursum, for whom making money is the "only effective way to keep from going insane in a changing world" (210). In contrast, the "Indians" with whom he deals insist on traditions and myth as a buffer between them and the culture by which they have been subsumed.[22] At the same time, the popularity of "cowboy and Indian" films, George's attempts to photograph the Sun Dance, and Karen's collection of books on Native Americans all illustrate the degree to which the native peoples become marketable products for mainstream America. King's attempt to rewrite those products (i.e., the "consumable" Native Americans) into the *consumers* requires his use of magical realism, as is discussed in more detail in the following section on popular culture.

The duality of their role as both consumers and the consumed is a popular theme in Native American magical realist texts. Although Erdrich's *Tracks* and *The Bingo Palace* also foreground the consumption of the indigenous peoples of the United States, Erdrich does not allow for a hopeful rewriting of history as does King. Instead, the whites "consume" the Native Americans and the land on which they live, to the extent that Nanapush finds himself manipulated by his lover Margaret, who is also a Native American and who saves her own land and not the Pillager property with the tax monies they collect. "Our trouble," Nanapush explains for all his people, "came from living, from liquor and the dollar bill" (4). Fleur's own tribulations begin, notably, in a store where she has been breaking even (always winning exactly one dollar) while playing cards with the white patrons. They brutalize her when she oversteps the boundaries of such meager winnings, raking in the pot filled with their entire week's earnings.

In *The Bingo Palace*, Erdrich reveals the outcome of the troubles Nanapush mentions in *Tracks*. The dollar, still almighty, has created a reservation full of people who, like Zelda's first love, "would hold down a low-pay job to support the bigger task it was to be an Indian" (47). Erdrich's depiction of "a little old Cree lady" who holds "a thin pocketbook" and "a wax cup of Coke"(9) seems a particularly fitting image for a people who can just barely manage to be consumers of the larger, mainstream culture. In stark contrast to this image is Lyman Lamartine, who "has run so many businesses that nobody can keep track" and who "is an island of *have* in a sea of *have-nots*" (16). But Lyman believes everything, even culture, is for sale. He even attempts to buy the ceremonial pipe that is Lipsha's inheritance; though on the surface his vision quest, in which Fleur speaks to him in her bear voice, seems more traditional than Lipsha's, its reassurance of his place in the capitalistic world seems a refutation of his Native American cultural ties. Lyman hears what he wants to, namely that his scheme to make money off of Pillager land has the more noble purpose of gaining back tribal land for his fellow Native Americans. Lyman's privileging of the consumer culture over his heritage is even evident in his grass dancing. Unlike his dead brother Henry, who "danced to move within his own thoughts," Lyman "danced for prize money" (162).

The consumer culture's hold on Lipsha undermines his vision quest by tempting him with Big Macs (196), but he is also visited by a skunk who tells him "*This ain't real estate*" after he thinks of putting money into one of Lyman's schemes. Any doubts we may have about Lipsha's non-traditional animal guide are undermined by the skunk's reappearance to Lipsha in his room; it is not in the woods but rather in his small room behind the bar that Lipsha finally gets his vision, one replete with images of wealth built on the land and bones of the Pillagers. The skunk's warning, "*Luck don't stick when you sell it,*" shows Lipsha that "[t]he money life has got no substance, there's nothing left when the day is done but a pack of receipts. Money gets money, but little else, nothing sensible to look at or touch or feel in yourself down to your bones"(221). What Lipsha learns through his vision, in stark contrast to Lyman, is that money has no heart and will not prove to be a balm for the Native American community's troubles. Though this is the first time Lipsha realizes it, he has already been taught this lesson by his easy winning at bingo. When his mother June, now dead, begins to appear to her son, the "guidance" she offers her son is through a bingo card with which he wins a van—a vehicle that is, in some respects, a consolation prize to her son for having taken back her Firebird. At first, like Fleur, Lipsha wins "just enough" money to exist on, but his big break winning the van proves no blessing. Instead, it brings him into direct contact with racism and pain, and when he discovers his uncle Lyman has stolen the money he saves, he doesn't get mad but "just stop[s] going to the bingo" (231). Erdrich, whose chapter titles in *The Bingo Palace* echo with the repetition of "luck," emphasizes that the reclaiming of the Native American traditions and pride cannot rely on luck *or* money.

Though the threat of the consumer culture does not always overrun Native American culture, Erdrich's representation of the consumer culture's attacks on Native American traditions in *Tracks* and *The Bingo Palace* calls to mind Morrison's consumed slaves of *Beloved* and the attempted consumption of the Indians in *Green Grass, Running Water*—though, like Erdrich in *The Bingo Palace*, King thwarts that commodification and suggests that the Native American culture will be strong enough to survive the attempts on its heritage. Conversely, the indigenous elements of the Canadian landscape in *What the Crow Said* have largely been consumed before the present day of the novel itself. When the drunken schmier players are "put on the Indian list[,] not one of them could, legally, be served an alcoholic beverage," uncovering not only the predisposition to stereotype the Native American (falsely so, since the true drunkards in this text are the whites of European descent) but also the intentional movement to exclude that population as consumers.

In Garcia's novel *Dreaming in Cuban*, even the most culturally marginalized characters rarely seem at risk of becoming consumed; instead, their appetites as U.S. consumers are perpetually fed, both literally and figuratively. Consider, for example, Lourdes's massive consumption of baked goods. Her appetite in the kitchen translates into a sexual appetite, and the "heavier she got, the more supple she became" (21).[23] Yet because she equates her dieting (during which she eats no food whatsoever) with transparency, "as if the hard lines of her hulking form were disintegrating," she loses interest in sex. Only when her "metamorphosis is complete," when she can fit into a size six designer suit, does she begin to eat again. "On Fifth Avenue, Lourdes stops to buy hot dogs (with mustard, relish, sauerkraut, fried onions, and ketchup), two chocolate cream sodas, a potato knish, lamb shish kebabs with more onions, a soft pretzel, and a cup of San Marino cherry ice. Lourdes eats, eats, eats, like a Hindu goddess with eight arms, eats, eats, eats, as if famine were imminent" (174).

Garcia also reveals the *lack* of consumption that is painfully evident in Cuba when Lourdes returns to Cuba to see her mother. Cuba, like the United States, revels in the consumer culture, but goods are hard to come by in Cuba—they are the toys of the privileged. But when Lourdes finally does visit her family in Cuba, the gifts she brings represent the degree to which Lourdes, as a "privileged" consumer, chooses not to share her good fortune. Though Lourdes has "crammed every inch of [her and Pilar's] suitcases," the gifts she brings are merely "cheap sneakers and tacky clothing from the Latino stores on Fourteenth Street" (217). Lourdes, an unwilling visitor, is also able but unwilling to provide for her family. In this way, she ironically mirrors her sister Felicia. Celia finds unused ration cards, for which Felicia, in her unstable state of mind, "had had little use" in the months before her death; instead, she and her children subsist on the coconuts she associates with Yoruba. Lourdes, who herself despises the subjugation under which she sees El Lider's Cuba suffering, refuses to hold her tongue during her visit. Pilar laments,

We've been in Cuba four days and Mom has done nothing but complain and chain-smoke her cigars late at night. She argues with Abuela's neighbors, picks fights with waiters, berates the man who sells ice cones on the beach. She asks everyone how much they earn, and no matter what they tell her, she says, "You can make ten times as much in Miami!" With her, money is the bottom line. (234)

Like Bursum in *Green Grass, Running Water,* Lourdes views money as the impetus by which she can distance herself from the "other," but, in her case, she denies her own heritage, her own "otherness" in so doing. When the family goes out to eat at a tourist hotel, Ivanito's insatiable hunger shocks Lourdes, who "knows that Cuba saves its prime food for tourists or for export to Russia. Degradation, she thinks, goes hand in hand with the certainty of deprivation" (223). She misses the fact that her own "diet" of deprivation similarly degrades her body.

In certain respects, though, the U.S. scene that Pilar describes is no better off. It is "-hell Open 24 Hours," as one Shell station (mis)spells it out (31). Fulton Street in New York, for example, is "just a run-down stretch of outdated stores with merchandise that's been there since the Bay of Pigs" (25), according to Pilar, who thus equates the "excess" with the United States's intervention into Cuban affairs. Lourdes's complaints about Cuba are not much different from her attitude in New York, where

all the neighborhood merchants hate her. "Where are the knobs, kid?" they ask me [Pilar] when her volume goes up. I don't think Mom's ever bought something and not returned it. Somebody somewhere must be keeping track of this. One day, she'll walk into a department store and there'll be camera lights and a big brass band and Bob Barker will announce, "Congratulations, Mrs. Puente! This marks the thousandth time you've come in here to complain!" (63)

Pilar sees her family's excess, especially Lourdes's, and wonders, "Like this is it? We're living the American dream?" (137). Of course, as Garcia demonstrates, the American dream is also alive and well in (or at least, well and imported into) Cuba. Celia once sold "American photographic equipment" in a Havana department store (35) where she prided herself on her ability to "gauge how much a customer had to spend on a camera. Her biggest sales went to Americans from Pennsylvania. What did they take so many pictures of up there?" (38). Her husband, Jorge del Pino, embraces the American dream to the extent that he jeopardizes his familial ties. While he works to prove to the gringos at the U.S. company for which he works that he is one of them, his travels as a salesman effectively remove him as both a father and a husband. As Garcia sees it, the American dream, whether at home or exported to other nations, cannot always meet the expectations of the individuals pursuing it in *Dreaming in Cuban*. Instead, the culture of consumers threatens to devour family ties. The infiltration of the supernatural into Lourdes's consumer world forces her to reevaluate those ties and to confront the irony of the Cubanized American dream. At the same time, Jorge's intervention in his daughter's life after his death seems to offer him penance for chasing that dream at the cost of his family.

If Garcia views Cuba as the ironic end of the pursuit of the American dream, her novel hardly paints a more promising view of the United States. Pilar's observation of the Shell sign (minus its "S") refigures the "paved streets of gold" into a very real "-hell" for the less fortunate. Arias invokes a similar portrait of the United States in *The Road to Tamazunchale* during Fausto and Mario's trek through Los Angeles: "They crossed the street, passed through an empty Standard station and stopped behind the telephone booth. The hard cover of the Yellow Pages dangled from a chain next to a Coke bottle with cigarette stubs floating on the bottom. Mario checked the coin-return slot with his finger, shrugged and caught up with Fausto" (26). The culture of Arias's Los Angeles is *consumed*, not consumable, and the American ideals of freedom, communication, sustenance, and profit are all markedly empty.

Celia's pre-marriage clerk and Jorge's traveler in search of the American dream conjure a particularly productive image for the North American magical realist: the salesperson. Like *Dreaming in Cuban*'s Jorge, Arias's Fausto Tejada chases the American dream by selling American products, but his success at sales does not seem to translate into a comfortable existence. In Foos's *Ex Utero*, shoe salesmen feed the frenzy for red high heels like the ones Rita wears on her talk show appearance. Even in a novel like *So Far From God*, where the consumer culture is less apparent, Castillo draws on the image of the salesperson. In one of the few passages about the consumption of goods, Sofi, who works in a *carnecería* or butcher shop, allows her family troubles to cause her to forget to charge a neighbor for her month's purchases. Other authors place much more importance on the role that selling plays in everyday life. In "The Jewbird," Malamud repeatedly identifies Harry Cohen as a "frozen-foods salesman" rather than by name, emphasizing not only his role as breadwinner for the family but also the consumer-based means by which he provides that sustenance. Not coincidentally, Schwartz's arrival is at dinnertime, and most of his requests revolve around his seemingly insatiable appetite, including a catalogue of predominantly Jewish delicacies. Cohen appears to hate Schwartz's consumption of free goods as much as anything about the bird. As Cohen begins his secret campaign of terrorizing the bird, he thinks, "The vacation was over, let him make his easy living off the fat of somebody else's land" (328). Unlike the incidental consumerism of *So Far From God*, the Jewbird threatens to take advantage of Cohen's role as breadwinner, suggesting that magical realism poses a significant threat to the consumer culture.

As with Garcia and Malamud, Foos places tremendous emphasis on the role of consumerism in her text. Yet *Ex Utero* transforms the consumer culture into the impetus for (and a menace against) the magical realism of the text. Foos refigures the shopping mall as the site of loss of womanhood for the main character. "Somehow, in her quest to achieve a versatile wardrobe, she'd lost her womb, the way some people misplace car keys or a pair of sunglasses" (2). Rita's pursuit at the mall symbolizes the stereotypical female desire in our consumer shopper—the desire to "shop till you drop"—only in this instance the "dropping" refers to Rita's uterus rather than to Rita herself. The red high heels she wears on Nodderman's show set off a spending frenzy; as one shoe salesman claims, "the fury over the lost womb has caused women to be far too interested in a product with little lasting value" (127). Rita's shoes simultaneously become the symbol of female sexuality, the hope for the longevity of that sexuality, and, since her heels no longer stimulate her husband, the failure of Rita's marriage.

While *Ex Utero* recasts the shopping experience into a quest, in Woody Allen's "The Kugelmass Episode," the reverse is true: Allen describes a character reprogrammed by the experience of buying goods in the contemporary culture of the United States. Emma Bovary's embrace of the culture into which Sidney Kugelmass inserts her includes a new love of shopping and room service. As her bills begin to mount "like the defense budget" (18), realizes that he has "created" a mistress who spends and acts just like his "troglodyte" wife. Because she is a relative novice in the consumer culture, Emma is as easily lured into shopping as she is into affairs. Emma, as a new inductee into capitalistic consumerism, finds the experience overwhelming but nonetheless falls into the web spun by the ability and desire to possess goods. Because we can "read" her as a fictional character who comments on and purchases "real" goods, Emma's sudden consumption is both amusing and supernatural.

Post-Civil War society creates an individual who is, arguably, as paradoxical for the South as Madame Bovary is to New York; the paradoxical nature of being a freed slave does not allow for the fact that this new citizen/consumer is dumped into a new system of reality. Because Paul D transforms into a consumer upon the death of slavery, Morrison emphasizes that his experience, though just as magically real as Emma's, is much less attractive. Rowe describes Morrison's works as "'postmodern politics'—that is, a politics that conceives of resistance and social reform as dependent on a critique of representation" (198). Indeed, Morrison's politics in *Beloved* relies on the critique and transformation of the *mis*represented slave. She writes a novel largely about the consumption of the "goods" of slavery, in which people are assets literally consumed by slavery.

Morrison best illustrates the consumer culture and what it represents to the newly freed African Americans of Reconstruction[24] in the scene in which Paul D makes his first purchase. Though the events Morrison relates are clearly not magical realist in the same sense, for example, as Beloved's appearance, she classifies Paul D's experience not as realistic but rather as extraordinary. Her third-person narration of his thoughts transfigures the exchange of money—particularly in the hands of a black man—into something magical.

Then came the *miracle*. Standing in a street in front of a row of brick houses, he heard a whiteman call him ("Stay there! Yo!") to help unload two trunks from a coach cab. Afterward the whiteman gave him a coin. Paul D walked around with it for hours—not sure what it could buy (a suit? A meal? A horse?) and if anybody would sell him anything. Finally he saw a greengrocer selling vegetables from a wagon. Paul D pointed to a bunch of turnips. The grocer handed them to him, took his one coin and gave him several more. Stunned, he backed away. Looking around, he saw that nobody seemed interested in the "mistake" or him, so he walked along, happily chewing turnips. . . . His first earned purchase made him glow, never mind the turnips were withered dry. (269; emphasis added)

Paul D's first purchase is more than his introduction to the consumer culture. It testifies to the irony of being black and being American, of life in the "land of the free" for the ex-slave. Atypical of the "ideal reader" for the consumer culture, he cites his purchase as a "mistake" and looks for witnesses. Like the wandering blacks along the roads after the Civil War who carry scraps of paper with loved ones' names on them, or like himself with the article Stamp Paid gives him, Paul D is "illiterate" in the ways of the (consumer) culture around him. Not knowing what his coin can buy (from a turnip to a horse) marks him as ill-equipped to survive in a capitalist society. Yet through Paul D, Morrison also illustrates the degree to which the ex-slave exists in an almost supernatural state, in that his definition of what is natural or proper is exceeded by his newfound freedom.

While Morrison paints Paul D's introduction to the consumer culture as magical, she makes Sethe's first transaction initially seem anything *but*. The only way Sethe can engrave her baby's tombstone is by transforming "her body into a commodity" (Lawrence 234), a commodification that gives a name to the magical realism of the text. "For Sethe, the price of [this] inscription is sexual degradation, and her sex is worth only the seven letters comprising the word 'beloved'" (Holmes 140). Beloved's appropriation of the name Sethe "buys" for her baby's tomb means that Beloved is, from that point on, directly connected with both degradation and death. Furthermore, her "consumption" (to the point of absorption) of the crawling-already ghost provides her with the ability to consume the mother figure in the text.

The single aspect of *Beloved*'s magical realism that signifies most on the consumer culture plays on the phrase itself. Beloved, in what is an extremely American gesture, consumes for her own benefit and to the detriment of others, most notably Sethe. When Beloved arrives, Sethe *stops* being a consumer—both of goods and of food—and is consumed instead by Beloved, who "ate up her life, took it, swelled up with it, grew taller on it" (250). Denver spends much of Beloved's stay worrying that whatever made it okay for Sethe to kill a child is still a threat, until Sethe vomits up something she had not even eaten. Her false consumption—Sethe's ability to produce something that she literally has not consumed—awakens Denver to the fact that it is Sethe, and not Beloved, who needs looking after. Though Beloved is not the only consumer in the text, her embracing of the consumer culture is the condition that finally demands her removal.

In *The Road to Tamazunchale*, Fausto, unlike Paul D, is "literate" not only in consumerism but also in the role that literacy has in his survival in the United States. A legal citizen, he uses the knowledge gained by his sales to "prove" his legal right to cross the border from Mexico back into the United States:

Then in his most exaggerated Oxford English, Fausto recited without a pause the Gettysburg Address, the Pledge of Allegiance and Franklin Roosevelt's death announcement. It was an old trick, but when the guard heard Roosevelt's name, he was convinced. Fausto was given his clothes and told to leave.
"By the way, where'd you learn that?"
Fausto stepped into his wrinkled trousers. "I used to sell books of knowledge . . . and that's one of the things you can learn. I sold a lot of sets that way." (966)

Though Fausto has a legitimate claim to his entry into the United States, he is required to draw upon "an old trick" in order to back up his claim—potent irony, considering that he is already tricking the guards into accepting as citizens the drunken Mexicans whom he has disguised as soldiers. Arias emphasizes the connection between ethnicity, (English) literacy, and the consumer culture. After all, in the United States, the bottom line (even for the supernatural) is money. Jess, who accepts the snow but not its magical appearance, responds to Fausto's declaration "[i]t snowed" with "Sure, how much did it cost?" (41). Jess is also the only Latino/a character in the text to reject his Hispanic roots. His nickname is the Americanized version of Jesús, his given name. Indeed, Jess seems to reject his spiritual *and* ethnic ties by appropriating his new name. More importantly, although Arias provides *The Road to Tamazunchale* with the authorial reticence Chanady requires of magical realism, he reserves the acceptance of the supernatural for the marginalized members of Los Angeles. Doubting is confined to those like the white motorcycle cop or Jess, characters who either stand outside the Latino/a community or reject that aspect of their culture.

Mario as thief outsmarts the consumer culture in which he lives by evading the issue of cost altogether. Though he drives the cars he steals until they are out of gas, he takes care not to scratch them. He "buys" milk by foisting off Fausto as his dying father, scaring the shopkeeper with threats of cholera and death. Mario searches his pockets and wallet, but the shopkeeper ousts them before he can pay. Mario mistakes Fausto's shuffling dance as duplicitous, part of their routine. "You know, we make a good team. I didn't think you'd do it. Man, you should've seen the pendejo's face! He was so scared we could've copped anything in the store" (26). Yet Fausto balks not at consumerism but rather at the border's effective separation of the "mojados"[25] from the consumer culture of the United States, and eventually, he recruits Mario for his cause. The supernatural evacuation of the theater during "The Road to Tamazunchale" emerges from Fausto's desire to save the Mexicans after their appearance in the culture. They are also illiterate in consumerism, and despite his efforts to help them cross the border, they are not granted the ability to become consumers simply by standing on U.S. soil.

"Pop" Goes the Culture

In *Dreaming in Cuban*, Garcia illustrates ways in which the consumer culture and the popular culture commingle. For Garcia, *what* Cubans import from their neighbor to the north is as important as *that* they import. Cuban characters eat, drink, wear, and play[26] the United States, even if they are unable or unwilling to live there. The coalescence of the consumer and popular cultures is a continent-wide (if not world-wide) phenomenon, particularly if, as Philip Simmons and others argue, "the consumer culture built on advertising" is a part of the larger mass culture (2). Yet, whereas popular culture is frequently rejected in Latin America because of its association with "the multinational capitalism that imposes a homogenizing mass culture" (David William Foster, "Popular Culture" 4), it is embraced for precisely the same reason by North American magical realists.[27] Popular culture itself seems willing to embrace magical realism, as evidenced, for example, by the publication of Michael Boccia's "Magical Realism: The Multicultural Literature" in the journal *Popular Culture Review*. Simmons's comment about Thomas Pynchon's *Gravity's Rainbow* seems pertinent for many of the magical realist texts considered below: "[T]he text's allusions to film, popular music, comic books, and other mass-cultural artifacts are a continual source of playful, comic disruption that suggests a possible realm of freedom to be found in the popular" (16). Though magical realists like Allen and King certainly epitomize comic freedom with their use of pop culture, other authors choose to explore the popular or "mass" culture as a "disruption" either to the text itself or to daily life.

From Jorge's and Lourdes's love of baseball to the Coca-Cola they keep in their fridge, the del Pinos in *Dreaming in Cuban* are shaped by the popular culture of the United States as much as they are by their own. When Jorge and Lourdes embrace this foreign element, it inspires them to move away from Cuba. Celia, by choosing to place her loyalty in El Lider, champions Cuba; her country is her spirituality. But Celia's encounters with her husband after death—especially her apparent sacrifice of herself, not to El Lider's campaign but rather to Jorge's image in the sea—seem to suggest that, unlike Morrison's perception of the South, at least as she describes it in *Beloved*, Garcia believes Cuba to be both magical *and* oppressive.

Like Garcia, Castillo sprinkles *So Far From God* with pop cultural references. From doña Felicia's Raider's cap to Rubén Blades, "one of *our* Rubén's pop culture heroes," Castillo allows her characters to experience both cultures that shape them. Yet for both Garcia and Castillo, the importance of these images frequently has less to do with the magical realist intent of the fictions and more to do with the fact that they are incorporated into such marginalized texts. Though the Hispanic origins of both the characters and the authors are driving forces behind the magical realism of Castillo's and Garcia's works, these authors, by reveling in (rather than separating themselves from) an admixture of traditionally U.S. popular culture with those Hispanic overtones, claim simultaneous places in the Latin American and North American traditions.

Some of the authors being considered here do rely more heavily on North American pop culture. Allen not only incorporates popular culture into its magical realism; the humorous tone of his "The Kugelmass Episode" depends on it. Kugelmass's leisure suit is evocative: "I love what you have on," Emma murmurs. "It's so . . . so modern." Kugelmass's response ('"It's called a leisure suit,' he said romantically. 'It was marked down'" [14]) tells us as much about his character as any other line in the text. Of course, leisure suits were modern in the late seventies of the story's setting, but taken out of the context of the popular culture, Kugelmass's clothing emphasizes how poorly he fits into what Emma terms "this crass rural existence" (14) at Yonville. Similarly, Emma's foray into New York would not seem so laughable if it were not so incongruous. At the same time, Allen also comments scathingly on the culture to which Kugelmass introduces Emma, a culture into which Emma is literally thrust when Sidney suggests they update their affair. Allen infuses their discussions, both in Yonville and on her visit to New York, with pop cultural references—slang ("cheesy," "sawbuck," "beat his time"), fashion (Halston and Saint Laurent), entertainment (discothéques, the Oscars, and Broadway), celebrities (O. J. Simpson and Jack Nicholson), and the places to see and be seen in New York (Elaine's, 21, and the Plaza). Of course, eventually, Emma discovers that "watching TV all day is the pits" (17) and considers pursuing an acting career. Emma's rapid absorption into the popular culture of Kugelmass's time spells immediate disaster for their affair, since his goal in pursuing their tryst is to escape a second wife (already immersed in the popular and consumer cultures) who has "let herself go" (11).

How Emma and Sidney transgress against fiction figures most importantly in the magical realm of the story. Though Emma never realizes she is a character in a novel, Kugelmass is very much aware of her fictionality: "'My God, I'm doing it with Madame Bovary!' Kugelmass whispered to himself. 'Me, who failed freshman English'" (14). Kugelmass takes it upon himself to rewrite the text of *Madame Bovary*, an inscription that also takes place on the body of the character herself. But Kugelmass forgets that he has an audience of readers. "What he didn't realize was that at this very moment students in various classrooms across the country were saying to their teachers, 'Who is this character on page 100? A bald Jew is kissing Madame Bovary?' A teacher in Sioux Falls, South Dakota, sighed and thought, Jesus, these kids, with their pot and acid. What goes through their minds!" (14). A fellow professor who identifies his colleague "as the sporadically appearing character in the Flaubert book" threatens to tell Kugelmass's wife (18); and a Stanford professor, at first finding "a strange character named Kugelmass" and then discovering Emma gone from the novel, declares, "Well, I guess the mark of a classic is that you can reread it a thousand times and always find something new" (16). By giving Kugelmass's indiscretions an audience, Allen creates a "fictional" character out of an already-fictionalized individual. In so doing, he not only revises the text of a classic novel but also challenges the identity of the readers—perhaps especially the abusers—of that text.

Just as Allen rewrites *Madame Bovary*, so too does King revise traditional texts and systems. In *Green Grass, Running Water*, he appropriates and rewrites *The Last of the Mohicans, Robinson Crusoe, Moby Dick*, the Bible, and even a radio-originated television character, the Lone Ranger.[28] The four Native Americans—who are the four originary women of the story (First Woman, Changing Woman, Thought Woman, and Old Woman) and who first reject the Christian myths of "Ahdamn" and Eve, Noah and the Flood, Mary's immaculate conception, and Christ (Young Man Walking On Water)—adopt their (male) names from the white Anglo texts and are responsible for establishing the narrative frame around the story. In the tale, then, King also irreverently modifies Native American myths, since he uses four cross-dressing, cross-naming women to effect changes in the "present" of the text and since Coyote, the audience for their tale, is traditionally the story-teller. Jeanne Delbaere says of magical realism that, "Like Coyote it can assume many different forms, appear and disappear in many different places and remain for ever [sic] elusive though magically alive" (100). But King's magical realism "out-Coyotes" Coyote, since it plays tricks with the trickster character. In fact, though Sanders argues for Erdrich's works that, "[i]f the magic is abused or bastardized, it fails" (280), King's warping or bastardization of the magic seems to be precisely the reason it can effect changes in the community. These same four characters turn up in the present-day of the narrative as escapees from a mental hospital. White texts are not the only ones King features in the novel, as Eli's white friend Karen forgives him "his pedestrian taste in reading" (181) and tries to push him to read about his own heritage:

Most of the books that Karen brought by were about Indians. Histories, autobiographies, memoirs of writers who had gone west or who had lived with a particular tribe, romances of one sort or another. Eli tried to hint that he had no objection to a Western or another New Woman novel, and Karen would laugh and pull another book out of her bag. Magic.

"You have to read this one, Eli. It's about the Blackfoot."

What amazed Eli was that there were so many. (180)

In his most important revision, King rewrites the classic John Wayne Western. King plays and replays the genre throughout the text, as various characters see portions of old Westerns on late-night television or on tape. Alberta turns one off in disgust: "Enough. The last thing in the world she needed to do was to watch some stupid Western. Teaching Western history was trial enough without having to watch what the movie makers had made out of it" (241). To Charlie, whose father,

Portland, wore a rubber nose in order to play a "more authentic" stock Hollywood Indian character, one of the films becomes the tool through which Charlie comes to identify with his father. The white television store owner sees one John Wayne classic as the movie most fitting for "The Map," his towering display of televisions in the shape of the United States and Canada. "Bursum doubted that even [college-educated] Lionel understood the unifying metaphor or the cultural impact The Map would have on customers" (140). For Bursum, *The Mysterious Warrior*,[29] the "best Western of them all" and a movie he has seen twenty times (211), emphasizes what he ultimately considers the "right" outcome—the triumph of the whites over Native Americans—in spite of his claims to help the Indians he had known his entire life.[30] Yet even Bursum cannot guess at the way the "cultural impact" of his "unifying metaphor" will be played out and resignified across his map of northern America.

When the Lone Ranger, Hawkeye, Robinson Crusoe, and Ishmael view Bursum's favorite Western, they find mistakes in the production.
    "The next scene," said Bursum, "used over six hundred extras, Indians and whites. And five cameras. The director spent almost a month on this one scene before he felt it was right."
    "He didn't get it right the first time," said the Long Ranger.
    "But we fixed it for him," said Hawkeye. (351–52)

The "predictable" (353) text then takes a turn for the different, though not necessarily worse. The four new "directors" of the movie colorize their version and remove the cavalry that charges in to save John Wayne. "There at full charge, hundreds of soldiers in bright blue uniforms with gold buttons and sashes and stripes, blue-eyed and rosy-cheeked, came over the last rise. / And disappeared. . . . 'What the hell,' said Bursum" (357). And

as Lionel and Charlie and Eli and the old Indians and Bill and Coyote watched, none of the Indians fell. John Wayne looked at his gun. Richard Widmark was pulling the trigger on empty chambers. The front of his fancy pants was dark and wet. . . . And then Portland and the rest of the Indians began to shoot back, and soldiers began falling over. . . . John Wayne looked down and stared stupidly at the arrow in his thigh, shaking his head in amazement and disbelief as two bullets ripped through his chest and out the back of his jacket. (358)

Bursum's response is to stab at the remote in an attempt to stop the revision, but "Charlie had his hands out of his pockets, his fists clenched, keeping time to the singing [of the Indians]. His lips were pulled back from his teeth, and his eyes flashed as he watched his father flow through the soldiers like a flood. 'Get 'em, Dad,' he hissed" (358). The four rewriters of history, at least the cinematized "history" Alberta scoffs at, change the tide of the cultural impact intended by the movie. They refigure the popular genre of the Western into a new genre, one in which the Portlands and not the John Waynes save the day. In doing so, they return to Charlie a father, as well as a culture and a history, of which he can be proud.

In *Green Grass, Running Water*, King revises what we believe to be the static text of film; in *The Road to Tamazunchale*, Arias uses that medium to play with our sense of what is real. When Fausto Tejada wanders onto the set of a movie being shot in Los Angeles, the reader momentarily has trouble deciding what is fact and what is fiction. The movie set seems more real than the main character's own sensibilities, and we "discover" where we are along with Fausto. Just as the play at the end of the novel will open gateways to new realities, the movie creates a "modern-day" seventeenth-century revolution in the middle of modern-day Los Angeles.

Hollywood, as a perpetuator of the popular culture, comes under fire in many of the afore-mentioned texts, but the new "stars" of popular culture in the United States are frequently on the small, rather than the big, screen. Simmons argues, "Together with popular film and advertising in all mediums, television is one of the primary means by which the postmodern conditions of knowledge are established within everyday life" (1). Of the many messages that Foos preaches in *Ex Utero*, the most significant in terms of popular culture is her indictment of the talk show genre. After she loses her womb, Rita makes the rounds of the syndicated talk shows, finally ending up on *The Nodderman Show*. Rod Nodderman is the quintessential talk show host, and Rita finds herself in *TV Guide*, along with Nodderman, whose Nielson ratings skyrocket after her appearance. One character and fan of the show, Adele,

likes to make love with her boyfriend Leonard while watching talk shows. There is something about the distant murmur of voices, she says, that never fails to propel her to orgasm. Some of the syndicated shows do the trick, but it is *The Nodderman Show* that drives her into a frenzy. Certain shows have sent her tearing at Leonard's hair and begging for commercials. She has been known to scream with pleasure at the opening strains of game show theme songs, writhing on the bed from the spinning of the Wheel of Fortune. (33)

But her sympathy for Rita's plight causes Adele's vagina literally to seal shut, and not even Leonard's hammering, drilling, and chiseling can reopen it. Women are not the only casualties of the media frenzy. Marty, a shoe salesman who cannot keep red pumps in stock after Rita's appearance on the talk show, thinks "perhaps it is the constant bombardment of wombs by the media that has driven him to [an] insatiable lust" (75). *Ex Utero* equates sexual excitement with both the female reproductive system and the "boob tube," and the novel's supernatural elements become a pawn in the production and reproduction of both the television industry and humanity.

Television plays a consistent role as popular cultural icon for other magical realist authors as well. In Castillo's *So Far From God*, for example, even the hundred-year-old doña Felicia keeps up "with her favorite telenovelas on Spanish cable T.V. in between 'patients' " (44); a friend of Francisco's uncle is named Sullivan after the *Ed Sullivan Show* by his grandma; and Fe attributes her constant screaming, after Tom dumps her, to being in touch with her feelings—"just like she had heard a panel of jilted ex-fiancées say on the 'Oprah Winfrey' show" (119). But Castillo shows us that television is not solely for female viewers, as evidenced by Domingo, who "was just sitting there all demoralized in his Lazy-boy in front of the television watching telenovelas, and shows like Cara a Cara . . . and fifteen-minute cooking programs sponsored by Goya Foods" (217). Loca picks up her father's "mindless habit of indiscriminate T.V. watching" after her sisters die. "And though no one would have ever thought of the television as any kind of psychic vehicle, one Sunday evening while Loca was staring at one of those 'news magazine' shows, Sofi got a premonition from it, and with a deep sigh, resigned herself to the fact that she was going to die alone" (219). Inevitably, then, Castillo adopts the television as a tool for her magical realism.

Yet television does not always play a prominent—or even significant—role in North American magical realist texts. In some cases, authors use television as a brief diversion or even as an interruption of the normal daily routine, rather than for its magical potential. The single time Kroetsch mentions television in the often timeless world of *What the Crow Said*, the reference is a telling clue as to its relative non-existence. "In the parlor, a TV set was turned too loud but no one was listening" (186). Indeed, no one is listening to much popular culture in the Municipality of Bigknife. In fact, the continuing progress of the outside world, with its "airplanes that flew without propellers [and] . . . highways that were made of solid cement but soared through the air" (142) are as foreign as magnets to Macondons. In *The Road to Tamazunchale*, Arias makes the intervention of the television just as fleeting and negligible. It is the vehicle through which the Americanized Jess seems to escape the more immediate concerns around him as he watches.

Jess was determined to go the limit with Monster Mulhoon, the Giant of the Ozarks. "Just a minute," he answered [Carmela's call for help], then saw the flying kick coming, heard the crack, and his spine broke like a saltine cracker. He fell to the floor and waited helplessly for another Mulhoon trick.

"Jess!"

"Alright, I'm coming." Rolling on his side, he socked the armchair cushion, ducked under the hairy eye-gouge and whopped the Giant on the ear. Mulhoon tumbled onto the coffee table. Jess bent over his victim, tweaked the handlebar moustache and skipped away toward the stairs. (44)

This pseudo-magical realist moment not only inserts Jess into the match; it also pulls the Giant himself into Carmela's living room in what seems to be an extremely telling, adolescent moment of indulgence for Jess.

Much more startling, and more important to the impact of magical realism in the text, is how Arias uses the interruption of *The Road to Tamazunchale* by the movie set. When Fausto with his pink cape and hoe and Marcelino in his Peruvian herder's clothes wander onto the set, they are still as out of place as they are on the streets of Los Angeles. "Wrong period," says a woman in cut-off Levis and sneakers who insists that she is only a "whore" (rather than a "Madame," as Fausto refers to her) and who had played a flower girl the day before. "We're doing seventeenth century" (51), she tells them. The director tells them that "one more take" and the revolution will be over. In a novel where Fausto's own mental wanderings take him on fantastic journeys into past histories, the most fantastic version is actually the one produced by Hollywood. Later Fausto explains the concept of movies to Marcelino:

> "It's a picture of people who move."
> "They talk too?"
> "Everything, they do everything we do . . . even fight."
> The nightmare swirled in Marcelino's head; he saw the midget lifting barbells, the dying man spewing blood, the machetes hackling at the blond, blue giants.
> "But there's a difference between them and us," Fausto said. "We can leave the movie, and they can't. They're trapped." (53)

In Fausto's mind, he and Marcelino are simply visitors in the surreal world of the movie, able to move in and out of the film. The "trapped" characters are indeed unable to leave; as fictional characters of the finished product, they are static, like the traditional version of *The Mysterious Warrior* in *Green Grass, Running Water*. The distinction between the two is that King's characters see the potential for re-writing that cinematic history; Fausto only sees the possibility for revising actual history, of taking the "mojados" to a place perhaps even better for them than the United States. Fausto's Quixotic quest works to "push away annoying reminders of time" like the telephone poles and billboards that remind him to which period he truly belongs (15).

Because *Beloved*, of all the novels included in this section, is historically bound to a scene in U.S. history that, unlike the contemporary influx of media, emphasizes little popular culture, it seems reasonable to conclude that in it Morrison would offer the least amount of commentary on pop culture. Although *Beloved* explores social, economic, even historical realities within the confines of its magical realism, the popular culture of the day seems particularly absent. In part, those social and historical realities that define it also exclude the characters in *Beloved* from participation in popular culture. No African American, particularly in the 1880s of *Beloved*'s "present," is quite free of the repercussions of slavery. Perhaps Morrison's only significant comment upon popular culture lies in her treatment of newspapers, specifically Paul D's assessment of the white papers and what they have to say about his race:

The print meant nothing to him so he didn't even glance at it. He simply looked at the face, shaking his head no. No . . . at whatever it was those black scratches said, and no to whatever it was Stamp Paid wanted him to know. Because there was no way in hell a black face could appear in a newspaper if the story was about something anybody wanted to hear. A whip of fear broke through the heart chambers as soon as you saw a Negro's face in a paper, since the face was not there because the person had a healthy baby, or outran a street mob. Nor was it there because the person had been killed, or maimed or caught or burned or jailed or whipped or evicted or stomped or raped or cheated, since that could hardly qualify as news in a newspaper. It would have to be something out of the ordinary—something white people would find interesting, truly different, worth a few minutes of teeth sucking if not gasps. (155–56)

If Sethe appears in the paper, she has to have done something "worth the breath catch of a white citizen of Cincinnati" (156), and it is therefore something Paul D does not want to acknowledge. Thus, Morrison not only makes Sethe's act of violence against her own child horrific enough to become the catalyst for the magical realism in *Beloved*, but she also makes it "newsworthy" enough to appear in white papers.

Through *Beloved*, Morrison challenges the "verity" of the printed word, particularly in relation to the African-American community; in so doing, she also reassesses the post-Civil War community of the southern United States, especially its mass culture's tastes, beliefs, and most popular medium. Dana Heller argues that "Paul D's inability to read the newspaper article describing Sethe's act of infanticide may suggest not that he has been deceived by Sethe, nor that he is ill-equipped to make sense of the world around him, but that the 'literate' culture's interpretation of her act is, and by necessity should remain, far removed from his own" (114). Similarly, Ashraf H. A. Rushdy notes that

Morrison provides a criticism of print media through Paul D's assessment of what newspapers will or will not write about black people. . . . Morrison criticizes the ideological imperative of print media in order to establish the value of oral historical relation. This criticism of print media is very much part of the overall revisionist motive in criticizing the historiography of slavery. (588)

Kroetsch, too, intends to critique the mass culture dependent on the newspaper as its primary news source. Kroetsch fills *What the Crow Said* with pertinent—often ironic—details left out of the articles printed in the *Big Indian Signal*. For instance, the newspaper's printed versions of Vera's accounts of her husbands' deaths avoid mention of the suicidal undertones at the crime scenes. Moreover, the name of the paper itself seems particularly ironic, given the limited interaction between the largely white readership of the *Big Indian Signal* and the indigenous group upon which the name signifies. The "signal" is not for Native Americans at all but rather for the mass, white populace. Liebhaber's editorial work eventually leads him to question the very signs by which he creates the *Big Indian Signal*; eventually his type has less and less meaning for him as he gains an awareness of its subjectivity.

All the capital letters in his collection of wood type were set in neat rows, arranged alphabetically. He couldn't bear that either. In terror at the domestication of those free, beautiful letters—no, it was the absurdity of their recited order that afflicted him: ABCDEFGHIJKLMNOPQRSTUVWXYZ—he . . . tried to disentangle himself from the tyranny of rote. The U, he argued aloud to himself, in the Middle Ages, was the final letter, held by the wisest of men to be only a rounded version of V. He tried to resay the alphabet and failed. I and J, he remembered, were once deemed the same: he tried to disregard one in his recitation and lost both. He tried again, the simplest changing of the alphabet—and heard himself making sounds for which he had no signs at all. (69)

But the most important magical realist aspect the paper brings to the novel is that it journalistically renders the supernatural events of the municipality: equally "factual" are the accounts of the year the snow does not melt, Liebhaber's drafting of Martin Lang's obituary before the event occurs, and Vera's dispassionate contributions—"*Mr. and Mrs. Bert Brausen are pleased to announce the engagement of their eldest daughter. The horses aren't shedding. Men are a bunch of useless bastards*" (19).

~

North American (and particularly the United States's) climb in global status has taken its toll on both Canada and the United States. According to Fath Davis Ruffins,

Between 1945 and 1975, Americans turned their nation into a global powerhouse of production and consumption. . . . Yet the same nation that was shown proceeding toward consumerist heaven in countless television commercials, Hollywood movies, and print advertisements was also riven by profound internal conflict, especially over questions of race and ethnicity. (379, 380)

As Ruffins suggests, the consumer and popular cultures are inextricably bound; they feed one another and have each become the other's best promoter. She also hints at the corollary between the growth of the consumer culture and the cost to the margins of the society. Because the discrepancies in the American dream introduce the specific need for both the marginalized and the majority to reassess their culture, magical realism seems particularly suited to the current situation for American writers. Although the particular needs of marginalized authors who invoke magical realism will be discussed in more detail in Chapter 6, the preceding discussion already begins to illustrate the degree to which this group comments upon the consumer and popular cultures by way of magical realist texts.

Debra Spark's lament about the paucity of magical realist works in the United States may be a bit rash, and her own difficulties using the mode on North American soil may ultimately hinge on a personal rather than communal difficulty. Zamora argues that "a crucial difference between U.S. and Latin American traditions of counterrealism" is that "[m]ost contemporary U.S. magical realists find a way to bring their ghosts above ground and integrate them into contemporary U.S. culture in order to enrich or remedy it" (*Usable Past* 118). Sanders concurs: "Contemporary [North] American Magic Realists . . . are concerned not with heightening confusion but with providing understanding and answers to the existing confusion"—a product of magical realism's evolution and adaptation into U.S. fiction (27). The magical realist mode allows a variety of authors to uncover inconsistencies in the popular and consumer cultures of northern America. Although the contradictions between haves and have-nots tend to be concentrated around the marginal figures of society—whether those individuals are marginalized by ethnicity or gender, or by quasi-legal or illegal status—they are also fodder for mainstream writers as well. Moreover, as such margins challenge the very terms "mass" or "popular culture," and since majority rules tend not to apply to predominantly diversified areas such as Los Angeles, the mainstream and the margin, particularly through the images of popular and consumer culture, seem to relocate to a more unified center.

NOTES

An abbrieviated version of this chapter appeared in *Publications of the Arkansas Philological Association* (26.2 [Fall 2000]: 45–60) under the same title.

1. Natty Bumppo might serve as an example here; in turn, the indirect connection between the frontier myth and magical realism seems to throw light on Thomas King's choice of "Nasty Bumpo" in *Green Grass, Running Water*.

2. Raymond Williams calls "culture" "one of the two or three most complicated words in the English language" (*Keywords* 87).

3. Rowe cites Homi Bhabha here; according to Rowe, Bhabha's work *Nation and Narration* explores the relationship between postmodernism and postcolonial studies in great detail.

4. That is, antirealism, counterrealism, fabulation, the fantastic, and surfiction (181).

5. Chanady, in "The Territorialization of the Imaginary," 144 n.32, provides an excellent and concise summary of Zamora's arguments in *Do the Americas Have a Common Literature?*

6. "Werner Sollers has now documented that the term 'melting pot' first became widely used as a result of a 1908 play [called "The Melting Pot"] by Israel Zangwill depicting the complications involved in a Jewish-Catholic marriage" (Ruffins 388).

7. See Seattle's "'Our People Are Ebbing Away' Like a Rapidly Receding Tide" for one Native American chief's take—albeit one filtered through the white editorial pen—on such "choice."

8. And some census predictions estimate that such marginalized groups might not remain the minority in the United States much longer, as their population growth outstrips that of whites.

9. The section in Chapter 6 entitled "On the Fringes of Magical Realism" pursues this line of argument in more detail and with specific examples from marginalized literature.

10. James Livingston defines the consumer culture "as the culture specific to corporate capitalism, which emerges circa 1890–1930 in the United States" (416), though the term has a world-wide application today.

11. Much the same work is being done in Latin America by contemporary authors, as Chapter 6 argues.

12. And as discussed in the introduction to *Rediscovering Magical Realism*.

13. Chapter 1 has already provided my rationale for using the Rio Grande as the border for "North American" magical realism.

14. Much as García Márquez refigures science as the fantastic in *One Hundred Years of Solitude* (see Chapter 3).

15. When discussing specific characters from the novel, *Rediscovering Magical Realism* follows the precedence set by King himself in referring to the Native-American characters as "Indians."

16. The irony is, of course, that Coyote—the predominant storyteller and creative figure in much of Native American culture—would need to be taught the story he generally tells.

17. Susan's communications with Helen and the other ghosts in *Out of Time* are equally private, as discussed in more detail later in this chapter.

18. Ultimately, though, of the texts considered "magical realist" in this chapter, *Dreaming in Cuban*'s link with the mode is the most tenuous.

19. Ude's criteria are as follows:

(1) They reject the narrow confines of traditional realism for a multi-dimensional, metaphysical reality; (2) They depict the mythical or legendary—as well as the historical—past as an actual presence in contemporary life; (3) They reveal an acute sense of esthetics, achieving—or at least seeking—poetic re-creations rather than mere imitations of reality . . . ; (4) They distort time, space, and identity as those elements are understood in conventional realism . . . ; (5) Their versions of human psychology tend to be based on Jungian archetypal theories rather than on either Skinnerian behaviorism or Freudian/surrealist notions of the single, isolated, agonizing psyche; and finally, (6) They demonstrate a firm belief in the validity of the realities they present; their persuasive, matter-of-fact tones and use of the everyday details of commonplace realism, mixed with magical—or mystical—elements are designed to produce in the reader an equally firm belief. ("North American Magical Realism" 23)

Ude's six "elements" provide interesting fodder for the definition of magical realism, and as with many critics' criteria for magical realism, his points are certainly within the limits of Chanady's own criteria. In his discussion of texts, though, he neglects the fact that religious events like "miracles" are, for the characters, authors, and readers, all accepted aspects of the supernatural's existence in "reality." Thus, magical realism cannot rely on these elements as the foundation for its own supernatural events.

20. Karl Oldenberg, quoted in Wyrwa, 436. "Oldenberg defined consumption as the satisfaction of human needs through economic means" (Wyrwa 436).

21. The easy availability of items on-line seems particularly ironic, since the "real" is even farther removed from the other side of the "glass" (i.e., the computer screen that separates us from the goods). Leach uses the phrase "difference between the real and the unreal" in his description of the ideological penetration of commercial culture into American life.

22. Notably, Bursum refers to the Native Americans around him as Indians, even though "you couldn't call them Indians. You had to remember their tribe, as if that made any difference, and when some smart college professor did come up with a really good name like Amerindian, the Indians didn't like it" (210). Interestingly, *Green Grass, Running Water*, in its indiscriminate use of the term "Indian" over the seemingly preferable tribal affiliation or even more politically correct "Native American," seems to side with Bursum.

23. Garcia references here the trend, one extremely popular in Latin American literature, of equating sexuality with food. Other texts with similar connections between the two types of appetites include *Dona Flor and Her Two Husbands*, *Like Water for Chocolate*, and *Señora Honeycomb*.

24. Though the use of the phrase "consumer culture" is perhaps anachronistic, given Livingston's claim that it is "a twentieth-century phenomenon" (416), Morrison's contemporaneity provides justification of this scholarly look at her characters as consumers and consumables of a nation on the cusp of (if not in the act of) embracing the consumer culture.

25. Or "wetbacks," as Fausto refers to the Mexicans. Fausto's use of the term seems almost an endearment; it is his dead wife Evangelina who thinks the United States has "too many mojados already" and who has forgotten her own first-generational Mexican roots (64).

26. Baseball is described in Cuba as "the national pastime."

27. See Chapter 2 for more on Latin America and its "take" on popular culture.

28. King, of course, does not stop at revising existing texts; he also revises history, as when Columbus's three ships and their "discovery" of the New World is reinvented as the destruction of the Parliament Lake Dam by three cars sailing on the lake—"a Nissan, a Pinto, and a Karmann-Ghia" (448).

29. Eli reads a novel with a character known by the same moniker.

30. Oddly enough, his claim that he is a friend to Indians is given in the context of his fight with the Indian who stands in the way of his development of Parliament Lake. When Eli Stands Alone decides to live in his family's cabin, which lies under the dam that creates the lake and holds up the building on lakefront property on a "legal technicality" (209), Bursum argues that Eli "[c]an't stay there forever." But Eli says he will stay "As long as the grass is green and the waters run" (295).

5

"Suspended Between the Nastiness of Life and the Meanness of the Dead": Beloved as the Physical Embodiment of Magical Realism

No gasp at a miracle that is truly miraculous because the magic lies in the fact that you knew it was there for you all along.

—*Beloved*

"Anything dead coming back to life hurts."

—Amy Denver, *Beloved*

Toni Morrison's *Beloved* ties together history, the supernatural, and the realities of life for African Americans in the 1880s into a rich package that teaches us things we would prefer not to know, about places we would never want to go. In addition, the novel is perhaps the single best illustration of U.S. magical realism known to the mainstream reader. The events in *Beloved* do not constitute the occasional magic Wendy Faris claims them to be ("Scheherazade's Children" 165). Instead, *Beloved*'s magical realism is pervasive: Denver will befriend it; Paul D will be ruled by it; Sethe, who is strangled and loved and tortured by it, lives with it. Yet the title character Beloved *is* magical realism. As a magical realist character, Beloved does more than represent Sethe's past or the history of slavery: Beloved "gives blood to the scraps" and *lives* them. By neglecting to distinguish Beloved as a character related to but ultimately independent of both the ghost and the "crawling-already?" baby, many readers also disregard the significance of the introduction of Beloved into the household of 124 and the surrounding community. Because Morrison draws on the distinctions between representation and actuality—on the interplay of symbolism and mimesis—to give literal and figurative flesh to Beloved, she allows this magical realist creation to play a complex, multifaceted role in the novel.

Critical perspectives on Beloved abound. She is described as demon, as possessed, as human, and as ghost-come-to-life. Most of these descriptions focus on
her representational form rather than her physical body; many who discuss the
corporeal aspect of Beloved still manage to connect her primarily with the ghost
that Paul D beats away from 124 at the beginning of the novel. Critics identify her
as the "ghost of the victim"[1] or refer to the ghost itself as "Beloved"—a particularly
ironic choice of wording, given that the baby has no name at all in the text until Beloved appropriates the word off the baby's tombstone.[2] Robert Broad, who calls
Beloved "a puzzled and puzzling, poly-generational, mnemonically tortured, un-
certain spirit" (192), must rely on the terms "spirit" or "ghost" to characterize
her—although he has an awareness of both Beloved's physicality and his terminology.[3] Ultimately, however, such readings seriously neglect (or, at least, neglect to
emphasize) that the ghost and Beloved are two separate and distinct characters.
While the ghost represents only the spiritual world and the rages of the crawling-already? baby, Beloved belongs to multiple worlds and multiple rages. In Denver's words, "At times I think she was—more" (266).

A few scholars have rightly begun to distance Beloved from the ghost itself, if
only slightly, as illustrated by Deborah Horvitz's "corporeal ghost" (93) or
Denise Heinze's "semiotic haint" (208). Indeed, any attempt to define Beloved
beyond "ghostly apparition" is a step in the right direction. An even clearer distinction is made by critics Ashraf H.A. Rushdy, who claims that Beloved is "the
incarnation of the ghost of the murdered daughter" (570), and Elizabeth Fox-
Genovese, in her evocative title "ghost-become-presence" (14); both distinguish
Beloved from the ghost by invoking the supernatural. Although defining the
magical—finding words to describe what Beloved is or is not—can test a writer's
semantic skills, several critics clarify Beloved's distinctions from and similarities
to the ghost by discussing her in the terms of the supernatural. Trudier Harris
calls her "the shape-shifter who takes on flesh-and-blood human characteristics"
(131), and Kristine Holmes argues she is "literally embodied as corporeal substance and sustenance" (141). She is a "grown-up zombie" to Martha Bayles (36),
and to Heinze, "part ghost, zombie, devil, and memory"(205), a "supernatural
memory" (209) that, in David Lawrence's words, "has the power to construct and
circumscribe identity . . . in the image of its own contents" (231). As memory,
Beloved most clearly connects with Sethe's infanticide. Indeed, Broad claims
that, in Beloved, Sethe and Denver both see only "their daughter and sister returned from the dead" (190), and Morrison herself argues that her novel is about
the "unburied" brought back to "living life" (Angelo 120).

Although "Morrison won't even let us capture Beloved's *bodily* identity without a
struggle" (Broad 195 n.1), those critics who do see Beloved as a corporeal character
are hard-pressed to "acquire" that body, if only temporarily, in order to write about
it. One popular interpretation refigures Beloved's body as the past, whether she is described specifically as the "external embodiment of Sethe's past" (Finney 105), as
"specific members of Sethe's family" (Horvitz 93), or, more generally, as "the material projection of slavery" (Moglen 208). As "Sethe's alter ego,"[4] Beloved is "the cus-

todian of the story that was not to be passed on" (Fox-Genovese 15). Lois Parkinson Zamora, calling Beloved "a symbolic and historical embodiment of both [Sethe's] past and her future" ("Magical Romance/Magical Realism" 501), links the supernatural not only to Sethe's individual past but also to her ultimate redemption and perhaps hinting that Beloved holds the key to both. As one of the "familial representations" that Dana Heller argues "take [shape] within historically-specific communities of women" (107), Beloved is the maternal ancestor returned. But refigured as a larger past, Beloved is "the embodiment of the past that must be remembered in order to be forgotten" (Rushdy 571), or "the inconvenient reembodiment of that which we would like to keep silent and submerged" (Holmes 145; emphasis added). Susan Comfort argues that bodily, Beloved "relives the past in the way a hysteric does" and connects her with the "transitional, liminal figures" described by Helene Cixous and Catherine Clement in *The Newly Born Woman* (123)—an apt title for Beloved herself. Yet Rebecca Ferguson believes Beloved approaches "most nearly Julia Kristeva's concept of the pre-Oedipal 'semiotic'"(117). Finally, "[i]n her most comprehensive context within the narrative, Beloved stands for all the ancestors lost in the Diaspora, demanding restoration to a temporal continuum in which the 'present' time encompasses much of the immediate past, including several generations of the dead" (Jessee 199).[5] In the end, we must accept Beloved as the "amalgamation" Holmes claims her to be (145)—but an amalgamation of *many* of these contingencies rather than the embodiment of any single theory or idea.

In a direct challenge to Beloved as the embodiment of anything, Elizabeth House expresses surprise at anyone who would believe her to be "unquestionably a ghost" or "a supernatural being of any kind" (117). House argues that Beloved's unlined feet and hands can be justified by Stamp Paid's hypothesis that Beloved is the girl from Deer Creek who had been locked away by a white man for her entire life. "This possibility would explain Beloved's 'new skin,' her unlined feet and hands, for if the girl were constantly kept indoors, her skin would not be weathered or worn" (120). Moreover, House contends, the scar on her neck could be from abuse. Yet when Janey, the Bowdin's maid, finds out that Beloved does not have lines on her hands, she draws her own conclusion that "Sethe's dead daughter, the one whose throat she cut, had come back to fix her" (255). In addition, Barbara Christian relates Beloved to her own Caribbean background, where ancestral spirits return to visit, eat, and drink in carnal form, yet differ "from the living in that while they do appear as bodies, their eyes and skin, like Beloved's, are those of new-born babies" (367).

If these verdicts neatly explained away or accounted for Beloved, this novel would *not* be magical realism. Under Janey's simple terms of revenge, Beloved could be accounted for as are most malcontented "haints"—as a punishment returned from the other side with unresolved issues or for past deeds, in which case Beloved would be a stereotypical ghost story. Yet Beloved wants *all* of Sethe, not just her remorse, but her love and attention and her life. If her sole purpose was "an-eye-for-an-eye" vengeance, she would have completed her strangulation of Sethe in Baby Suggs's field and have been done with it. Janey's hypothesis is understandable; indeed, Ella and others in the community put forth the same theory. Similarly, Christian's context allows a plausible explanation for the new skin (if not the scars) on the young woman's body. Only House, who contends that Beloved is merely the girl from Deer Creek, must warp both history and the novel to supply support for her claims. Not only does she claim that Beloved could have been a passenger on the slave ships (a near impossibility, since the slave trade to North America was nonexistent by the early nineteenth century); she even invents a second pair of earrings for the mother the girl left behind in Africa. Perhaps more disturbing is the fact that, beyond the earrings, she never accounts for Beloved's intimate knowledge of the household and its inhabitants, particularly her ability to put the single word on a tombstone together with Sethe and her crime. Finally, House simply disregards the magical aspects of the character. If we are to believe that Beloved is the escaped girl, her supernatural qualities—the disappearance in the shed, her removal of and sexual assault on Paul D, even her apparent need of Sethe in particular—must be attributed to illusion, lust, and chance.

In order to reach her conclusions, House must ignore the evidence, physical and otherwise, that Beloved has an immediate connection with Sethe's past. In dismissing the similarities between Beloved's scars and those of the crawling-already? baby, she discounts signs that transcend coincidence and refuses Beloved that portion of her reality that should be regarded as a homecoming. Most important is that she misses what Morrison is attempting to tell us by embodying Beloved but also by leaving her a nearly blank slate. Beloved's smooth hands and feet lack not weathering, but rather the finger, palm, and sole prints that make us individually distinguishable. Lacking these marks allows Beloved to be more than House wants to admit, more than any *individual* person could be, and, at the same time, less than human.[6]

Identifying what Beloved is *not* is at least as important as pinning down what Beloved *is*: Beloved and the ghost that haunts 124 at the beginning of the text are not synonymous. They are, at least to an extent, two separate and individual characters. Beloved cannot simply be the ghost that many claim her to be, nor is she the human Elizabeth House argues for. Comfort suggests that "Beloved's power and magic derive from her discursive liminality: she is both a child and a woman but neither, both a ghost and a living human being but neither" (123). Certainly, one aspect of her magical realist quality revolves around what she *might* be—the possibility that she is a real girl from Deer Creek, or that she is somehow Sethe's mother returned, or any number of other possibilities. In short, she cannot be confined to any one of the above descriptions. As a ghost, the crawling-already? baby is, and is only, the murdered child haunting 124 who can do little more than demonstrate her anger. When Beloved encompasses that spirit, however, she takes on new hurts and needs, as if becoming "real" involves taking on the world's problems, including, as Heinze suggests, the readers' own need to purge themselves of what Morrison calls the "national amnesia" (208) that has disassociated us from the history of slavery.[7] Just as Sethe's re-memories are more tangible than memories, Beloved is more tangible than a ghost.

Beloved's palpable physicality does not make her less ephemeral. "Beloved can never be fully conceptualized because she is continually in a state of transition" (Heinze 208); "she assumes the shape of something slightly different to all who embrace her. She is their worst fear and their most profound need combined" (Heller 115–16). Significantly, Denver asks "*What* is that?" (51; emphasis added), rather than "who," when she sees Beloved sitting on the stump. In his review of Morrison's novel, Thomas R. Edwards says

Beloved thus proposes to be a ghost story about slavery, and Morrison firmly excludes any tricky indeterminacies about the supernatural. This ghost of the elder daughter is no projection of a neurotic observer, no superstitious mass delusion. . . . Morrison provides us no cozy corner from which to smile skeptically at the thrills we're enjoying. If you believe in *Beloved* at all you must accept the ghost in the same way you accept the other, solidly realistic figures in the story. . . . But then Morrison, with even more daring indifference to the rules of realistic fiction, brings to Sethe's house a lovely, historyless young woman who calls herself Beloved and is unquestionably the dead daughter's spirit in human form. (79)

Sally Keenan, too, notes, "Morrison's text . . . draws attention to its decidedly fictive quality by constantly transgressing the bounds of even realist fiction" (49). Though we might quibble with Edwards's "unquestionable" notion of Beloved's origin, he spells out the dilemma over reading *Beloved* as a ghost story. After all, were this an actual ghost story, we should be frightened of Beloved's "haunting." The fact that we are not indicates her position as a supernatural force that descends on the complacent, accepting remnants of Sethe's family. Instead, we are more afraid of what she represents for the inhabitants of 124 Bluestone Road.

Beloved is haunted by more than one ghost. Sethe hears the Miami who ride the wind above the pig yards as she is walking home. Stamp Paid discovers that the voices surrounding 124 "like a noose" (183) are from the "people of the broken necks, of fire-cooked blood and black girls who had lost their ribbons" (181). Hence, Baby Suggs all but dismisses the ghost in their midst: "Not a house in the country ain't packed to its rafters with some dead Negro's grief. We lucky this ghost is a baby" (5). Christian says that "for African Americans, at least until the recent past, the experience of spirits communicating with the living was a natural one rather than a weird, unnatural act" (366). While ghosts are not anomalies in this text, Beloved nonetheless defies convention. When Beloved violates the rules of the dead by assuming both shape and attitude, the neighbor woman who had helped Sethe when she first arrived feels obligated to assist her again: "As long as the ghost showed out from its ghostly place—shaking stuff, crying, smashing and such—Ella respected it. But if it took flesh and came in her world, well, the shoe was on the other foot. She didn't mind a little communication between the two worlds, but this was an invasion" (257).[8] Like Ella, *Beloved* "is not concerned with the claims the past may make upon the present, but with how far those claims may conceivably be met and on what terms" (Ferguson 111). Baby Suggs is prescient not of the baby's death or even of its reappearance as a haint; her fears and premonitions focus on the trouble in "the high-topped shoes she didn't like the look of" (139). Like the "angel" in Gabriel García Márquez's "The Very Old Man with Enormous Wings," Beloved no longer conforms to the stereotypes assigned to the supernatural and becomes an object of anger and rejection.

Because Beloved challenges the notions of a traditional ghost story, one goal of many critics has been to reclassify both Beloved and the novel accordingly. Heinze claims, "Beloved is Morrison's most unambiguous endorsement of the supernatural; so rife is the novel with the physical and spiritual presence of ghostly energy that a better term than supernatural would be the uncanny, defined by Schelling as 'the name for everything that ought to have remained ... secret and hidden but has come to light'" (205). Similarly, Ferguson evaluates Beloved by Freud's definition of the uncanny: "She is, in Freud's words, 'something repressed which recurs,' something supposedly 'dead' returning painfully to life, through the supernatural at work in the 'world of common reality,' yet 'in reality nothing new or alien, but . . . familiar and old-established in the mind' " (113). Granted, in spite of the novel's own decree that "[i]t was not a story to pass on" (274–75), Beloved cannot remain secret or hidden if Sethe is to heal. But Sethe, to whom Beloved should be the "familiar and old-established in the mind," does not recognize Beloved until well after her appearance on the stump in front of the house. What is more, Denver initially identifies Beloved as her returned sister, kindred spirit to the exiled ghost, but eventually finds her to be "more" than the familiar or expected.

The "more" of Beloved and its title character is magical realism. While such scholars as Bayles and Francis Joseph Schaack have taken the first step and connected Beloved with magical realism, they have done very little to defend their points of view.[9] Indeed, Bayles's primary intent is to show that, "[b]y embracing the genre, Morrison[, who may be the first to combine black folk culture with the romantic impulses of magic realism,] also embraces its willful romanticism, which, in the context of black America, leads to the corollary that the most marginal people are the least corrupted by the false values of the dominant white society" (38). She sees this as reverse racism, "excusing Sethe from lasting blame" and "almost equat[ing] her infanticide with Sixo's pilfering" (40). Finally, she says, "[i]n Morrison's mind there seems to be only one crime, that of slavery itself, and no person who lives under it has to answer for anything. So intent is she on showing the inhumanity of the master, she dehumanizes the slave" (40). Yet Heller argues that Morrison "unsettles the definitional boundaries of the Western European traditions of family romance and novelistic realism" and that "experienced readers of African-American fiction" will see her work as a de-romanticization of the black family romance, a result of the "complex forms of economic and psychological oppression that black women and men have experienced both within the nuclear family and within the larger economic structure" (106–7). Halle, the ironic and mysteriously M.I.A. father and husband, is no longer himself when he "deserts" his family. In a way, then, he is no more to blame for deserting his family than Sethe is for killing their child. Like Sethe, Halle is a victim of the institution; the "rape" of Sethe's breast milk undoes his noble ideas for both of them. The scene Paul D recounts of seeing Halle covered in butter and clabber (another form of "mother's milk"), though, suggests that Halle is broken more easily than Sethe can be, even after she kills one of her children. Rather than having "betrayed the black family by failing to shoulder responsibility for restoring to it an image of wholeness and unity" (Heller 105) as media and critics like Bayles suggest, *Beloved* returns the father figure to the text in the end, providing Sethe with a man who is strong enough to put Sethe back together. Bayles's reading of Morrison's magical realism also fails to connect Sethe's crime with Beloved's reappearance. Much like the community that ostracizes Sethe for eighteen years, Beloved symbolizes the "payment" for Sethe's actions; both disallow Sethe to forget her crime. Bayles does not acknowledge Beloved as both muse to and incarnation of the magical realism in the text.

Beloved (novel and character) not only relies on magical realism for its present but also connects magical realism with the past. Helen Lock's notion that Sethe's "rememory as narrative principle . . . enables *Beloved* to mediate between past and present realities, blurring the distinction between them and remembering the disremembered" (205), provides a valuable tool for describing the magical realism of the novel. The use of magical realism as a narrative mode enables Beloved to mediate not only between past and present realities but also between the natural and supernatural worlds. "*Beloved* is also a novel that constructs the ideal 'listener.' Denver will tell and re-tell the story that she now understands. . . . Denver represents the implied community of ideal readers, the 'aural being'" (Rushdy 586), sentiments that echo Amaryll Chanady's discussion of the implied reader and authorial reticence.[10] Morrison takes the edge off what even she has described as a "ghost story" by turning the events into matter-of-fact realities that are as believable as the atrocities that the black characters suffer at the hands of Southern whites.

Schaack's discussion of magical realism notes that "almost every critic of the fantastic mentions the supernatural event as issuing from and dependent on and reflecting a particular 'worldview'" (31 n.10), and Beloved is no exception. Sharon P. Holland and Michael Awkward believe that "while Sethe needs an alternative worldview to survive in and out of slavery, it can blur her perception of events affecting her approach to living. *Beloved* consistently addresses this sense of paired realities and the choices each person is responsible for making in relation to existing or created space, reality, and time" (51). Arguably, Beloved is the physical manifestation of Sethe's own skewed worldview; in any event, she does issue from, depend on, and reflect "a world with limited notions of reality" (Heinze 206).

Because Paul D exorcizes the ghost from Sethe's house,[11] he robs the supernatural of its ability to function within the realm of the natural world. He tampers with the balance between the customary supernatural and everyday in this community, and by doing so he arguably threatens the magical realism in the novel. To maintain the magical realism and to intervene in the real world more directly, the spirit must assume a human shape, must become a physical presence in the novel. Once she does, her actions are harder to "classify" since, as a ghost, she displays typical ghostly behavior: she rants, she knocks things around, she haunts through noise and color and tantrum-like displays. Paul D forces Beloved to "grow up," though with Beloved perhaps the more appropriate term is "grow out."

Although logically Beloved should focus her rage on Sethe, she initially diverts it toward Paul D, the aggressor who rids 124 of its baby ghost. Beloved's revenge on him for intervening in Sethe's life is a very grown-up one, in that she manipulates him with sex. After Beloved discovers sex through the turtles in the creek, the following chapter begins, "Paul D began to tremble" (106). Although the sentence refers directly to the flashback of his days in Arnold, Georgia, the words carry an ominous foreshadowing of Beloved's use of him. But Beloved's seduction of Paul D is more than revenge on her mother or Paul D. Sex stresses her fleshly shape, and it gives her a power over him that the ghost did not have. Paul D is unable to exorcize this new form from his bed or the house from which she slowly removes him. He only *thinks* her out of the house and she "strangles" on a raisin, planting her more firmly in Sethe's and Denver's sympathies. Even Paul D feels wrong about trying to remove her from 124: "It was one thing to beat up a ghost, quite another to throw a helpless colored girl out in territory infected by the Klan" (66). Ironically, Beloved is not merely a "girl," and because she is actually less helpless now than if she were a ghost, it takes something stronger than Paul D (i.e., the humming anger of the female neighbors) to expel her the second time.

Once Beloved, with the inadvertent help of Stamp Paid, removes Paul D from the house, she concentrates on Sethe. Beloved wants to be Sethe's daughter and double. Although her imitations certainly show Beloved's desire, she fails because she is not real in the sense that counts—she is born not of Sethe but of water, and her connections to the supernatural are at odds with any human qualities she has. "Beloved's double presence, for all its potency, suggests equally powerfully a kind of absence. Being in both realms, she seems to exist fully in neither" (Ferguson 114). Beloved's double presence in the text is perhaps best symbolized by the name she appropriates off the tombstone, a name that cannot truly represent the crawling-already? baby, since her name either never existed or was absorbed by the tragedy of her death. Being nameless keeps the ghost in the world of the supernatural; she has lost touch with her human form, and because we never learn the baby's name, we get the sense that she was never human, either. "The loss of name, [Hortense] Spillers argues, is 'a metaphor of displacement' for the cultural and social practices lost in the Middle Passage. The naming by Morrison summons up this profound absence in the historical record" (Comfort 123). In a sense, though, Beloved invents herself through self-naming. By her "misreading" of the message on her gravestone, Beloved simultaneously constructs her own existence as human being and compromises any sense of what her "person" really means to Sethe and Denver. Her mother trades sex for Beloved's name merely because she does not think to bargain for "Dearly" as well, and the words themselves are put into Sethe's mouth by the minister at the funeral, not by the emotion she has for her unnamed, dead daughter.

Perhaps because of her connection with Sethe's dead daughter, Beloved's body seems subject to the forces of both the spiritual and the natural worlds. "The only relatively sure thing about Beloved is her bodily identity" (Broad 190), that is, that she has a body representative of Sethe's act nineteen years earlier. When Beloved says, "I am Beloved and she is mine," we see her need to possess both the body of the character Beloved and the spirit. As Ferguson points out, Beloved spends considerable time and effort "holding herself together, defending herself from being engulfed or exploding in the space between the two worlds in which she simultaneously exists" (114). Ferguson illustrates her point via the shed scene where Beloved is "eaten alive by the dark" (114), but the passage where she loses a tooth and fears flying apart is likewise exemplary. Beloved's physical and spiritual aspects do not always work in tandem, and at times her struggle is made manifest in her relationship with others. For example, the spirit (rather than the logical, easier-to-manage-and-manipulate body) is what chokes Sethe in the clearing; the body kisses the wounds. Ironically, before Beloved's arrival, "the ghost [is] the only member of the family who seeks the intimacy of physical contact" (Lawrence 237). Even though the contact the two make with the living is violent in nature, Beloved and the murdered daughter are nonetheless linked by their mutual need to touch.

We can associate Beloved with at least three forms in the text, then—the baby girl, her ghost, and the physical form called "Beloved." In spite of this ironically reconfigured "trinity," Beloved's return is no religious journey. Instead, hers is a stagnant characterization. For one thing, each of these forms maintains the same emotional maturity. In spite of the scope of her physical growth, a physicality suggesting the grown-up daughter herself had she survived Sethe's attempt to "save" her from slavery, Beloved cannot duplicate that growth mentally. She still behaves like the two-year-old ghost throwing tantrums in the house. "There is always that aspect of the child and of the dislocated being in Beloved which cannot be mediated, even though it so powerfully communicates with Sethe and Denver" (Ferguson 118). Indeed, everything about Beloved attests to arrested mental development, even given the contradictory evidence of her physical progression. She has the "lineless and smooth" (50) skin of a newborn, but her well-aged scars are remnants of the crawling-already? baby's experience. She looks and acts sick but can lift a rocking chair by herself. She attempts to strangle Sethe and then bathes her neck with kisses. She embodies "resurgent desire" (Lawrence 232) but is unable to satisfactorily convey her needs. Furthermore, in spite of Sethe's repeated confessions, she offers neither forgiveness nor an explanation for her presence and behavior.

Another telling aspect of Beloved's fleshly existence is how she is nourished in the text. Beloved does grow, even if that growth is not emotional maturation. Aside from Beloved's sweettooth, she is fed by Sethe's storytelling, by her love and attention, but most importantly by her pain. When Sethe stops going to work, both she and Denver begin to starve, but Beloved grows plump and glows with good health because "Beloved ate up [Sethe's] life, took it, swelled up with it, grew taller on it" (250). Like sex, consumption emphasizes her physicality. Beloved's apparent pregnancy seems less the consequence of her rape of Paul D than her saturation with Sethe's misery. As the ultimate nourishment for this dead thing who hurts, Sethe's anguish and attempts to make up with Beloved only feed her evil side.

Because of Beloved's supernatural status and her vendetta through most of the text, she is a character with whom it is most difficult to sympathize—an irony, given the pasts through which she seems to have suffered. Whatever her connection with the dead baby, the incident in the woodshed robs both the child and Beloved of any innocence. Like Baby Suggs, we see only trouble in the new hightop shoes. At the same time, we begin to sympathize with Denver's dilemma—her dual urge to protect her sister (her only companion, in her opinion, and whose blood "nourished" her as she drank her mother's milk) and her mother.

If Beloved's afterlife (as described in the chapter told from her point of view) conformed to the constraints and glories of heaven or hell as we know them, we might see her story as one of angels or devils walking the earth. If the entrance and exit of Beloved were timed with Sethe's psychological or emotional epiphanies, we might be able to read this work as a didactic tale. Were the actions of Sethe less complicated to understand, we could accept Beloved as a purely physical symbol of her mother's guilt. Had the ghost simply disappeared after Paul D's exorcism, or had Beloved's reappearance not pervaded the rest of the book, we might see certain incidents or characters as "occasional," as Faris claims. Morrison leaves none of these options clearly open for us; instead, she muddies the waters with Beloved's seduction of Paul D, with Denver's love for her "sister" and Denver's own development into a strong young woman, and by making Beloved's destruction a communal occupation. Beloved, as the title suggests, will encompass Sethe's story, and she does so with magic that bumps up against the very real existence that Sethe is trying to carve for herself.

In spite of the wealth of magical realism centered at 124, all supernatural events are confined to the present and recent past of the novel. Morrison refrains from painting the South of her novel in terms of magical realism. The Southern scenes, with Sethe and Paul D (among others) as slaves under the yoke of whites, are, simply, realism—extremely graphic, unsettling reality. Mr. and Mrs. Garner, the nephews, and Schoolteacher all represent the old ways, slavery at its best and worst, but the narrative connects them to the individual price of slavery. Mr. Garner robs his slaves of their manhood even as he "confirms" that they are men; the nephews rob Sethe of her complacency and her ability to be a mother when they steal her milk. Paul D reflects on Mr. Garner's naming of his slaves and wonders what he meant. "Garner called and announced them men—but only on Sweet Home, and by his leave. Was he naming what he saw or creating what he did not?" (220). Moreover, Sethe, while telling Paul D about the tree on her back, stresses not the whipping she received for telling Mrs. Garner about what the nephews did, but rather what she feels is their true crime:

"They used cowhide on you?"
"And they took my milk."
"They beat you and you was pregnant?"
"And they took my milk!" (17)

Were this scene, or any event collected and recollected from Sethe's and Paul D's pasts, to incorporate the supernatural, Morrison might take away from that harshness, might compromise the vividness of the very real subjugation she depicts. Instead, she incorporates magical realism into settings where African-Americans are still fighting the system but doing so as apparently free people.

There is no juxtaposition of supernatural and natural in the South of *Beloved* because the slave's situation is as straightforward as it is deplorable. Instead, it is in the North of pre-Civil War America's history where the African American's identity is ambiguous—freed without freedom, covert racism rather than the "in your face" prejudice of the South—and, thus, only in the North does magical realism seem to live and breathe. The characters "are, as the figure of Baby Suggs highlights, physically and notionally free but not psychologically free. They have just managed to escape from the fact of slavery but have not been released from its effects" (Keenan 50). It is a more frightening position to be in, in some ways, because the freed black does not know who his or her enemies are. Sethe's infanticide and her attempted attack on Bowdin at the end of the novel illustrate the paradoxical nature of the free black's existence. In spite of the harsh way of life Sethe endures before her escape, it is the juxtapositions of the free North that drive her to attempt murder. She intends to save her children not only from a return to slavery but also from a life where the possibility of that return will always exist.

Sweet Home and Georgia, though lacking in magic themselves, are introduced within the framework of an extraordinarily supernatural text. While the contrast between what is real and what is magical might be most striking were the events of the novel laid out chronologically,[12] Morrison chooses the piecemeal fashion of *Beloved* to tell this story.[13] Beloved and her story are like Baby Suggs's patchwork quilt, pieced together by Sethe, by community, by history, even by Morrison herself as she invented Beloved. "[B]it by bit I had been rescuing her from the grave of time and inattention. Her fingernails maybe in the first book; face and legs, perhaps, the second time. Little by little bringing her back into living form. So that now she comes running when called—walks freely around the house, sits down in a chair; looks at me" (Naylor and Morrison 593). Beloved's retelling, then, brings her to life both inside and outside the fictive realm. Repetition—and particularly the repetition of Sethe's and Beloved's stories—is a valuable tool, painstakingly revealing more complete versions each time a new speaker takes hold of the narrative. This approach both mediates the brutality and "allows the readers to respond to Sethe's act with an understanding of its fully complicated historical context" (Jessee 204–5). Morrison's magical realist text breaks the linear march of history. In doing so, it "questions our attitude toward history as a form of order and coherence" (Birat 324).

The disordering of *Beloved* creates a balanced, magically realist text. Were the story presented chronologically, beginning with the spiritually deficient South, the supernatural elements of the text would not appear until well into the second section of the book. But her reorganization also allows us to feel the sort of disruption that Morrison intends for her reader: "[T]he *in medias res* opening that I am so committed to here is excessively demanding. It is abrupt, and should appear so. No native informant here. The reader is snatched, yanked, thrown into an environment completely foreign. . . . Snatched just as the slaves were from one place to another" ("Opening Sentences" 91–92). Thus, the "complex narrative strategies of the novel reflect the way in which Toni Morrison sees slavery as a disruption of all the normal relations and processes of human experience" (Birat 324). *Beloved* confronts this version of slavery by revisiting the past, by proposing "an alternative to [that] past" (Lock 202), and by revising slavery's effects on individuals. Since Beloved "also contains the *effects* that slavery had, its profound fragmentation of the self and of the connections the self might have with others" (Ferguson 114), she is the alternative to the past. She is also the embodiment of "a particular historical contradiction" who "also represents the threat of being engulfed by that past" (Keenan 74). If Sethe and the community allow Beloved to engulf their present, they can no longer hope for a future. Thus, the "dangerous power of [the myths of slavery] to rigidify meanings and fix identities" (75) and the linear progression of history must both be exploded in order to reorder the community.

In their own attempt at "reordering" the past, the members of the community endeavor to exorcize Beloved one final time. But is Beloved's existence explained away? Faris notes that

right at the end we get what could be interpreted as a disclaimer concerning her magical existence. The people who had seen her "forget her like a bad dream," and finally "realized they couldn't remember or repeat a single thing she said, and began to believe that, other than what they themselves were thinking, she hadn't said anything at all." In the final analysis, though, her existence remains shadowy, for we can—and perhaps should —discount this disclaimer, this after-the-fact-rejection of her magic, and consider that just because the people "began to believe" this, it is only part of the whole story. ("Scheherazade's Children" 183)

Arguably, rather than discrediting Beloved's existence, such belated denials, ironically, only emphasize her existence. The community illustrates the ultimate power of Beloved's psychological impact when they attempt to rationalize her away *after* the fact and not during her tenure at 124. Similarly, the townspeople asking questions about whether Beloved really existed does not serve to diminish the effect of the magical realism in the text. Instead, like the official version of the Banana Company massacre in *One Hundred Years of Solitude* that sweeps everything under the rug, it stands as commentary on the willingness (and perhaps even the need) for people to force things to conform in order to deal with them or even to do away with them entirely. Just as "there haven't been any dead here" in Macondo (García Márquez 313), there hasn't been a Beloved ("any dead") here in a community that chooses to "quickly and *deliberately* forget her" (274; emphasis added). Both are ways of dealing with "impossibilities," and yet neither ultimately discounts the truth nor explains the disappearances away. Comfort notes that "the novel speaks of her absence in the same moment that it evokes her continued presence" (130). After physically exorcizing Beloved, the community (through language or pre-language) attempts a psychological exorcism, an effort to remove her even from memory. But while it is not a story to "pass on," the community cannot "pass" on Beloved, either.

Beloved's presence in the text is a reality while she is there. Furthermore, she is privy to information outside the immediacy of Sethe's present existence, including her knowledge of the crystal earrings—ornaments that simultaneously represent Sweet Home and exclude the present, where the earrings are no longer a reality. Her *being* is more significant than the community's attempts to explain her away after she is gone. Because no one ever tries to modify or justify her existence until she no longer exists, she is not merely symbolic.[14] Although we can read Beloved as a negative symbol of Sethe's psychological baggage, she will also have been an ironically positive force in Denver's and Sethe's lives in addition to existing as a physical entity. At no time in the text does Morrison give us the *reason* for Beloved's existence. The extent of Beloved's success is left a mystery because we never fully know what she wants of Sethe. She seems to need her love and her destruction at the same time. We know something about what motivates her, just as we know something of Sethe's motivations as she cuts her baby's throat, but we are never told the full story.[15]

It seems that Sethe does not understand the game in which she is a pawn. She does not identify Beloved as her daughter when the young woman appears on the road, an appearance that Lawrence argues triggers for Sethe a reenactment of "Beloved's natural birth" (239).[16] Beloved's appearance is all the more supernatural for *when* it takes place in the novel. Sethe lives a life of few pleasures and still seems to be serving time for her sins. Not until Sethe lets down her guard and attends the carnival will Beloved make her reappearance. Notably, " 'everybody who attended the carnival associated it with the stench of the rotten roses' [on the lumberyard fence. Thus, t]he possibility of a new life juxtaposed with the sickly sweet aroma of imminent death anticipates Beloved's image and the confrontation of the living and the dead that her arrival occasions" (Heller 110). In fact, the symbol of rotten roses is the first in a long line of "deadly" associations for Beloved and Sethe. However, "Beloved's arrival at this pivotal moment [also] suggests both her desire to be included in this family-like group, and her infantile need to sever Sethe's newfound lifeline lest her memory be reconciled and her name forgotten" (109). In other words, by arriving immediately after the carnival, Beloved fills her own agenda as much as she *fulfills* Sethe's projected guilt and penitence. Sethe already lives in the shadow of her sins; Beloved's return is not solely responsible for or representative of Sethe's guilt.

To the extent that Beloved personifies Sethe's own skewed sense of redemption, her appearance represents or embodies Sethe's psyche. It would, however, be a mistake to read Beloved as the living symbol of Sethe's deeds. A brief comparison of *Beloved* with Nathaniel Hawthorne's "Rappaccini's Daughter" better illustrates the difference between the symbolic and the magically real. Like the crawling-already? baby, Beatrice is a child whose life is literally at the mercy of a parent. Her father, in his pursuit of science, recreates her into a magical, mortal version of the purple flower in his garden. Indeed, Beatrice is the living personification of his science. Though her beauty originally convinces Giovanni to overlook the evidence against her, his attraction to her threatens to be fatal. Rappaccini's and Sethe's actions both isolate their children from the community; in this respect, Denver, the crawling-already? baby, and Beatrice are all affected by their parents' needs to gain control over the natural world. As slavery epitomizes the ultimate evil in *Beloved*, science fulfills a similar role for Hawthorne. Yet the difference between these two parents and their seemingly callous use of their children also comments on the distinctions between Sethe's unwilling participation in slavery and Rappaccini's ardent embrace of science. Rappaccini chooses, and even prefers, science; Sethe's actions are a direct reaction against the ultimate evil. Hawthorne attempts to symbolize the psychology of the parent, while Morrison attempts to move beyond the symbolic. Unlike Hawthorne's didactic intentions for "Rappaccini's Daughter," symbolism is not the primary means by which Morrison intends to make her point. Furthermore, whereas any supernatural elements are mitigated by scientific, rational explanations in Hawthorne's short story, Morrison's novel successfully muddies the waters, refusing to explain away Beloved or any other supernatural element. Reading Beloved as a primarily symbolic character compromises the magical realism of the text, since such symbolism would rationalize her existence, imposing an authorial intent that Morrison never intended over the supernatural elements.

That Beloved is not merely symbolic is illustrated by her slanted interpretation of Sethe's past and needs. Sethe "projects Beloved in a maternal and filial fantasy as a perfectly dutiful daughter who 'came right on back like a good girl' and 'understands everything already,' effectively denying Beloved the expression of *her* anger at the savage separation" (Ferguson 116). Sethe takes to heart Baby Suggs's advice when she tells her congregation "that the only grace they could have was the grace they could imagine. That if they could not see it, they would not have it" (88). As Baby Suggs says, Sethe literally sees the "grace" she imagines for herself (i.e., the physical form of Beloved). "Rather than a divine state of being that descends from above, grace is a humanly conceived, embodied experience" (Lawrence 235) for Sethe. Only when Sethe allows herself to imagine that she might be worthy of Paul D's love does Beloved appear on the scene. But Beloved's tainted redemption is the only grace that Sethe feels herself good enough to receive. To Heinze, Beloved's own spitefulness ultimately seems more a projection of the punishment Sethe imagines she deserves than a reincarnation of her daughter (206).

Sethe's self-imposed penance begins long before Beloved arrives on the scene, and her actions signify on her own sexuality, motherhood, and illiteracy. Lawrence argues, "In order to acquire the inscribing power of the white man's chisel, [Sethe] must transform her body into a commodity[,] . . . must temporarily 'kill off' her own body (she lies on a headstone, 'her knees wide open as the grave') to purchase the text that she thinks will buy her peace" (234–35).[17] This ritualistic suicide illustrates Sethe's own self-loathing. "For Sethe, the price of inscription is sexual degradation, and her sex is worth only the seven letters comprising the word 'beloved' "

(Holmes 140). Beloved and the crawling-already? baby are both "born out of" this sex, since both are absent from and nameless in the text at the time of Sethe's act and the engravement.[18] Beloved's appropriation of the name that Sethe "buys" for her baby's tomb requires Sethe's own (temporary) death, foreshadowing Beloved's attempts on and continuous absorption of Sethe's life during her stay. Sethe's knees being "wide open as any grave" also references not only this sexual act—ironically referred to as "the little death" in Europe (Holmes 140)—but the act of giving birth as well; both of Sethe's actions symbolize the grave of the crawling-already? baby, whose mother robs her of the very life she gives to her.

Finally, her efforts to engrave the tombstone equate Sethe's sexuality with her illiteracy, and not for the only time in the text. When Paul D makes love to Sethe, he "reads" the scars on Sethe's back, a feat of which she is incapable. "Because reading as a form of knowledge privileges visuality, Sethe's inability to view this inscription on her own body leaves her illiterate with regard to her body's text and thus vulnerable to the readings of others" (Holmes 139). Sethe is disempowered by her incapacity, since *Beloved* consistently relates "the question of authority over one's own body . . . to that of authority over discourse" (Lawrence 233). Likewise, when Paul D says "You got two feet, Sethe, not four" (165), he inadvertently resurrects Schoolteacher's journal and his discursive (as well as literal) attempt to own Sethe's body. His reaction to her secret threatens to rewrite her 'on the animal side of the page,' the very fate from which she hoped to spare herself and her children when she escaped Sweet Home. Fox-Genovese argues that Paul D "ultimately shares Schoolteacher's view of Sethe's deed as the deed of an animal" (14). But Paul D's next thought is of the calves of Sweet Home and Beloved's use of him. "How fast he had moved from his shame to hers. From his cold-house secret to her too-thick love" (165). Paul D recognizes, even if Schoolteacher cannot, that "we cannot entirely divorce the murder of this baby from the slavery that shaped its murdering mother's life" (Fox-Genovese 16). Like Paul D's thoughts of Sweet Home, Beloved's multiplicity suggests that the crimes of slavery continue to add up.

As with Paul D, Beloved evokes the memory of Schoolteacher in her relationship with Sethe. "In her insistence on absolute possession of her mother, Beloved resurrects the slavemaster's monopoly over both word and body, enforcing the internalized enslavement that has become a legacy of institutionalized slavery" (Lawrence 240). That Beloved and Sethe cannot seem to get enough of each other is clear enough in the text; that this destructive obsession will not serve any purpose for either is less obvious, perhaps only hinted at through Beloved's conversations with Denver and other foreshadowing in the text. For example, Beloved hovers like a "familiar, . . . never leaving the room Sethe was in unless required and told to" (57). Unlike the three shadows that walk to and from the carnival hand in hand, Sethe's and Beloved's "shadows clashed and crossed on the ceiling like black swords" (57). As Denver realizes early on, neither Beloved's revenge nor Sethe's explanations will settle anything. Their "mutual hunger for a loving union" and "their inevitable struggle for control" perpetuate the pre-oedipal cycle of love and hate between mother and daughter until it threatens to destroy them both (Mathieson 212). Of the two, Beloved is playing the more dangerous game. Beloved is, Denver rationalizes when Beloved plays her own version of hide-and-seek on the very site of the baby's death, "[a] magical appearance on a stump, the face wiped out by sunlight, and a magical disappearance in a shed, eaten alive by the dark" (122–23). This image solidifies Beloved's magical status and brings her full circle; not only has she assumed Sethe's psychological projections of her crime, but she has also taken on the role of Sethe's past and of the baby who, because of her and her mother's "darkness," is "eaten alive" by the teeth of the saw in this same shed.

According to Susan Willis, for Morrison "the psychological, like the sensual and sexual, is also historical"(102), and Sethe's present psyche in *Beloved* is most definitely linked with her historical past. The novel invokes "the supernatural as both a figurative and actual means to reunion with the past" (Heinze 210). In order to survive, Sethe believes she must forget the painful events from her past. "Supernatural to a world with limited notions of reality, Beloved is nothing more or less than a memory come to life that has too conveniently been forgotten" (Heinze 206). Indeed, "Beloved 'haunts' her mother and the others because they work at repressing the painful memories of being under slavery" (Jessee 199). Though Sethe is haunted by her past later in the story, we ultimately realize that she is pursued by it actively when she first shows up on Bluestone Road. It is the past and not any lack of motherly love that prompts her flight to the woodshed when Schoolteacher shows up. "She just flew. Collected every bit of life she had made, all the parts of her that were precious and fine and beautiful, and carried, pushed, dragged them through the veil, out away, over there where no one could hurt them. Over there. Outside this place, where they would be safe" (163). Indeed, "in the face of slavery's destruction of the mother-child relationship, she insisted upon its dissolubility" (Keenan 71). *Beloved* foregrounds "the varying ways in which a people tries to impart human love in inhuman times[,] . . . about the ability, the willingness of those who were not beloved, to love" (Denard 42–43).

Sethe's day-to-day reality has more to do with her past than with the present or even her future. "To Sethe, the future was a matter of keeping the past at bay" (42). In fact, she finds that she has no imagination for drumming up notions of any future for herself. Sethe's brain has no room to ponder the future because it is so loaded down with the past (71). "For Sethe, in particular—whose name echoes Lethe, the mythical river of forgetfulness—*re*memory provides the key to unlocking, and ultimately transforming, a past her rational memory has repressed" (Lock 203).

Eventually, of course, Sethe *must* revisit her past (literally and figuratively) in order to discover a future in which she can exist without Beloved. The novel does not describe Sethe's growth as a character in psychological terms but rather by providing the site of the re-enactment of her past. Sethe takes "a crucial step towards self-ownership in directing her protective violence against the oppressor (Schoolteacher in the form of Bowdin) instead of against her own flesh and blood" (Lawrence 242). Her "visceral reenactment [when white men return to her yard] enables Sethe to see past the 'facts' and place the blame for her daughter's murder where it belongs, exorcizing at least part of the guilt (and, finally, the ravenous Beloved) herself" (Lock 204). If, in the act of killing her baby, Sethe lost the self-claim she asserts by escaping Sweet Home and crossing the Ohio River (Rushdy 584), she *reasserts* that claim by redirecting at least part of the blame for her crime. This redirection refigures "Sethe's response [to Schoolteacher's arrival in her yard as] one extreme point in a range of possibilities in which mothering or the rejection of it becomes a register of female resistance to the condition of enslavement and the commodification of the female body" (Keenan 67). In other words, Sethe's past defines her as *more of*, rather than *less than*, a mother. Morrison chooses to signify on Sethe's mothering abilities by linking Sethe's escape and the female cycle of fertility. Although Rushdy is careful to note that Sethe is free for twenty-eight days (584), he does not point out that Sethe's "freedom" to claim her own body lasts for the typical length of a menstrual cycle, a cycle that her deliverance of Denver would once again have set into motion. By arriving in the yard just as her menses comes to an end, Schoolteacher seems especially to emphasize the end of Sethe's cycle of freedom and to reassert his claim over her as a reproducing product of slavery.[19] As we examine Sethe's past and not merely the effects of her past on her present but also its causes, we begin to discover "what constitutes justifying a murder that arises out of the paradox of a mother's love (for her child) and hate (for slavery)" (Reyes 78). At the same time, Morrison "wants readers to understand that while blacks were often driven to excess by the cruelties of slavery, slavery was not allowed to excuse those crimes" (Denard 46) or the individuals who are driven to them.

While the community will not allow slavery to excuse Sethe's crime, they are also reluctant to celebrate an individual's triumph over slavery. Witness their ousting of Baby Suggs after her feast for ninety: "Loaves and fishes were His powers—they did not belong to an exslave . . . [who] had, in fact, been *bought out* of [slavery] by a doting son and *driven* to the Ohio River in a wagon" (137). The community is eager to remember Baby Suggs's place because it reestablishes her at their level, solidifies their mutual pasts at this tenuous border between freedom from and domination under whites. Sethe believes Beloved to be "the one and only person she felt she had to convince, that what she had done was right because it came from true love," (251) the love that Paul D says is "too thick." When Sethe finally guesses at Beloved's identity (or at least a part of it), Sethe does not read the situation as a return of her past so much as a sign that she can be forgiven and forget that past. Yet she forgets the strength community can provide, and, more important, the punishment (withdrawal) it dispenses if it feels it has been wronged. Sethe never realizes that the community feels she owes *them* an explanation or apology. "[T]hough the horror of slavery seems a reasonable cause for a violation of ethics, it does not exempt from punishment the violators of the community's codes" (Denard 43). At the very least, they reason, she should act more repentant, as befits her crime. Her neighbors turn their backs on Sethe because they demand either her explanation or her humility—neither of which she provides. The community intervenes in Beloved's case for two reasons: first, because the community does not send Sethe "a warning which might have prevented the slaughter of one of their own" (Lawrence 237), and in neglecting to do so, implicate themselves in her crime. Second, the women intercede in order to displace Beloved, reaffirming that, while forgetting the past is simply not possible for Sethe, finding some sort of peace with that past *is*.

Because the crawling-already? baby dies a victim of her mother's perception of slavery, she never allows her mother to *escape* to the North; Sethe remains "haunted" by slavery. The "other side" for this text can mean either the afterlife or the North, as when Sethe crosses to the other side of the river, the free side. No matter what, Sethe intends for her children to know only "the other side"; she is even willing to kill them to ensure it. Baby Suggs cannot "approve or condemn Sethe's rough choice" (180) because she knows what she is choosing between.[20] Halle's purchase of his mother's "freedom"—a freedom that represents geographic rather than psychological distance from slavery—shows that slavery followed Baby Suggs and every other ex-slave across the Ohio River. Halle, by buying his mother's freedom, displaces himself—her eighth and final child—away from her just as slavery has done with her other children. Halle seems to think he can remove the burden by granting freedom, but for Baby Suggs, slavery and freedom effect the same removal from family.

Like Baby Suggs, who understands that freedom out of slavery is not enough to rescue her heart, Sethe learns that her escape will never be enough to set her free. Sethe and Denver accept the supernatural forces in the home, initially, because they see both the ghost and Beloved as Sethe's penance. Her attempt to kill her children ultimately intrigues readers—who, like Paul D, cannot stay away from her or quite pass judgment on her, even when we know all the facts of her actions. Stamp Paid, who sells her out to Paul D, later tells him, "She ain't crazy. She love those children. She was trying to out-hurt the hurter" (234). Like Helene Moglen, we realize she is "implicated in the cycle of violence by which she was herself produced" (210). Whether we see her as wrong, loving, crazy, or a mixture of these, we are unable to dismiss her. In fact, we find ourselves hoping that Paul D and Denver can "revive" her, freeing her from the past and offering her a future in which she can truly live.

While Beloved is perhaps first Sethe's past, she also represents the past itself, including that inhumane chapter in history known as the Middle Passage. "Sethe's killing of her already-crawling baby is not only the killing of that individual baby but also the collective anguish African women must have experienced when they realized their children were cut off forever from their 'living dead,' [ancestors] who would never be called upon, remembered, or fed" (Christian 369). Of course, Beloved's connection with the Middle Passage means "that we cannot entirely cast the murder of a baby as an act of heroic, if tormented, resistance" (Fox-Genovese 16). Sethe must acknowledge her act, accept responsibility for her individual actions, and recognize "the reason for her act within a framework larger than that of individual resolve. . . . [Thus,] Morrison insists on the impossibility of judging an action without reference to the terms of its enactment—the wrongness of assuming a transhistorical ethic outside a particular historical moment" (Rushdy 577). Were Beloved not spurred by Sethe's own tortured memories of her past actions, she would not exist in the novel. Were she solely the history of slavery incarnate, she would haunt everyone in the community and not just Sethe. Still, this story of one family evolves into a communal history, and Beloved's association with the Middle Passage and other histories illustrates the degree to which Sethe's infanticide is tied to slavery's transgressions against the human spirit. If the Middle Passage is the *first* in a long line of atrocities, Sethe's act represents the "final" one—and suggests perhaps the only way in which the slave could take back a child from the master.

Geoff Hancock claims that magical realism absurdly recreates history while working with a collective sense of folkloric past (36); *Beloved*'s ability to work within these confines on the past, as well as Morrison's attempts to explode them, creates a distinct magical realism that is at once aware of the past as past and at the same time not yet willing, or able, to part company. By "demanding to be remembered" (Keenan 72), Beloved takes Sethe hostage and represents the very real danger of the past overcoming the present (Daily 145, Keenan 74)—no surprise, according to Christian, since children represent both past and future, particularly in African cosmology (369).[21] Beloved attempts to rewrite the past in present tense, but the past cannot be relived, only *relieved*. The past can only be "internally confronted and externally shared through the telling and exchanging of stories. So why then the echoing of the final line, 'This is not a story to pass on'? Perhaps this is a warning that the cycle of separation and loss must not be repeated" (Heller 116).

Beloved takes the reader beyond this cycle of history by delving into the supernatural. While "Toni Morrison writes *Beloved* in direct response to the atrocities of slavery and its aftermath" (Faris, "Scheherazade's Children" 180), her topic emphasizes the dichotomies of slave-life, and in doing so, allows for magical realism to flourish in the text.

> By centering in her narrative a black woman who is, not incidentally, a mother, Morrison documents the tragic human cost of being "other," and takes us into the dim regions of desubjectification and undifferentiation that were not explored by Freud or by Lacan. As a result, she refuses the conventional oppositions of realism and the fantastic, of the Symbolic and the Imaginary, and of the sociopolitical and the psychological. (Moglen 205)

Beloved's fascination with color (particularly "darkness" and the lack of color) suggests that race issues traverse the border between the natural and supernatural; she dwells on "color" because, based on her experience(s), that feature of reality is what precipitates death. The afterlife, at least for the soul(s) not at rest, is a more gruesome kind of existence than that conceived of in most religions; as Beloved's stream-of-conscious passages illustrate, the evils of the natural world continue to haunt the dead. Beloved's recollections of the "other side" are the supernatural reflection of the South (and of the Middle Passage spawned by the South's commodification of black flesh) in the text. Sethe's house on Bluestone Road is the middleground, the only place in the text where the two realms meet, and thus where both magical realism and the contemplation of color occur.[22] Baby Suggs spends her last days studying the colors like blue that cannot hurt—unlike black, which she learns brings pain. And the hurt generally comes in the form of men without skin, as Beloved refers to whites, who are "colorless" because they are missing their black covering. It is a lesson Beloved knows well, since the crawling-already? baby is killed because her color compromises her freedom, as her mother knows.

Perhaps the magical realism of *Beloved* does for slavery what the fairytale or folklore ethics of Uncle Remus does—it puts a storyteller's spin on an historical event that is so graphic, so dehumanizing that it "cannot involve any form of closure which would bring healing and order sufficient to counterbalance the initial disruption" (Birat 324). *Beloved* "invites in the ghosts of slavery's horrors" (Daily 141). In addition, Beloved is certainly a symbol of the dehumanizing effect of slavery on people. She represents her mother's need to find her children safety no matter the means. Sethe and the crawling-already? baby have both been dehumanized by the whites who come into the yard. Beloved is left not quite ghost (once she appears in physical form on the doorstep) and not quite human, and all because Schoolteacher happens to consider her and her mother his property.

Beloved never asks Sethe why she was murdered, and, in so neglecting this question, seems to prove that her "anger stems from a trauma completely different in time, place, and nature from the expected one" (Broad 191). Beloved's return, then, symbolizes not just Sethe's past, but the community's—Ella's child, the runaway captive from Deer Creek, Middle Passage. "This communal reclaiming is exactly what happens when Beloved returns to 124 Bluestone Road: Looking for their 'beloved,' Sethe and Denver get their people, too. All sixty million of them" (Broad 192). Beloved's stories and actions suggest that "whoever Beloved is, and whoever she is for others, her longing is the longing and her rage the rage of all children abandoned in untimely separation from their mothers and oppressed as others in an alien culture" (Moglen 211). *Beloved* "signifies on history by resurrecting one of its anonymous victims" (Rushdy 578). Yet, as a character, Beloved defies the anonymity of the past.

The naming by Morrison, like the naming by the Mothers of the Disappeared [in Latin America . . .] enables her to 'harness the magical power of unquiet souls' in order to imagine and affirm a living community of resistance. Thus, the name 'Beloved' evokes not only the dead child, not only those who have died in the Middle Passage, but also the living African-American community. (Comfort 122)

If, as Karen E. Fields argues, "the essence of slavery was the creation of free-standing individuals, not families or communities" (163), then the task for former slaves upon arriving in the North was to reestablish those communities and families. Ultimately, that is the work that the magical realism of *Beloved* undertakes.

"In *Beloved* family and language must be jointly reconstructed" in order for the family and community to be "mutually restored" (Heller 110, 116); thus the voices Stamp Paid hears swirling around 124 are a confusing mass of murmurs. The work to reconstruct this family, their history, and their language has yet to be completed, and this work must be done before the rift within the community can be repaired. No one from the community warns Baby Suggs and hers of the coming of the strangers, thereby investing in Beloved's death before it happens (Fox-Genovese 15), since those who know the South know its dangers on Northern soil. But the roaring that drives Stamp away does not emanate solely from within the house. "Beloved magnetizes 124, attracting all the lost life now returning to lay claim to its own" (Lawrence 239), but she evokes more than the ancestral generations lost in the Diaspora. When "Paul D relates her bewildered state of mind and the slow and painful spelling of her name to his recollections of the crowds of stunned, exhausted Negroes wandering the roads after the Civil War had ended" (119), he links Beloved with another "critical transitional point in black history," that is, with Reconstruction (Jessee 199). Thus, Paul D associates Beloved with other "lost souls," the post-Civil War African Americans who, though neither dead nor enslaved, were both literally and figuratively *lost* to their severed family ties, as well as to the society that granted them judicial but not absolute personhood.

Just as Beloved cannot be contained by one past, the magical realism of the novel bearing her name cannot be limited. Moreover, although Beloved and magical realism go hand in hand in the text, Beloved is not the only supernatural element at work. Denver's deafness, the white dress kneeling beside Sethe as she prays, Baby Suggs's return near the end to push Denver off the porch and into the community again—each represents a portion of the supernatural tapestry sewn throughout the story. From almost the beginning of Sethe's life on the outskirts of Cincinnati, magical realism plays a role in her life and the lives of those she loves. Not incidentally, most of those magical realist elements in the text are tied either to Beloved or to the baby whose place she takes. The house at 124 Bluestone Road, like Beloved herself, reflects the influence of magical realism behind its doors. It begins as a "spiteful" place when it is merely haunted, progresses to the "loud" spot that Stamp Paid hears from the road, and subdues into the quiet home that Denver, Sethe, and Paul D make of it by the end. Of course, Beloved's supernatural talents are not confined to the house, like the crawling-already? baby ghost. Beloved takes over the shed and even Baby Suggs's clearing in her attempt to control Sethe and those who love her. In fact, the Clearing is the only place where Beloved directly and physically abuses Sethe after she returns. Still, the house bears the brunt of the violence done by and to Sethe after she escapes Sweet Home; the women's growing seclusion in the house ensures that Sethe is constantly present for Beloved's "feedings."

When Denver goes deaf from hearing about her mother's deeds, only the baby ghost's noises on the stairs can wake her from her soundless world. Chronologically, this moment is perhaps the first instance of magical realism in the novel. We are not to believe that Denver *imagines* her hearing loss, nor does the text give us any viable explanation for it, other than her hearing Nelson Lord's inquiry and linking it with the jail cell she shared with her mother—certainly not a scientific explanation, even if the psychological readings of the situation might suggest otherwise. Denver is literally (and without much fuss over the fact) deaf. It makes sense that, unlike Sethe and her "sister," Denver, even after her hearing returns, does *not* want to know her mother's history "pre-Denver." Not only does Denver not figure into that past; she has also already lost (been exposed to the ramifications of) that past in a way that Sethe has not—because Denver gets *her* mother's milk but at the cost (and physical ingestion) of her sister's blood. Denver's hearing loss, once reversed, makes her a keener listener. She is the one who filters Sethe's articulation of her reasons for killing Beloved; she hears Sethe's words to Beloved and is finally convinced herself. Most importantly, she learns from listening "that because of a larger communal history, her mother's deed might not be so heinous as she had at first thought" (Rushdy 583).

Denver's recognition of the complexities of her mother's choice forces her to give up her "willful isolation" (Rushdy 580) and to rejoin the community she left at such a tender age. She buys her mother's freedom from Beloved much as her father Halle bought Baby Suggs out of slavery (Heller 115). When Denver takes "her mother's milk right along with the blood of her sister" (152), she consumes "both the life-giving nourishment and the act of violence which was the condition for her future as a free woman" (Keenan 76). She also becomes a metaphor for the larger community, "the post-Civil War black family [that] was nourished by the combination of these essential elements: mother's milk, the blood of relations lost to the violent reality of slavery, and the stories that are passed down to each subsequent generation, even if they require raising the dead" (Heller 114). Denver "is the site of hope in Morrison's novel. She is the daughter of history," "signifyin(g) history" (Rushdy 571, 579) in the text. Although Denver does not initially conjure up much compassion in the reader, her growth is the most hopeful aspect of *Beloved*, and by the end of the novel she shares as much "space" in the text as either her sister or her mother. Denver saves her family and herself by pulling them out of willful isolation. Because they reconnect with the neighbors, Sethe and Denver can now confront the historical and psychological baggage that Beloved brings upon herself and into the community.

Each of the events that can be construed as magical has in common a link—and generally a very direct one—to history. The historical in this text is frequently, and effectively, brought up into the present by the supernatural. Morrison offers us a scene that is at once historical and current, and uses magical realism to connect the two. We live through such powerful images of slavery and the lengths to which it drives her characters that Morrison allows us to see the supernatural in an almost pragmatic light. The specter of Beloved seducing Paul D and torturing Sethe pale in comparison to Paul D's earlier subjugation or Sethe's victimization at the hands of the young white boys who steal her milk. Because we see slavery in such a light, because Morrison forces us to deal with hatred and racism and evil, two things happen for the reader: we can forgive Sethe's actions, and we can accept Beloved's presence as easily as the main characters do. After all, this spirit plaguing the text, comparatively, is neither fantastic *nor* terrifying.

Beloved refuses, however, to prescribe magical realism as a balm for the past. By using the mode as a vehicle for her resurrection of the past, Morrison illustrates that, "[h]owever compelling the claims of the past may be—and this novel never ceases to make them so—it cannot interpret itself for us" (Ferguson 123). The use of the past, the history (whether shared or individual) of the characters, is one way in which Morrison shows the excessiveness and horror of a reality that makes the supernatural almost tame by comparison. At the same time, Sethe's past is what provides the fear that drives her to infanticide, and her actions will breathe life into Beloved's magical, real form. But the novel refuses to equate *belief* in the supernatural with *capitulation* to that magic. P. Gabrielle Foreman argues, "*Beloved*'s most basic premise lies in the magical: it is the community's shared belief in magic that enables them to save Sethe from [Beloved's] magical effects" (299). Ultimately, Beloved is not a champion of the present but rather a remnant of the past. She is "the last that remained of a past whose annihilation had not taken place because it was still in a process of annihilation, consuming itself from within, ending at every moment but never ending its ending" (García Márquez, *One Hundred Years of Solitude* 409). "If history is what happened, then literature . . . is what what happened *means*" (Denard 40). Morrison's literature rewrites the "what happened" of slavery into the magical realism that is *Beloved*.

NOTES

1. Fox-Genovese, 15. Many other critics, including Robert L. Broad, Susan Comfort, and Kristine Holmes, refer to Beloved's character as "a" or "the" ghost— whether or not they will elsewhere argue that she is more than or different from a ghost. In doing so, they blur the lines between the haint in 124 at the beginning of the novel and Beloved herself.

2. In fact, although readers can assume from the baby's age that she was called by *some* name, we cannot even be certain that she had one. Even in the flashbacks dealing with Sethe's escape from Sweet Home, the baby is referred to as the "crawling-already?" baby.

3. Broad quotes David Bradley's *The Chaneysville Incident*: "Ghost isn't the right word. Ghost is a word that was invented by people who didn't believe. . . . Ancestors is a better term" (189). His realization that "the spirit that inhabits Beloved's body is more than that child's soul, more than Paul D, Sethe, or Denver ever bargain for" (190) also illustrates that his definition of Beloved moves beyond a simple word like "ghost." Though "[a]ll the empirical evidence, in other words, points to a good, old-fashioned, unified spectral identity, when we gain access to her thoughts, with the benefit of the interior monologue beginning on page 210, . . . this tidy conception [flies] apart" (190).

4. Heinze, 207. Though Heinze discusses Beloved as a psychological projection—Sethe's double—she does not seem to rule out the physicality of the character in doing so.

5. Kristine Holmes points out that embodiment "implies a connection between lived (bodily) and literary (representational) experiences" (135). Perhaps it is because Beloved puts the physical body in "embodiment" that so many critics rely on the term as they attempt to interpret Beloved—including, of course, the author of this text. (The purpose of this chapter, after all, is to argue that Beloved *embodies* magical realism.) For example, still other scholars see Beloved as "an embodiment of resurgent desire"(Lawrence 232), of "*story*

itself" (Holmes 145), or of the " 'social imaginary,' an emergent and/or residual social subject that disrupts discursive limits" (Comfort 123).

6. Paul Neubauer reaches a similar conclusion regarding Beloved's humanness (or lack thereof).

7. If the ghost represents action, Beloved represents the word—specifically, the story that can't be "passed on."

8. Ella and Sethe's own mother share in common the "throwing away" of babies forced on them by white men. Once Ella sees this common bond between Sethe and herself, that is, makes the connection between these babies who have been resigned to the afterlife by their mothers, she convinces herself that enough is enough. It takes Beloved's physical form, however, to push Ella into this stance.

9. Bayles—who claims that Morrison's "embrace of magic realism has led her to neglect her strengths and indulge her weaknesses—traces what she sees as Morrison's growing trend to incorporate the supernatural in her texts and then asks, "Now, what does all this have to do with magic realism?" (37). Unfortunately, Bayles never satisfactorily answers her own question.

10. For more on Chanady, see Chapter 1.

11. Or, as Sethe sees it, "ran her children out and tore up the house" (22)—suggesting Sethe's acceptance of the ghost form of her baby as one of her children, a recognition she will not give Beloved until well after Beloved has become a permanent fixture.

12. Brian Finney begins his article by ordering the events of the two principal periods—1850–1855 and 1870–1874—chronologically (104–5).

13. Piecing together these fragments, Lock argues, requires the reader to mimic the oral memory process in order to "extract individual meaning from the narrative" (204).

14. Heinze agrees: "While the double can explain Beloved in psychological terms, it cannot explain the fact that Beloved is visible and real to the other characters as well. . . . But the fact that she can be seen at all is testimony to her power as a supernatural force" (208).

15. "Denver thought she understood the connection between her mother and Beloved: Sethe was trying to make up for the hand saw; Beloved was making her pay for it. But there would never be an end to that" (251). Denver's perceptiveness here notwithstanding, no simple explanation defines the exact nature of Beloved's return. For this reason, she helps the text to fulfill Chanady's requirement for magical realism in that the text does not explain her existence away.

16. Rushdy, who sees Denver and not Beloved as the ultimate "daughter signifyin(g) history," points out that "later, in a retrospective moment, [Sethe] remember[s] this scene in trying to discover who Beloved could be. What is worth noticing, though, is that at that precise moment she does not remember the birth of Beloved but the birth of Denver" (578).

17. The actual passage Lawrence references here reads, "The welcoming cool of unchiseled headstones; the one she selected to *lean* against on tiptoe, her knees wide open as *any* grave" (5; emphasis added).

18. A term that has particular resonance of its own, simultaneously conjuring both the grave and the word "Beloved" on it.

19. Sethe's menses and its connection with both blood and the end of the fertile cycle would be ripe subjects for future criticism, particularly in relation to Beloved's death.

20. During her journey to the North, Sethe's persistent desire to bring her milk to her baby and her equal determination not to be "a crawling graveyard for a six-month baby's last hours" prove her true feelings toward her children much more clearly than her few minutes in the woodshed. She does not think dying on her way North would be so bad, "but the thought of herself stretched out dead while the little antelope lived on—an hour? a day? a day and a night?—in her lifeless body grieved her so she made the groan that made the per-

son walking on a path not ten yards away halt and stand right still" (31). Here, her motherly love gives both Sethe and her baby a chance to make it to Ohio.

21. Christian explains,

> When one views the novel from [an] African cosmological perspective it is especially significant that the embodied past is represented by a girl-child who is simultaneously a woman, the character Beloved. It is not surprising, then, that the spirit who is the most wrathful and most in pain is that of a child who dies in a violent, unnatural way, for the child represents the sustenance of both the past and the present, as it becomes the future, not only for an individual family but also for the group as a whole. (369)

22. Since both the South and the afterlife get very little "playing time" in the text, they heighten the real and supernatural qualities, respectively, of the work without overshadowing the magical realism in the novel.

6

MARGINALLY MAGICAL: MAGICAL REALISM INFRINGING ON THE MAINSTREAM

They don't know our literatures for the very same reason that we know theirs. Theirs are important, canonical, the core of the core curriculum; ours are marginal, exotic, frilly, not part of anyone's cultural literacy program.

—Roberto González Echevarría, "Latin America and Comparative Literature"

The role of the marginalized author is much the same no matter the location; as González Echevarría claims, while such authors are "exotic" to mainstream readers, they are largely unread, unappreciated, and unimportant in mainstream criticism.[1] As the scope and variety of these writers and their works have grown over the past, however, so too has critical (and curricular) interest in their texts, and there is good reason for the increased interest. Carlos Fuentes, for example, argues that "the role of marginal cultures is that of guardians of memory. A memory of what the West sacrificed in other cultures through imperialist expansion and what it sacrificed within its own culture" (122). Certainly, we have seen the notion of margins as caretakers of culture and memory played out on the pages of *Beloved*, as Chapter 5 illustrates. Moreover, Lois Parkinson Zamora's *The Usable Past* claims a similar role for the writers with whom she deals. The writers she cites "engage American historical experience thematically—colonization and independence, *mestizaje* and melting pot, domination and self-determination—and they also question how these historical experiences have created and fostered American literary forms and traditions" (xii). She adds that "America's ideas about history and its own historical identity are, of course, profoundly rooted in European philosophy," a relationship that continues to be problematic (4). At the same time, the "historically motivated anxiety" that equates residency with the "political and social responsibility of the writer to his or her own culture and country . . . is uniquely American"; we cannot even imagine such debates taking place in England, France, or Germany (11–12).

> Although questions of national and cultural identity are now relatively rare in comparative studies of Western European literatures, they are current in areas where national identity is in more formative stages of development, as it is in Latin America, and where it is undergoing deep and historic diversifications, as in the U.S. In these regions, literary criticism is effectively redefining concepts of canonicity and collective identity; indeed, postcolonial theorists questioning the very possibility of collective identity have repeatedly taken cultural practices in the Americas as their testing ground. (4)

In other words, writers and critics in the Americas are redefining our very "American-ness," how we perceive ourselves as parts of a larger whole in the New World—a fluid perception that is predetermined by our peripheral status. "There can be little doubt that nationalism as a founding ideology is a characteristic peculiar to marginal and dependent societies" (González Echevarría, Voices of the Masters 11). Ironically, though Americans value "individualism," collective social identities like nationality seem to prevail over individual ones. As K. Anthony Appiah notes, "If what matters about me is my individual and authentic self, why is so much contemporary talk of identity about large categories—gender, ethnicity, nationality, 'race,' sexuality—that seem so far from individual?" (149).

In fact, though these collective identities drive many marginalized authors' works, this fringe is also attempting to reclaim both collective and individual identities of which they can be proud; but this reassertion proves to be a daunting literary task. What constitutes marginalization itself is a problem that needs reconsideration, particularly given the diverse groups subsumed by the word "margin." In fact, the condition of being marginalized is not necessarily brought on by mainstream readers. For example, marginalized groups like women and gay and lesbian writers "do not fit easily into any academic categories. In some cases, the marginalization is geographical. Paraguay, Central America, and Brazil are frequently ignored in the history of Latin American literature" (Williams, Postmodern Novel 109). Thus, critics seem to remarginalize the margins by refusing to include them in the canon, effectively excluding them not once (at the level of mass culture) but twice (at the levels of both mass culture and critical culture or academia). Such exclusion ensures that many writers share "the multiple political agenda of postmodern writers. . . . Some of these marginalized writers . . . question the historical bases of dominant ideologies and search for methods to subvert literary and political traditions" (126). Indeed, political writers have a new significance for contemporary literature. "In the U.S., as in Latin America, to write politically now is to write about the interactions of cultures and cultural forms" (Zamora, Usable Past 198) because the "American energy to amplify and include stems from an awareness of the processes of cultural transmission in colonized or seemingly marginalized contexts" (199).

For many writers from marginalized groups, questioning the centered discourse of literature encourages (and perhaps occasionally even requires) a marginalized mode. "Most commentators of magical realism have underscored its function as a differential mode of literary expression that valorizes a discourse whose perceptual orientation is essentially non-Western, or that at least diverges from the logocentric tradition of mainstream Western thought and literature" (Erickson 425). Indeed, "we have seen [the decentered wholes] encoded *formally* in the converging strains of counterrealism that we now regularly refer to as magical realism" (Zamora, *Usable Past* 199). As Stephen Slemon points out, "The incompatibility of magic realism with the more 'established' genre systems becomes itself interesting, itself a focus for critical attention, when one considers the fact that magic realism, at least in a literary context, seems most visibly operative in cultures situated at the fringes of mainstream literary culture" (408). As a critical tool, "magical realism can . . . signify resistance to monumental theories of literary practice" and can call into question the more mainstream traditions—though, ironically, in doing so magical realism itself is at risk of becoming a "monumentalizing category for literary practice" (408–9). The tendency of the criticism available on the magical realist mode toward mainstreaming or obfuscating magical realism, as Chapter 1 emphasizes, has already threatened to take the mode out of commission as a critical term.

The marginal writers who practice magical realism in their own writing confront this threat simply by continuing to write in the mode. Yet what their use of this narrative mode *does* for the fringes is as important as the fact that they persist in creating magical realist works. "Magic Realism with its cultural impetus," Karla J. Sanders argues, "seeks to disclose marginalized beliefs and religions" (205). Jean-Pierre Durix, too, claims, "Through 'marginal modes' of expression, writers [search for their own roots and rediscover] those myths which might help them to transcend this marginal position" (148). Magical realism is not only challenging the center, it is also allowing the margins to rediscover their historical and mythical past.

In addition to uncovering—or *recovering*—the myths of the margins, magical realism (perhaps especially as it is practiced in the Americas) tackles the very idea of boundaries. Edward A. Shannon calls American magic realism "an aggressive literature [that] explores the most polarizing issues of our age: race, gender, ethnic, and religious difference" (3). Jeanne Delbaere argues that "marginality and silenced voices—Canada vis-á-vis the United States; women and animals vis-á-vis male domination—[are] the issues most often addressed in magic realist fiction" (97–98). She adds, in the words of Theo D'haen, that "it is precisely the notion of the ex-centric, in the sense of speaking from the margin, from a place other than 'the' or 'a center' that . . . seems an essential feature of that strain of Postmodernism we call Magic Realism" (98). She then surveys the application of magical realism in relation to discussions of marginality and finds many critics in agreement with D'haen's claim. Drawing from several such critics, Delbaere explains:

There is broad consensus on [the fact that magical realism speaks from the margins]. Noting that magic realism comes from the south of the United States and from Canada but that "there's not a lot of it in the United States itself[,]" Linda Kenyon also wonders whether it does not develop more frequently on the margins; Stanley E. McMullin analyses the phenomenon in terms of heartland and hinterland; [Jean] Weisgerber and Stephen Slemon both remark that in a literary context magical realism is most obviously operative in cultures situated at the fringes of the mainstream literary traditions[;] and Robert Kroetsch sees the very strong South American oral traditions of storytelling as an expression of "the energy of the margins." Margins, he thinks, "are interesting places, because that's where different forces are mixing, on the margins instead of at the centre." (98)[2]

Delbaere's discussion, though perhaps a bit shortsighted in terms of the magical realist efforts in the United States, challenges the traditional perception of the margin, specifically its geographic limits, and, as others have done for magical realism itself, urges that the conditions that determine marginalization be reexamined.

It is important to mention here that magical realism is not restricted to writers on the margins. Though being "part of the Third World [has been] a condition long thought necessary to the currency of the term in regard to literature" (Slemon 407–8)[3], magical realism is—as the first chapter of *Rediscovering Magical Realism* suggests at length—a geographically and stylistically adaptable mode that still manages to reflect the needs and idiosyncrasies of the authors by whom, and regions in which, it is practiced. In fact, Delbaere implies, it is when "magic realism occasionally spills over to the centre" that it must change most drastically (98). Magical realism "is a means for writers coming from the privileged centers of literature to dissociate themselves from their own discourses of power, and to speak on behalf of the ex-centric and un-privileged (with the risk of being judged 'patronizing' by those on whose behalf such writers seek to speak)" (D'haen 195). Such mainstreamed magical realism is "either characterized by ex-centricity of genre, gender and setting . . . or feature[s] marginal characters" (98), an observation that will indeed hold true for the more mainstream writers considered later in this chapter.

At the same time, criticism of magical realism has been much more centralized than the marginalized writers it critiques. Magical realism "came into common usage in the late 1960s, a time when intellectuals and literary critics were often involved in Third-Worldism, civil rights and anti-imperialistic protests" (Durix 116). In other words, interest in magical realism coincided with an interest in the margins—but that interest (as illustrated by the commodification of Latin American literature during the Boom) came predominantly from mainstream groups.

Because colonialism both presumed and perpetuated for the imperialists the notion of an other separated by geographic, physiological, and ideological space; the postcolonial societies that have been subjected to imperialism, forced assimilation, and the other homogenizing forces of cultural imperialism are directly implicated in the revision of the margins. Thus, "[f]or postcolonial writers, . . . it is important to distinguish between 'marginality' as a term in academic discourse and the *actual conditions of marginality* that sustain or disdain their very lives and create or destroy the very conditions of their artistic work" (Katrak 666–67). Furthermore, because "Postcoloniality itself overdetermines the 'choice' to migrate[,] . . . post-colonial peoples embody a hyphenated condition of identity . . . —the phenome-non of having too many roots, too many locations" (649), conditions with t which they must reconcile on a daily basis. Another difficulty for postcolonial writers is that, in many postcolonial societies, differentiation between eras or ages is compli-cated by how, "in some cases, the two exist side by side and simultaneously. In much West African literature in English[, for example], there is no clear separation between the old beliefs in the supernatural and the new 'scientific' age" (Durix 82), yet such duality is a condition we see repeated in Latin America, as well as around the postcolonial world. Indeed, says Durix, "*One Hundred Years of Solitude* illus-trates this precarious hold that post-colonial people sometimes have on reality" (128), or, more specifically, on Western reality.[4]

In order to negotiate such marginalization, many writers are turning to modes that function as "code breakers" for the redefinition of status *post* colonialism.

One only needs to think of the major contributions to world literature made by Salman Rushdie from India, Gabriel García Márquez from Colombia, or Tahar ben Jelloun from Morocco to realize that the former colonial territories, which used to depend on the "mother-countries" for their cultural nourishment, are now beginning to invert the process. (Durix 4)

What is perhaps more significant for our purposes here is that all three writers Durix mentions are noted magical realists. "Postcolonial literature not only attacks colonial attitudes, but also seeks for alternative positions for the indigenes to oc-cupy. One effective strategy of this enterprise is the deployment of the device termed 'magic realism'" (Baker 55). But this literature may not merely exist side by side with the dominant discourse:

To write ex-centrically, then, or from the margin, implies dis-placing [the discourse of the privileged centers.] . . . [M]agic realist writing achieves this end by first appropriating the techniques of the 'centr'-al line and then using these . . . to create an alternative world *correcting* so-called existing reality. . . . Magic realism thus reveals itself as a *ruse* to invade and take over dominant discourse(s). It is a way of access to the main body of "Western" literature for authors not sharing in, or not writing from the perspective of, the privileged centers of this literature for reasons of language, class, race, or gender. (D'haen 195)

For example, "[t]he exclusive attention given to Anglo-American modernism is in itself an indication of 'privileged center' discourse. In this respect, then, merely to talk of magic realism in relation to postmodernism is to contribute to decentering that privileged discourse" (D'haen 203). Since the goal is generally not to regurgi-tate Western literature or themes but rather to celebrate the differences, "[t]he po-litical agenda for any such marginalized group, therefore, is to appropriate the dominant language and use it for [its] own purposes, while still retaining an indig-enous discourse" (Baker 55). Thus, the "postmodernism or postcolonialism in the inter-Américas context ought never to be viewed as a static and homogenous phenomenon" (Saldívar, *Border Matters* 20), but rather as an opportunity for the margins to subsume the center. Magical realism, as D'haen notes, is optimally suited for derailing the dominant discourse.

Postcolonial writing subverts the colonial traditions on which many of those postcolonial nations have been built (or, as is perhaps more appropriate, rebuilt over the site of other cultures). According to Durix,

Besides the polarities which separate the colonizer and the colonized, the metropolitan and the indigenous artist, a number of post-colonial writers are developing aesthetic theories based on certain aspects sometimes related to "magic realism" in order to define their hybrid cultures. These are to be found especially in the English-speaking and French-speaking world and constitute a theoretical basis for a practice of literature which differs from the old imperialistic binary opposition between "them" and "us." (148)

Thus, "Post-colonial writers have brought a major contribution to the revitalization of outdated genres such as realism" and "have demonstrated with much authority that reality can be multifaceted" (189). In fact, "by inverting totally the whole concept of Magical Realism," says Philip Swanson, one could argue "that the magical is a construct of alien, imperialist, dominant or exploitive forces which transforms simple realities into myths" (12). On the other hand, Slemon claims that "the concept of magic realism can provide us with a way of effecting important comparative analyses between separate post-colonial cultures" and "can enable us to recognize continuities within literary cultures that the established genre systems might blind us to; continuities, that is, between present-day magic realist texts and apparently very different texts written at earlier stages of a culture's literary history" (409). In either case, magical realism works to reestablish indigenous and other marginalized histories as a site of "truth" in literature.

Of course, as Brian Conniff suggests of *One Hundred Years of Solitude*, the threat of colonization is not always an "alien" one; it can come from external (international) or internal (*intra*national) threats. Fernanda represents the internal colonizer's failed attempt in Macondo. When she equates her inland upbringing with "high" culture and tries to bring that to Macondo after she marries into the Buendía family, Fernanda represents the confrontation between the urban and rural domains. Yet, as she travels back to her inland home on the train, she does not realize that the banana groves she is passing symbolize the extent to which outer, imperial forces will prevail over her own "intranational" attempts at imposing order. "At this point," Conniff explains, "it is clear that she has failed in her attempt to colonize Macondo with the manners and rituals of the inland cities; but her 'internal colonization' has been superseded, without her noticing it, by the brutal imperialism of the banana company" (176).

The commodification of Latin America, as represented by the Banana Company in *One Hundred Years of Solitude*, is not a recent phenomenon, but capitalistic imperialism did not limit itself to exporting traditional goods. In their literary exploitation of Latin America (as symbolized by the Boom and discussed in Chapter 2), these economic imperialists were just as interested in Latin America as commodity. Indeed, the Boom was as responsible as North Atlantic imperialists for maintaining Latin America's marginal status, if not more so. Borges, whose work is what Gerald Martin calls "a highly marketable finished commodity, albeit a minority one" ("On 'Magical' and Social Realism" 98), "describes himself as positioned simultaneously in the mainstream of Western culture and on its colonized margins" (Zamora, *Usable Past* 83). Of course, the capitalization on Borges's talent somewhat compromises claims that he is a "marginal" writer, just as it has for García Márquez, Toni Morrison, and other formerly marginalized authors whose fame has pushed them into the mainstream. Such authors, of course, by challenging the *idea* of the margins, are revising the discourse of the center in ways outside their texts. And, as Morrison and other "mainstreamed" margins prove, these writers are also in a unique position to tackle extremely sensitive and marginalized themes because of their dual status.

In spite of the international status of a handful of Latin American writers, many critics continue to insist that all Latin American authors are marginalized by geography alone. González Echevarría, who claims marginality for even the most mainstream of Latin American literatures, thus embraces such masters as García Márquez and Borges as "marginalized" writers. Roberto Fernández Retamar, Cuban essayist and poet, similarly argues that Latin America is a peripheral society defending itself against the neocolonialism of northern America and against devalorization by Europeans. But he sees the defense as a force uniting the various groups of Latin America (Aínsa 36). "From a North Atlantic perspective, the history of Latin America's literature, in fact, is a continuum of marginality. Excluded for generations from the canon of Western literature, all Latin American writers, from the two centuries since the independence, have been, technically speaking, writing in the margins" (Williams, *Postmodern Novel* 110). Gerald Martin agrees: "[I]n Latin America all writers are from the periphery and all narratives, inevitably, bear the imprint of this origin in their structure" (*Journeys Through the Labyrinth* 127).[5] Unfortunately, the attempts to consolidate Latin America's "autonomy vis-á-vis the colonial and neocolonial powers, have created a unifying and reductive ideology," one that excludes or silences the specific identities of groups like the Afro-Hispano-American or the Amerindian (Chanady, "Latin American Discourses of Identity" 45).

Ultimately, Latin America as a marginalized commodity is being (as it should be) challenged from within its borders. The constraints, both international and intranational, that critics and the publishing industry enforce are urging many writers to revise marginality. "More and more, it is women, gay writers, and [other] writers at the margins who have assumed the responsibility for questioning and destabilising received pieties" (Franco 353). Finding themselves silenced inside the discourse of "marginalization" that claims to provide them a voice, indigenous, black, gay, and women writers hope to reassess the history that puts them at risk of being edged right off the literary maps of Latin America. For example, Richard L. Jackson, who wrote *The Black Image in Latin American Literature*, says that "the black experience in the Hispanic world is as momentous a subject as the indigenous one" (ix). Yet, in order to determine "the nature of race relations and the kind of prejudice prevalent in Latin America," the current trend subjects "the area to a comparative analysis of historical and current patterns of race relations in the Americas, with particular emphasis on the United States and the West Indies" (Jackson xi–xii). In this way, Latin America's attitude toward blackness corresponds to the theory of Tzvetan Todorov that "[e]ven if the discovery of the other must be assumed by each individual and eternally recommenced, it also has a history, forms that are socially and culturally determined" (247). Though the "pressures and effects of white racism in Latin America, especially as far as the man on the black end of the color spectrum is concerned, are as harsh and virulent as in the United States," at the same time "the critical difference between [race relations in] Latin America and [the] United States . . . lies in the more favorable attitudes in Latin America toward the mulatto, that is, toward the group that is somatically closer to whites" (Jackson 11, xii).[6] Ann Cook, an author "who has traveled through Latin America only to return disillusioned with the reluctance to identify with blackness there, encountered much anti-black consciousness reflected in directly translatable phrases that are so much a part of the culture in the United States" (Jackson 8).

This is not to say that blackness is not celebrated in Latin America or that it is only a topic for black authors. But certain regions and authors are more interested in drawing from the African traditions, particularly in relation to what Alejo Carpentier referred to as "*lo real maravilloso.*" Jackson argues, "*El reino de este mundo* shows, in effect, how blacks like Mackandal held a strong fascination not only for other blacks but for the author as well, a fascination which helped shape Carpentier's well-known theory of '*lo real maravilloso,*' manifest, to a large degree, in the many incredible evocations of Africa in America" (Jackson 65). Yet interest that is restricted by area or by topic (as when Carpentier limits his discussion of black culture by concentrating on the link between the blacks in the West Indies and Africa) relies on a perspective of black Latin Americans as "other" and further emphasizes the somatic distance between the races.

Somatic and geographic difference both play key roles in the idea of "border writing." Border writing, D. Emily Hicks says, "emphasizes the displacement of antinomies ('original and alien cultures') by narrative strategies that 'translate' multiple cultural and linguistic codes in the work itself" (qtd. in Zamora, *Usable Past* 8). Though Zamora argues that her emphasis in *The Usable Past* "will be on unresolved antinomies," border writing seems to conjure the same *resolvable* antinomies that Amaryll Chanady discusses in reference to magical realism. As a tool for border writers and other margins, then, magical realism may indeed be one of the most innovative narrative strategies to define the cultural codes of the Americas.

Of course, American marginalized groups share much more than the threat of white racism and magical realism as a mode of expression. According to Zamora, Latin America and the United States "share a common characteristic: their lack of resolution" about the past, but "if the U.S. has too completely assimilated its past, rendering it inaccessible, Latin America has incompletely assimilated its history, to the same effect" (*Usable Past* 15). The work to be done at the margins, then, is to reconcile with America's past. Zamora, like Fuentes, believes "that Latin America's unresolved history can only be encompassed by an inclusive mythic vision and its consequent narrative modes" (16). Zamora suggests that modes like magical realism will prove the cure for Latin America's under-assimilated history. "Read as a form of postcolonial discourse, the magic realist texts [that Slemon works] with . . . comprise a positive and liberating engagement with the codes of imperial history and its legacy of fragmentation and discontinuity" (422). Arguably, the magical realist works of marginalized authors like Isabel Allende and Toni Morrison are challenging these assimilated or unassimilated pasts and are reconciling the history of the Americas with the reality of the present. Moreover, as in the United States and Canada, the "heterogeneity of Latin America, which seemed deplorable to many members of the intelligentsia in the nineteenth century, is now seen as its greatest strength" (Franco 353).

Our shared colonial history and sense of boundaries have perhaps always led the "two" Americas to contribute to each other's literatures in myriad ways—by way of what René Prieto calls "the literary traffic that flows between the Americas" (317)—and magical realism provides yet another means for such cross-cultural exchanges. Moreover, while our understanding of each other's histories and literatures is severely limited, the onus falls to Latin America to know more about the culture north of the Rio Grande. As noted in Chapter 2, José David Saldívar and others argue that such discourse between the two continents must begin with an overhaul of Canadian and U.S. curricula that exclude the other.

It is generally accepted that the (postmodernist) magic realist movement in the Americas led by Alejo Carpentier, Carlos Fuentes, Gabriel García Márquez, Manuel Puig, and, more recently, Isabel Allende has had a powerful influence on a diverse group of post-contemporary United States writers of color [such as Toni Morrison, Arturo Islas, Maxine Hong Kingston, Helena María Viramontes, and Alberto Ríos]. . . . While the works of these United States writers of color have been widely praised for their oppositional, feminist, gay, and minority discourse poetics, and for their powerful supernatural lyricism, their use of (postmodern) magic realism has received little attention in our largely Anglophonic Departments of Literature, owing to an inadequate understanding of a vast and rich literary and cultural movement in the Americas that began over forty years ago. (Saldívar, "Postmodern Realism" 522–23)

As critics and readers, authors and teachers, we must incorporate the history of the "other" America into our vocabularies and our courses. In literary terms, the modes that are beginning to rescue marginalized groups from social and historical amnesia are also gaining a certain cultural status. "In Latin America, [because] the badge of magical realism has signified a kind of uniqueness or difference from mainstream culture[, it] . . . gives the concept the stamp of cultural authority" (Slemon 407).[7]

As *Rediscovering Magical Realism* illustrates, however, U.S. and Canadian marginalized writers also wear a badge of authority that distinguishes them from "mainstream" writers. As Phil McCluskey notes, "Given the 'stamp of cultural authority' that the concept of magic realism maintains within a Latin American context, it is hardly surprising that claims for its appearance outside of the continent are accompanied by declarations of marginality, 'ex-centricity,' and otherness" (89–90). For Latino/a writers in the United States, literary maturation has required them to leave behind the "direct Steinbeck style of social realism" [8] in order to foster an increased interest in other techniques—including the magical realist mode (Walter 103). Yet the dearth of criticism on magical realism as it has extended north of the Rio Grande suggests that the notion of Latin America as the site of magical realism is planted rather firmly in the critical subconscious of North America, even if the many Canadian and U.S. practitioners of the mode are proving otherwise.

ON THE FRINGE WITH MAGICAL REALISM

When we categorize a writer's work as marginal, the issue often becomes a question of "nature or nurture"—is the author's natural (biological or geographical) marginality the deciding factor, or does the theme or subject matter "nurtured" in the text determine whether the work is a peripheral one? Criticism that addresses this question tends to choose "natural" marginalization as the more dominant feature. Marginalized writers tend to produce marginalized works, whether they intend to or not, because the very conditions at work on the authors similarly affect judgments of their texts. While Louise Erdrich argues that classifying her writing as Native American marginalizes it (Sanders 6), the themes she chooses also decenter her works even before critical opinion is brought into play. Although Erdrich herself had Western-based schooling, her "fiction reflects ideas and values of both the Ojibwa (Chippewa) culture and the more dominant American culture" (Sanders 6),[9] so Erdrich seems to be reacting (and rightly so) to the notion that its marginality outweighs its mainstream qualities. But Erdrich's penchant for a "reconstruction of the world to include magic alongside mimetic reality illustrates the importance of a cross-cultural methodology for Magic Realists like" her (279). Erdrich's magical realism and the blatantly marginalized status of her Native American characters within the community of her texts suggest that, whether she admits (or realizes) it, her work demands attention and categorization as marginalia. Moreover, the "contradictory messages" (196) that Erdrich must balance in her own life are the same contradictions that must be balanced by *any* marginalized group. Ultimately, since Erdrich (herself marginalized) has chosen to develop characters who are themselves living on the boundaries of the mainstream, her argument against her work being marginalized seems to embrace both the "nature" and "nurture" features of such literature.

Our classification of a work as thematically marginalized is generally a question of intent. Most readers and scholars would classify James Fenimore Cooper's works as "mainstream," even given such Native American characters as Chingachgook. In contrast, Erdrich clearly intends for her reader to absorb and consider the aspects of marginalization that her characters face on a daily basis. That Cooper never intends to establish or maintain such a focus could be as important a factor in our decision (not, that is, to classify *The Last of the Mohicans* as a marginal work) as whether or not Cooper himself was a marginalized author. The fact that other mainstream writers create texts that do address marginal subjects, and that they do so with success equal (or perhaps even superior) to that of Erdrich, suggests that critics must not automatically validate marginalized writing simply because it originates with a marginal author. Thomas King, whose Canadian and Cherokee roots have both been challenged, may provide the better example of an author whose works prove "marginalized" whether or not he himself belongs to the cultural fringes of society. Conversely, it would be difficult to argue that the mainstream work of an author of international fame, a text *not* given over to themes of marginalization, would be classified as such; Julio Cortázar's *Hopscotch*, with its focus on urban and European (or Europeanized) subjects, would not be considered a marginalized work, in spite of Cortázar's Argentinean roots.[10]

Canadian Robert Kroetsch may not himself be marginalized,[11] but there is no question that he deals with ambiguous borders in his work *What the Crow Said*. As Slemon notes, "*What the Crow Said* . . . thematize[s] a *kind* of postcolonial discourse: one involving the recuperation of silenced voices as axial to a 'positive imagined reconstruction of reality'" (420). The novel features multiple forms of marginalization, perhaps most especially because of its physical location.

The Municipality of Bigknife lay ambiguously on the border between the provinces of Alberta and Saskatchewan; no one, due to a surveyor's error, had ever been able to locate conclusively where the boundaries were supposed to be. The south end of the municipality, beyond the poplar bluffs and the fields of grain, faded into bald prairie and a Hutterite colony; the north end vanished into bush country and an Indian reserve. (36)

According to Luca Biagiotti, "Kroetsch very carefully locates his fictitious town between two 'conflicting' toponyms, one imperial (Alberta), the other indigenous (Saskatchewan), and explicitly declares his difficulty in giving its exact place on the map" (105). Geographically, then, the township of Big Indian rests in a state of limbo of sorts, an area much like Macondo, where the outside world has not yet managed to make much of a dent.

Ironically, in a town named "Big Indian," the only Native American character to hold any position of importance in the text is the Cree Joe Lightning (with whom Cathy is in love and whose flight with the eagle will end in tragedy). In this township, with its Big Indian Hotel and *Big Indian Signal* newspaper and its having been "named after a little Cree trapper who could sweep eight quarters off a beer table with one swing of his hammer" (119), the Native Americans have been so marginalized that they rarely rate more than a casual mention. *What the Crow Said* only mentions in passing that Liebhaber writes an article citing Walking Eagle's prediction for a mild winter (45) or that "a handful of Indians, solemn and quiet, filed into church and sat together in two back pews" at the marriage of Joe Lightning and Cathy Lang (103). The biggest insult to the schmier players is that "every white male over the age of twenty in the Municipal District of Bigknife" is "put on the Indian list: not one of them could, legally, be served an alcoholic beverage" (115) and illustrates the degree to which the racism of a town built around the "idea" of the Indian has remained a constrictive factor. This list is a remnant of a code that is no longer able to enforce its order on the world, for after the decree against the white males only "Indian males over twenty were . . . allowed to purchase alcoholic beverages" (119). As for Native American women, who are not even mentioned in the text or the town, they are pushed so far onto the margins as to have become invisible.

Even the white women exist on the fringes of Big Indian, though this is not true of the narrative, since the story itself revolves around a houseful of white women, mothers and daughters. Tiddy Lang's decision to go into the Big Indian Hotel bar shocks the men, since "[i]t was against the laws of the municipality for a woman to enter the beer parlor" (18). The men subsequently attempt to keep her quiet in an effort to regain the top hand, to marginalize her through silence if not through physical ostracism. "Tiddy, again, tried to speak; the men, not letting her be there. Nothing was so important as her not being allowed to violate their secrecy. [They] . . . excluded her from the misery of their loss and their terror and their loneliness" (20).

Authors writing on and/or about the margins are not limited to the traditional novel by their use of magical realism. Such narrative genres as the short story or cycle, *testimonio* and *transa* fiction, and documentaries are favorite mediums for magical realists or marginalized writers (or both) and provide the space in which these authors explore the margins. For instance, Saldívar notes, "Mary Louise Pratt suggests that the formal marginality of short story cycles enables them to become arenas for the development of alternative visions and resistances, and often introduces women and children as protagonists. . . . Marginal genres such as the short story are also often the site of political, geographical, and cultural contestation" ("Postmodern Realism" 536). Thus, Major Aranda's hand, in Mexican author Alfonso Reyes's short story by the same name, points to the degree to which our preservation of specific versions of history—in this case, the "severed hand, testimony to a glorious deed" in battle (135)—can pervert or diminish the reality of that history. After a while, "it ceased to be a relic and entered into domestic circulation" as a paperweight and "the children of the house ended up by losing respect for it" (137). Eventually, it "really 'got out of hand' " (138), until it begins to read and discovers its own metafictionality, "that it was only a literary theme, a matter of fantasy already very much worked over by the pen of writers" and "let itself die" (142). What we realize, though the hand does not, is that it holds a place in the magical realist mode rather than in the fantastic—in part because it derisively alludes to the latter tradition. Of course, the short story is not the only genre to receive increased attention from marginal writers and their critics. Debra A. Castillo notes that this heightened attention has also increased the awareness of and interest in the *transa* (or "con novel") and *testimonio* genres, novelistic forms that challenge the boundaries of authorship. García Márquez's background in journalism and documentary writing could provide yet another example of genres that garner special interests within marginalized groups.

Because a genre like the short story is familiar to most readers, it increases the author's ability to juxtapose the magic and the real and, thus, such genres often retain particular charm for marginalized writers who are interested in magical realism. They provide magical realists, even more "mainstream" artists like García Márquez, with an additionally rich capacity to reinvent the margins using these types of writing.[12] One of García Márquez's techniques for resolving the antinomy between the supernatural and natural worlds is by assuming a journalistic "telling-it-like-it-is" tone. In "A Very Old Man with Enormous Wings," for example, García Márquez's matter-of-fact tone allows readers access to a marginalized community that is completely foreign to many of his readers. In this short story, he creates a geographically isolated community much like Macondo, one cut off from the realities of everyday modern life. Rather than infusing this scene with a sense of the mysticism that angels typically inspire or conforming to the subtitle's suggestion that the story will be a "fairy tale" for children, García Márquez details the events surrounding the mysterious old man's appearance as if he were reporting for the local newspaper. In just as uniform and logical a manner, he also introduces and then discounts various theories and events that might alternately prove or disprove the angel's authenticity.

The parish priest had his first suspicion of an imposter when he saw that [the angel] did not understand the language of God [Latin] or know how to greet His ministers. Then he noticed that seen close up he was much too human: he had an unbearable smell of the outdoors, the back side of his wings was strewn with parasites and his main feathers had been mistreated by terrestrial winds, and nothing about him measured up to the proud dignity of angels. (107)

Yet the angel seems to perform miracles on the sick who visit him, although "the few miracles attributed to the angel showed a certain mental disorder, like the blind man who didn't recover his sight but grew three new teeth, or the paralytic who didn't get to walk but almost won the lottery, and the leper whose sores sprouted sunflowers" (110).

Brazilian author João Guimarães Rosa adopts a similar technique in "A Young Man, Gleaming, White," which begins with the tone of (and actually references) a journalistic report: "On the night of November 11, 1872, in the district of Sêrro Frio in Minas Gerais, there occurred eerie phenomena which were referred to in contemporary newspapers and registered in the astronomical tables" (99). Only the "excited" Negro José Kakende (103)—the "odd . . . former slave of a halfwitted musician[, who] had been touched in the head ever since a shock he had suffered during the calamities in the country" (101), thereby damaging his credibility—and his report to "wild descriptions of a cloud, flames, noises, round things, wheels, a contraption of some sort, and archangels" (107) allow us to connect the catastrophic events or phenomena with the arrival of the brilliantly white youth who is nameless, naked, and speechless. Though Kakende's descriptions appear to mark the events as the arrival and departure of what seems to have been an alien, the fact that the phenomena are "registered in the astronomical tables" makes the supernatural impossible to discount as mere science fiction. Like García Márquez's very old man, Rosa's youth causes miracles (Hilário Cordeiro's wealth, Duarte Dias's emotional transformation) and, at least according to José Kakende, "[goes] off on wings" (107). The townspeople (though not charged admission) "came to inspect him" (101), and after he leaves they "doubted the air they breathed, the mountains, the very solidity of the earth—but remembered him" (107). Reality has become less accepted and less believable than the supernatural.

In *One Hundred Years of Solitude*, García Márquez peoples Macondo with groups who, in addition to their geographic and technological marginalization, are also marginalized by race and gender. Macondons are, in short, a group as close to the fringes as we might expect to find. Yet, there is something familiar in the community he describes, because he chooses the magical realist mode to make the unknown *comfortable*. When he chooses the voice of the documentary or of journalism (generally with a generous dose of humor) for his tone, then, García Márquez manages to "unexoticize" the exotic.

We might also consider here Ti Noel or Mackandal from *The Kingdom of this World* or the mestizos in the Brazilian novel *Dona Flor and Her Two Husbands*; in both texts, the exoticism of voodoo is defused through magical realism. Unfortunately, Jorge Amado's work divides almost neatly into two sections—one that features magical realism and one that does not—and thus cannot qualify as the sustained use of magical realism that Chanady's definition demands. As opposed to Amado, Carpentier uses both magical realism and marginalized characters to effect a reviewed (if not revised) Haitian history. In *The Kingdom of this World*, as Oralia Preble-Niemi argues, "the *loci* of magical realism [is] the outcast classes which hold values consistent with an ancient, matriarchal, gyneolatric period. . . . [T]he supernatural incidents generally relate to beliefs in African cults that touch the lives of the characters" (105). Like García Márquez, Carpentier qualifies the exotic in *The Kingdom of this World* by choosing the magical realist narrative mode for the text. For Carpentier, what redeems the magical realist events from the suggestion that spiritual powers are at work is that they are not successful, that they are not the end-all means of survival for the slaves. "In the marginalized community, 'magic' fails to achieve the slaves' ambition to assume a patriarchal stance as warriors and claim the equally patriarchal privileges of authority and power" (Preble-Niemi 107). In other words, the failure of voodoo and other African beliefs to overpower the enslaving culture (especially during Henri Christophe's reign, when both the oppressor and the oppressed are relying on voodoo) calls into question the *powers* of the supernatural without disputing the magical realism itself. Voodoo and other indigenous traditions—like the Hispanic *santería* featured in Ana Castillo's *So Far from God*, the Christian faith King dissects in *Green Grass, Running Water*, or the powers of the Native American vision quest Erdrich depicts in *The Bingo Palace*—through the lens of magical realism, become ordinary or even absurd.

Magical realist texts make use of such traditions as voodoo and vision quests not as salvations or excuses for the presence of magic but rather because magical realism is concerned with the revision of *many* traditions, even those of the margins, particularly those that comfort us with the expected. In other words, magic has many forms in our everyday reality, and we have expectations of that supernatural, whether it is voodoo- or *santería-* or Christianity-based. Magical realism works to overturn our expectations of the supernatural, just as it forces us to reconsider reality.[13] The Catholicism of Ana Castillo, the Native American heritage of Louise Erdrich, and the African beliefs in *The Kingdom of this World* are no longer the familiar. And yet, when authors like Castillo, Carpentier, King, and Erdrich reevaluate these traditions using the magical realist mode, they still *read* like the familiar. We are equally unable to excuse or exoticize these as religious or spiritual rationales.

Some critics see magical realism as an inappropriate choice for minority authors rereading and revising their status. In her review of *Beloved*, Martha Bayles intends primarily to show that, "[b]y embracing the genre, Morrison[, who may be the first to combine black folk culture with the romantic impulses of magic realism] also embraces its willful romanticism, which, in the context of black America, leads to the corollary that the most marginal people are the least corrupted by the false values of the dominant white society" (38). She sees this as reverse racism, "excusing Sethe from lasting blame" and "almost equat[ing] her infanticide with Sixo's pilfering" (40). Bayles's most outrageous argument is that "[i]n Morrison's mind there seems to be only one crime, that of slavery itself, and no person who lives under it has to answer for anything. So intent is [Morrison] on showing the inhumanity of the master, she dehumanizes the slave" (40). But Bayles's claim that *Beloved*'s margins are *least* corrupted, that Morrison suggests they are somehow outside the value system "of the dominant white society," only decenters the novel's characters more. Bayles equates Morrison's magical realism with escapism, and in doing so aligns herself with the magical realist critics who see magical realism as purely self-referential. Without the crime of slavery, true, there might be no *Beloved*, but without Sethe's crime (the ramifications of which follow her for years, excluding her from the community) there would be no Beloved to deal with, either.

Magical realism is *not* a means for implicating "the false values of the dominant white society" to the exclusion of the marginalized. What is striking about the magic of *Tracks*, for example, is that Pauline uses it. She is neither fully a peripheral character nor fully Native American; unlike most of the characters in the novel, she is both at once. Her warped powers, as illustrated when she vicariously pleasures herself by willing Sophie to copulate with Eli, are especially revealing in a novel where the supernatural is more frequently turned against the white, male aggressor. Fleur's storm-inspiring rage crushes the very men who had raped and abused her, but like Sethe, Fleur is never refigured as martyred or above sin. If anything, it marks her as "different" to the community. Indeed, Erdrich continually proves

Pauline to be an abuser herself, for *Love Medicine* opens with a scene in which she abuses her own daughter. Pauline disrupts all "mainstream" systems of order—Catholic, Native American, relational, communal—in Erdrich's works.

Many marginalized characters in magical realist works are verbally marked as such by those around them. In Ana Castillo's *So Far From God*, Francisco el Penitente is known to his buddies in Vietnam as Chico, but

> He didn't like Chico—which back home meant a roasted corn.
> Or just a hard kernel.
> He didn't like Chico no more than the Navajo who was also in his platoon went for the nickname "Chief," or the Puerto Rican from Rio Piedras, just shy of finishing his Ph.D. when he was drafted, liked to be called "Little Chico." Francisco . . . was a lanky six feet in height compared to Little Chico's five feet eight inches, and to the white and black soldiers all "Spanish boys" were "Chico." (94).

The white soldiers—and, interestingly, the black ones as well, who would undoubtedly endure their own nicknames in such a situation—mark the cultural boundaries of the platoon with these derogatory terms, humping their racism along with their backpacks. "La Loca," which becomes a sort of endearment, begins as a communal observation and serves as a marker of Loca's place on the fringe, a reminder that Sofi's daughter does not conform to accepted religious, physical, or even superstitious doctrines.

In *The House of the Spirits*, Chilean Isabel Allende frequently places the emphasis on the oppressor rather than on the marginalized and/or oppressed, most notably illustrated in her decision to describe numerous scenes from Esteban Trueba's point of view. We often learn of Trueba's exploitation of the peasants on Tres Marías firsthand. Even his more considerate deeds, though, are tainted with his need for class structure: Trueba "aspired to the day when all the children and adults of Tres Marías would know how to read, write, and do simple arithmetic, even though he was not in favor of their acquiring any additional learning, for fear they would fill their minds with ideas unsuited to their station and condition" (59). During the elections, the conservative party to which he belongs

> piled the peasants onto wooden carts and hauled them off to vote, under careful observation. . . . It was the one time in their lives they showed the peasants a trace of intimacy: pal this and pal that, don't worry, *patrón*, I'm on your team, you can count on me, that's the way I like it, pal, it's nice to see you have a patriotic conscience, you know the liberals and radicals are all a bunch of morons and the Communists are atheist bastards who eat little children. (70)

The expected outcome, the success of the Conservative Party, Trueba holds up as

> "[a]n example for this continent of Indians and Negroes who spend their time making revolutions to overthrow one dictator and install another. [Chile] is a different country. This country's a genuine republic. We have civic pride . . . and we don't need a general to

keep things orderly and calm, not like the neighboring dictatorships where they kill each other off while the gringos walk away with all their raw materials," Trueba declared. (70)

Trueba's strongest test, though, is Clara, whom he loves, who "had summoned him with the power of her thought, and . . . had already made up her mind to marry without love" (90). Perhaps most important to the magical realist aspect of Allende's text is that Clara's abilities make it impossible for him to own her.

> He realized that Clara did not belong to him and that if she continued living in a world of apparitions, three-legged tables that moved of their own volition, and cards that spelled out the future, she probably never would. . . . He wanted far more than her body; he wanted control over that undefined and luminous material that lay within her and that escaped him even in those moments when she appeared to be dying of pleasure. (96)

To Trueba, Clara's talents stand in the way of her loving him, and her powers dismember him in the sense that he no longer feels like the man of his own "house of spirits."

Unlike ethnicity or nationality, being a woman is almost always a visible mark of marginality, though some (like George Eliot for example) may prove elusive enough to deflect the stinging effect it tends to have on women writers. As Appiah might add here, "Gender and sexuality, unlike [religion or ethnicity or race] are both grounded in the sexual body" (150). It is no wonder, then, that the body factors so prominently in female discourse, and this is no less true for magical realist texts. Instead, though, the body is re-bodied in very supernatural ways.

M.O.M.A.S. AND DAUGHTERS OF MAGICAL REALISM

Just like ethnic and national groups, women writers have long been edged out of the mainstream, but unlike their male counterparts, they are doubly marginalized if they happen to belong to a "marginal" ethnicity. "For obvious reasons," Zamora argues, "writers from marginalized racial and ethnic communities are impelled to recuperate cultural and historical differences and create inclusive structures to express them. And many of these writers are women" (*Usable Past* 206). Moreover, "[m]any Latin American women share with their First World counterparts what [Linda] Hutcheon calls the postmodern valuing of margins" (Williams, *Postmodern Novel* 16). Because it is possible for a woman who is, for example, an indigenous Latin American author, to be on the margin of a marginalized margin, it becomes startlingly clear why women have begun to appropriate not only the voice of marginalia but also its literary modes.

For the marginalized female writer, magical realism is frequently the optimum mode of choice because of its flexibility and marketability. As recently as the early 1980s, "Isabel Allende became Chile's first mass-marketed modern writer, beginning with her initial imitations of Gabriel García Márquez's magic realism in *The House of the Spirits*" (Williams, *Postmodern Novel* 71). In a sense, Allende and other

Latin American women are "cashing in" on a mode that was creating international recognition for their male counterparts. "Recently, women writers, such as . . . Allende and Laura Esquivel, have benefited from the commercial interests in magic realism and the Latin American Boom" (109). More importantly, they have "placed women writers in Latin America in the spotlight for the first time in the history of the region" (110). Notably, the Boom "created a public both inside and outside Latin America for women's writing" (Franco 342). Perhaps the most significant development from the Boom and post-Boom, and the slowest in coming, has been that women could write from and about margins (perhaps even using a marginalized mode) and yet, for once, be heard throughout Latin America and the world.

Women writers are using their own commodification not only as a means to be heard but also as a way of revising their own marginal status. Philip Swanson argues, "Allende's aim is . . . to push the marginal into the mainstream. . . . This politicisation . . . includes sexual politics and brings us closer to a Kristevan model of marginality based on all 'that which is repressed in discourse and in the relations of production. Call it "woman" or "oppressed classes of society," it is the same struggle, and never the one without the other' " (147). Like magical realism and the Boom itself, this Kristevan model challenges us to reassess marginality, to understand it not only in terms of the end product of marginalization but also in terms of the means to that end, in the sexual and discursive processes through which people are pressed into marginalization, that is, the process by which the fringes are distinguished. Morrison, Erdrich, Allende, and other female authors who are attracting the attention of the mainstream by writing about the margin have reinserted themselves into the discourse by which marginalization is achieved. They are reacting to a system in which

marginalized groups like women and the working class are actually central to the process of reproduction and the capitalist economy: [Toril Moi says] "it is precisely because the ruling order cannot maintain the *status quo* without the continual exploitation and oppression of these groups that it seeks to mask their central economic role by marginalizing them on the cultural, ideological and political levels." The main strategy in this programme of marginalisation . . . is the creation of an illusion of a unified individual and collective self, a given universal world order in which male, white, middle-class, heterosexual experience passes itself off as "nature." (Swanson 148)

Women writing from a magical realist perspective undermine this illusion, as noted earlier, by disrupting our notions of what is "natural" or ordered, but magical realism—and those who practice it—are still very much at the mercy of those who capitalize on their marginality. The commodification of female writers, whether through the Boom or post-Boom or via other forms of commercialization, creates universal recognition and a wider forum but continues to be a mixed blessing.

Magical realism allows women writers who themselves exist on multiple planes to create worlds that can address all of those levels within a single work. Through magical realism, for example, Erdrich challenges her upbringing as a Catholic, as a Native American, and as a woman. "Magic Realism is a literary genre directly tied to writers whose cultures have been threatened or destroyed by a more powerful or dominant one" (Sanders 18), and it "is the embrace of a *both/and* rather than an *either/or* mentality which helps to make Magic Realism an attractive genre for Erdrich[, for example,] who brings her ancestral culture to bear on the contemporary settings of her texts" (22; emphasis added). This all-encompassing, "both/and" fixture of magical realism means that Erdrich can challenge the multifarious forces intent on overpowering her at once.

Though women magical realists are attempting, through their fiction, to shift the balances of power, this shift encompasses mixed blessings of its own. Women writers embrace magical realism as a means for countering the dominant discourse at risk (ironically) of challenging their own sense of worth and of silencing the feminine voice in their texts. For Erdrich, for example, the cost has been a sort of cynicism about the power both of magic and of the female figure. "From a feminist and North American perspective, . . . Erdrich's fiction both values and distrusts the existence of the (m)other who has been killed or marginalized in the mainstream white, male texts. In [her] Magic Realism, magic functions in much the same way. Like the mother, belief in magic has been killed off or marginalized" (Sanders 92). Allende provides an exceptional illustration of this distrust of the powerful, magical mother figure (Clara, from *The House of the Spirits*) through her use of the first-person narration of Esteban Trueba. He is the site of the memory *and* the forgetting of the supernatural, as Allende proves when she leaves memory in his keeping. His realization that the hatbox with which Alba plays contains the head of her grandmother shows that, though the hatbox "contains" one of Clara's stories, Esteban is the only means of carrying it to the next generations. Even before her death, the violence men visit upon the female form has brought about Clara's silence, first when her sister's dead body is violated by the doctor's assistant and finally when Trueba knocks Clara down in anger. What ultimately silences Clara, though, is Trueba's distrust of the supernatural; as a phenomenon outside the empirical (in every sense of the word) world, and thus out of his control, magic threatens his power. Unfortunately, Allende compromises her reader's belief in the magical realism of her novel when she emphasizes Trueba's voice at the cost of Clara's.

Counterbalanced with this marginalization and silencing of the (m)other is the fact that women are cultural impetuses for the supernatural. Women provide magical realism with several things—children, homes, and rebellion being only a few of their offerings—as Morrison, Erdrich, Allende, and others detail in their literature. What happens when a mother figure is imposed on the magical realist realm? After all, motherhood has long been associated with a sort of magical realism: the Child —at once god and man—born out of the Virgin Mary, who is herself a chiasmus: the Wedded Maid and Virgin Mother. In Christianity, Motherhood fulfills its ultimate purpose without soiling its hands at the fountain of sexuality. In some ways, then, motherhood allows the text, and the magical realist text in particular, to reconcile the virgin/whore dichotomy—without giving up the qualities of either.

In some magical realist texts, the primary mother figure, like the Virgin Mary, will be only implicated in the sexual act rather than participating directly. In Macondo, though sexual relations abound, García Márquez creates a near sexless existence for the matriarch and patriarch of the family. Úrsula perpetuates a line of descendants, but her coupling with José Arcadio Buendía exists largely outside the scope of the text. García Márquez gives us the story of the chastity belt: "At night they would wrestle for several hours in an anguished violence that seemed to be a substitute for the act of love, until popular intuition got a whiff of something irregular and the rumor spread that Úrsula was still a virgin a year after her marriage because her husband was impotent. José Arcadio Buendía was the last one to hear the rumor" (*One Hundred Years of Solitude* 21). We also see José Arcadio Buendía's ultimate decision to risk fate by mating with his cousin, in spite of the curse of incest and in spite of the tragic circumstances that precede the actual act of intercourse:

So the situation went on the same way for another six months until that tragic Sunday when José Arcadio Buendía won a cockfight from Prudencio Aguilar [and then kills Prudencio]. . . . That night, as they held a wake over the corpse in the cockpit, José Arcadio Buendía went into the bedroom as his wife was putting on her chastity pants. Pointing the spear at her he ordered: "Take them off." Úrsula had no doubt about her husband's decision. "You'll be responsible for what happens," she murmured; . . . they were awake and frolicking in bed until dawn, indifferent to the breeze that passed through the bedroom, loaded with the weeping of Prudencio Aguilar's kin. (21–22)

But these acts are pre-Macondon history. The Adam and Eve of García Márquez's text never copulate in the garden. In its own way, the deliberate exclusion of their acts makes Macondo all the more magical; it (and the Buendías) become all the more supernatural. García Márquez invents a world where the mother figure perpetuates an entire line; culminating in the fated birth of a child who fulfills the curse of the pig's tail, but where the mother figure is never again associated with her sexuality.

The definition of women's roles, whether sexual, domestic, or maternal, is frequently handed down by the men in magical realist texts. That women's roles are not always clearly defined for them is revealed tellingly when *So Far From God*'s Esperanza begins going to tepee meetings of the Native-American Church with Rubén. He ends up

teaching her the dos and don'ts of his interpretation of lodge "etiquette" and the role of women and the role of men and how they were not to be questioned. And she concluded as she had during their early days, why not? After all, there was Rubén with his Native and Chicano male friends always joking among themselves, always siding with each other, and always agreeing about the order and reason of the universe, and since Esperanza had no Native women friends to verify any of what was being told to her by Rubén about the woman's role in what they were doing, she did not venture to contradict him. (36)

In *The House of the Spirits*, Clara hears similar lessons, this time from a group of women in her community who seem to be speaking on the men's behalf and using masculine language.

Since when has a man not beaten his wife? If he doesn't beat her, it's either because he doesn't love her or because he isn't a real man. Since when is a man's paycheck or the fruit of the earth or what the chickens lay shared between them, when everybody knows he is the one in charge? Since when has a woman ever done the same things as a man? Besides, she was born with a wound between her legs and without balls, right, Señora Clara? (106)

Both Esperanza and Clara are locked into cultures that preach the same message. For Esperanza, "no kind of white woman's self-help book" will, in fact, help more than the "courage she got from the sweat lodge and which she surely needed now more than ever" (47). Esperanza looks to the traditions, certainly, for her healing, but she does not look to her *own* traditions. By having her character relying on Native American "cures," Castillo puts an ironic twist on the ways in which her Hispanic female characters attempt to recover what their marginalization has cost them, because she insists that they will not find help within their own margin.

Like the failure of "white woman's self-help books" for Esperanza, Pilar Puente is similarly failed by the school systems and psychiatry that stands outside her world in *Dreaming in Cuban*. Her psychiatrist

Dr. Price told Mom that we should start some mother-and-daughter activities, that I was starved for a female primate, or something like that, so she enrolled us in a flamenco class in a studio over Carnegie hall. Our teacher, Mercedes García, was a bosomy woman with jackhammer feet who taught us how to drop our heels in time to her claps and castanets. Our first lesson was all stamping, first as a group then individually across the floor. What a thunder we made! Mercedes singled me out—"A proud chest, yes! See how she carries herself? *Perfecto! Así, así!*" Mom watched me closely. I could read in her face that we wouldn't return. (59)

Of course, the more important failure here is of Lourdes as mother to Pilar. Her mother later takes great pride in the dance she shares with her nephew Ivanito in Cuba, but she is unable (at least at this point in the story) to share either her pride or her culture with Pilar. This lack is also evident in her consistent berating of Cuba, to which Pilar would like to return to learn more about her grandmother and her heritage. Pilar finds that trusting her own instincts, as her Cuban grandmother taught her, "is a constant struggle around my mother, who systematically rewrites history to suit her views of the world" (176). Later, when Lourdes sticks up for Pilar's painting of a punk Statue of Liberty before falling to the floor in an "avalanche of patriotism and motherhood," Pilar discovers, "And I, I love my mother very much at that moment" (144).

Frequently, the imposed order of the mainstream needs to be revised in order for mother and daughter characters to survive the margins. M.O.M.A.S. (Mothers of Martyrs and Saints) does this for *So Far From God*; for a people "so far" from the God of Catholic religion, the "rules" of martyrdom are bent in order to honor the children whom the Hispanic mothers are losing. La Loca's death experience and visit to Hell reenvision what the priest understands his religion to be, but her experience grants her mother a privileged position in the community of other marginalized mothers. Pilar Puente manages to get herself kicked out of the Catholic school to which she refers as "Martyrs and Saints" (*Dreaming in Cuban* 58). Furthermore, in *The House of the Spirits*, Clara proves to be a blessing to her family, rather than the possessed devil the priest pronounces her to be when she, too, questions the system of Christianity. During a dramatic pause in one of the priest's apocalyptic sermons, in which "he described the torments of the damned in hell, the bodies ripped apart by various ingenious torture apparatuses, the eternal flames, the hooks that pierced the male member, the disgusting reptiles that crept up female orifices, and the myriad other sufferings that he wove into his sermon" in an attempt "to rouse the conscience of his indolent Creole flock . . . the voice of little Clara was heard in all its purity. 'Psst! Father Restrepo! If that story about hell is a lie, we're all fucked, aren't we' " (7).

Clara, though refusing to be constrained by the rules of dominant society, is still situated on the fringes of that society. When Clara goes "everywhere with her little girl clutched to her breast, nursing her constantly without a set schedule and without regard for manners or modesty," her motherly instinct marginalizes her further, for now she is "like an Indian. She did not want to swaddle [Blanca], cut her hair, pierce her ears, or hire a nursemaid to take care of her, and least of all to use milk manufactured in some laboratory, as all the ladies did who could afford such luxuries" (101). Breast-feeding, as a marker of class status, simultaneously makes Clara's bond with Blanca stronger and "low class." The message is clear: being a good mother cannot be reconciled with the high society to which Trueba so desperately wants to belong.

Laura Esquivel challenges the notion of the "good mother" altogether when she makes Tita the only good mother in her text *Like Water For Chocolate*. She plays the perfect midwife to her sister Rosaura though she has never before delivered a baby. When Rosaura has no milk and the wet nurse is killed, Tita is able to nurse her nephew. Her response is brought on equally by her love for her brother-in-law Pedro and his child, and by her love of feeding people, because, "[i]f there was one thing Tita couldn't resist, it was a hungry person asking for food" (76). Tita is denied her own rights to motherhood by the family tradition that insists the youngest daughter will never marry and will care for her mother in her old age. Rosaura threatens to carry out this family "curse" with her daughter Esperanza, suggesting she is no better or sympathetic a mother than Mama Elena. In spite of her refusal to bond with Esperanza by nursing (since she fears she too will be taken away), Tita ends up so attached to her niece that Rosaura can punish Tita for her affair with Pedro by refusing to let Tita feed the baby. Moreover, Mama Elena, who returns to curse Tita during her pregnancy, seems to deny Tita her final chance at motherhood by triggering a miscarriage.[14] In place of the "natural" but negative mother figure, Esquivel inserts a character who represents positive, *super*natural motherhood.

Singled-Out Mothers

In many of the magical realist works with which *Rediscovering Magical Realism* deals, the male or father figure is missing—literally or figuratively—from the family core, leaving the women in the home alternately to mourn and to revel in the loss. José Arcadio Buendía becomes a supernatural pet of the household; the clabber-covered Halle never arrives from the South; and Sofi's gamble doesn't pay off "since no one had seen hide nor hair of [her husband, Domingo] since he'd left Sofi and the girls" (*So Far From God* 21). Less obvious examples of the missing male figure include Jorge del Pino—who, while he does not actually desert his wife and children, travels for his job for an American company, keeping him out of the house "five weeks out of six" (*Dreaming in Cuban* 6); Martin Lang, whose concerted efforts to stay out of the house make his death in *What the Crow Said* seem less of a loss than a continuance; and Pedro Muzquiz, who is "absent" in his marriage to Rosaura, since it is purely a means for being closer to her sister Tita. While Karla J. Sanders argues that Erdrich makes her positive "father figure magical by connecting positive paternity to the trickster characters of Nanapush and Gerry, and by giving these fathers magical capabilities" (137–38), by and large, fathers do not figure prominently in Erdrich's texts and are more frequently missing, as with Eli, whom Fleur essentially cuts out of the picture entirely. In Lulu's case, not only is the father figure missing, but the mother figure also demands that this be the case.

Domingo is a husband who is initially introduced and dismissed in a single page. His return halfway through the text is not a homecoming but rather a home-disrupting. Domingo's absence prior to most of *So Far From God* seems to have been prophesied by the fact that their "marriage had a black ribbon on its door from the beginning," since no one in Sofi's circle of friends and family approves of him. Ironically, he is the missing father who returns, and, like Wakefield in Hawthorne's story, he never explains either the disappearance or what he does during it. But La Loca, who has never really known him, gets to know him by sniffing him and quickly establishes a bond:

" 'Jita," Sofi asked her daughter one day when they were alone, "what is it that you smell when you smell your father?"

"Mom," La Loca said, "I smell my dad. And he was in hell, too."

"Hell?" Sofi said, thinking her daughter, who didn't have any sense of humor at all, was trying to make a joke.

But instead Loca replied quite soberly, "Mom, I been to hell. You never forget that smell. And my dad . . . he was there too."

"So you think I should forgive your dad for leaving me, for leaving us all those years?" Sofi asked.

"Here we don't forgive, Mom," La Loca told her. (41)

Rather than providing her father with a religious explanation for his disappearance, though, La Loca's reasoning merely connects him with the daughter whose own "miraculous" death and resurrection defy conventional Christian beliefs. Sofi, who "had not been taken out for close to a quarter of a century" (103), cannot forgive and must be re-courted by Domingo when he returns, even though the apparent ease of their routine belies the length of their separation.

> He had come home last fall and Sofi and he in an unspoken way had picked up as husband and wife again as if only a day of estrangement had passed between them and not nearly twenty years. They acted like a couple who had actually been together for the better part of their nearly thirty-five-year marriage and had become so used to each other that they didn't even notice one another no more, like an old chair in the corner of the room. . . . They slept not only in separate beds but in separate rooms, and hardly shared a meal together. (109)

Later we learn that Sofi had greeted his reappearance with a dry "Did you forget something?" and that "she had let him return, he was after all her husband and the father of their children, but he was sad to accept the reality that his presence was little more than tolerated" (110). Domingo chooses to "court" Sofi by leaving again, this time to build Caridad a little adobe house. When he gives up the deed to their house to pay a gambling debt, she remembers that she was the one who had made him leave the first time, and she decides "to send Domingo out of her life once again" (215) by divorcing him. In the end, we discover that Sofi, like Fleur, is the one who sets the terms for the father's absence.

    What the Crow Said is replete with missing husbands, literally and figuratively. Martin Lang, a Rip Van Winkle character "who was always in town when he was needed, always in the beer parlor in the Big Indian Hotel, doing anything but farming" (9), is as absent alive as he is dead.[15] After his death, though, even his dead body goes missing when he slips from the back of John Skandl's sleigh on their ride into the undertaker's, until he is found thawing in the church basement. Skandl, who becomes Tiddy's second husband, also deserts her, this time for politics, and dies in a plane crash. Mick O'Holleran, a hired hand for the Langs and future son-in-law, is missing in a figurative sense, in that he does not possess private parts or a right leg. But when the second daughter, Rose, reveals that she is pregnant, "without the slightest argument, [he] admitted that at times he not only felt the presence of his missing leg and private parts, but could actually use them" (66–67). Equally absent is the father of Gladys's child, conceived the night of a fight at the skating rink. When Liebhaber asks who the father is, Tiddy Lang tells him "Everybody" (75). In this communal fathering, no one is required to take the "blame" of fathering Gladys's child, and as with the bees in Vera's pregnancy and Theresa's claim that a ghost fathered her child, the community provides an explanation—no matter how unsatisfying those answers may be—but no husband or father. That is left up to the creative force of Tiddy Lang, who after each pregnancy proclaims, "Someone must take a wife." A final, ironic example among the Lang women is Jerry Lapanne, the escaped convict who is "an emblem of incarcerated desire" and who "repeatedly tries to escape *into* the site of the text toward Rita Lang. . . . But the police are always there on the borders of the municipality to stop him; and his one breakthrough results in his death" (Slemon 418). The one man who tries hardest *not* to be missing is the one who is incapable of entering the text.

In what perhaps might be the ultimate missing husband scenario, two of the novels considered here incorporate artificial insemination, "AI-ing, this was called, to Liebhaber's immense satisfaction" (*What the Crow Said* 70). Artificial insemination, at least on the surface, seems to be the height of noninvolvement on the father's part. Yet, though the process of "AI-ing" in *What the Crow Said* involves cattle, it leads to Nick Droniuk's impregnating Anna Marie Lang. Instead of the father being absent for artificial insemination in Kroetsch's world, then, Nick seems to be inspired by the process to take on the role in reality. In *Green Grass, Running Water*, the process is similarly introduced—"When Alberta was small, she had seen cows artificially inseminated. There was nothing wrong with it, she guessed, for cows, but even there it had seemed . . . mechanical" (195)—but it has drastically different outcomes. Her own decision to be artificially inseminated is complicated by the fact that she is single. "I just want a child. I don't want a husband," Alberta argues (198). Again, Alberta's act seems to represent the definitive missing father, since she wants a baby without having to deal with the baby's father. Apparently the disappearing father must "disappear" himself; Alberta learns that even in modern society, no woman wants to be responsible for cutting him out of the picture herself.

Conversely, the definitive *present* father could be represented by the Christian God who is *omnipresent*, but Thomas King even revises the immaculate conception, much as he revises other aspects of Christianity. When A. A. Gabriel (whose business card lists him as a Canadian Security and Intelligence Service agent *and* as the Heavenly Host) appears to Thought Woman, the interviewer attempts to rename her Mary, to require "virgin verification," and to take her picture next to a "snake" who is actually Old Coyote. When she refuses him and floats away again on the ocean, A. A. Gabriel shouts after her: "There are lots of Marys in the world. . . . We can always find another one, you know" (301).

Infertile Magic

Perhaps worse yet than the missing husband is the revision or displacement of the womb or womanhood. The single most drastic case of the womb becoming a viable force in the magical realist text also sets off the entire chain of events in *Ex Utero*. Foos begins, "Rita is lying in bed one night when she realizes she's lost her uterus" (1). Although she recovers the missing organ by the end of the text, Rita discovers it has been used by someone else. "There in the tiny pink shape she sees the dents that have given the womb an odd curvature around its middle, the once-furious pink now dulled to a dusky rose. . . . She can see traces of blood around the sides of the womb and at its pale center. Someone has gotten to it, she realizes, before she's had a chance to fill it" (177). What is more interesting, perhaps, than the use Rita's womb gets without her is how others use Rita when she is without her uterus. Rita, via her appearance on Rod Nodderman's talk show, becomes a celebrity. A fan puts it succinctly: "'She's more than just a womb,' the woman says, her eyes narrowed in disgust. 'You men had better think about that'" (57). In fact, however, even the women in the text—though sympathetic with her—see Rita as lacking. A pregnant audience member tells Nodderman, "My womb,' [she] says, . . . looking straight at Rita, her eyes round and full of hope, 'is everything I am' " (33), and the fan mail she gets is largely sympathetic about her "loss." Rita's talk show appearances also set in motion the other magical events in the text. Adele is driven into a sexual frenzy by television shows, particularly Nodderman's talk show. "Certain shows have sent her tearing at [her boyfriend] Leonard's hair and begging for commercials. She has been known to scream with pleasure at the opening strains of game show theme songs, writhing on the bed from the spinning of the Wheel of Fortune" (37). But when she sees Rita on Nodderman's show, her vagina seals shut in sympathetic response to Rita's loss. And Lucy has a flood of womanhood in response to the other two stories. Her menses refuses to stop; she is ironically in a perpetual state of infertility, with her body in continuous preparation for fertility.

If her womb is important to Rita, it seems vital to her husband, who can no longer get an erection. George searches the house inside and out, certain that her uterus could not have gone far. Eventually, George is reduced to drawing pictures of his once-erect penis and selling them in the mall parking lot. Leonard, too, equates his manhood with his sex-life with Adele and sets about to "correct" her impairment: "Leonard lays his tools down on the hardwood floor, takes out a tape measure and begins jotting down dimensions. A chip to the left, some heavy chiseling in the center, perhaps a drill will do, he says" (40).

Just as female reproductive organs prove the impetus for the action in *Ex Utero*, so, too, do wombs play an important role in the ending of *So Far From God*:

To be a member of M.O.M.A.S. [Mothers of Martyrs and Saints] of course you had to have issued the *declared* santo or martyr from your own womb, coming out of that very place that some malcriado, like Saint Augustine, had so disgracefully referred to back in the fourth century as "being between feces and urine"! . . . But for a long time, a rumor followed las M.O.M.A.S. that the appointed board member Mothers were made to sit on chairs much like the ones that popes back in the beginning of their days were made to sit on after a woman who passed herself off as a man had been elected pope. In other words, a chair that was structured to *prove* that you were in fact a "mom" or, at least, could have been. What happened to that woman pope way back when, by the way, was that she was not only thrown off the throne for not being a man, but dragged through the streets and stoned to death. Nothing like that never happened among the M.O.M.A.S.! ¡Hiho! Imagine las M.O.M.A.S. taking things that far to make sure that they all had wombs!
After all, just because there had been a time way back when, when some fregados all full of themselves went out of their way to prove that none among them had the potential of being a mother, did it mean that there *had* to come a time when someone would be made to *prove* she did? (Castillo 251–52)

Though indeed one of Castillo's goals is to satirize "our collective desire to codify the sacred" (Faris, "Scheherazade's Children" 169), the overriding mission of such passages is to satirize our perceptions of the female body, of motherhood, of membership in a kind of club being granted through sexual organs. In both *So Far From God* and *Ex Utero*, the presence or lack of a womb figures a woman's worth in her world. Rita becomes a pop culture sensation because of her lack of womb. Although the female pope in Castillo's version cannot fulfill her religious pretensions because she is *pro utero*, the M.O.M.A.S are accepted into their religiously based organization for the same reason. Tellingly, it is not the actuality of the womb in either text that grants its power; it is its *potential* that offers both Rita and the mothers in the club their status in the worlds in which they live.

The "potential" that Sethe's womb represents to her dead child and Beloved is the potential for death. Rita's comment to her friend Adele in *Ex Utero* that her "womb . . . is now not an instrument of life, but of death" (134) proves just as apt for Sethe. As noted in more detail in Chapter 5, for *Beloved* the womb is symbolic of the tomb, as illustrated by Sethe's "payment" to the engraver. The tombstone "she selected to lean against on tiptoe, her knees wide open as any grave" is as "[p]ink as a fingernail" (5). The color of the stone even recalls the womb, then, just as Sethe's actions evoke the grave. In fact, it is only after Sethe delivers the afterbirth that Denver utters her first cry. The umbilical cord, the twenty inches of cord that once connected the two, must be completely severed before Denver is willing to live, as if she, too, realizes the danger of being connected with Sethe's womb.

Castillo's satirical portrayal of the religious portents of the womb comes sharply into contrast with other authors' much more worldly consideration of female sexuality. While Foos concentrates on the womb as the site of desire, Castillo defines the womb as a magical connection with one's child; this theme is also carried out in *Beloved* and *One Hundred Years of Solitude*, though for Morrison such a link can be a dangerous one for Sethe's children. *Dreaming in Cuban* also links wombs with danger and children. When Lourdes's sister loses touch with reality, "Felicia feels herself getting younger in her sleep, so young in fact that she fears she will die, be driven beyond the womb to oblivion" (82). After she tries to kill herself and her son, she is deemed "an 'unfit mother,' and accused . . . of irreparably damaging her son," and she is told "that she must find meaning in her life outside of her son, that she should give the revolution another try, become a New Socialist Woman" (107). Because of her unusual behavior, her twin girls, Luz and Milagro, call her "not-Mamá" (121). Erdrich also creates a "not-Mamá" character, June Morrissey, in *Love Medicine* and *Tracks*. June's failure as a mother seems to be linked with the failure of her own mother to protect her from the attacks of her mother's boyfriend, Leonard. When he rapes her, June decides never to be held down again. Lipsha realizes that, when she made an attempt on his life during his childhood, "she did the same that was done to her—a young girl left out to live in the woods and survive on pine sap and leaves and buried roots" (217). For Lipsha, even Shawnee Ray's sexuality begins to be tied up with her role as mother, as when he reflects,

it occurs to me that being a smart woman and a good mother are two things I never valued quite enough in Shawnee Ray either. What I think about more than anything else is sex—day in and day out those thoughts preoccupy my brain. But now, I put my mind onto her other qualities. . . . I want everything about Shawnee Ray, even her motherhood. Only, I want her to mother me, to heal me. (165–66)

As Morrison's version suggests, some authors argue that the womb carries its own involuntary memory of that connection with the child. When Sethe sees Beloved sitting on a stump near 124,

for some reason she could not immediately account for, the moment she got close enough to see the face, Sethe's bladder filled to capacity. She said, "Oh, excuse me," and ran around to the back of 124. Not since she was a baby girl, being cared for by the eight-year-old girl who pointed out her mother to her, had she had an emergency that unmanageable. She never made the outhouse. Right in front of its door she had to lift her skirts, and the water she voided was endless. Like a horse, she thought, but as it went on and on she thought, No, more like flooding the boat when Denver was born. . . . But there was no stopping water breaking from a breaking womb and there was no stopping now. (51)

Here, in one of the richest and most symbolic passages of the novel, Morrison conjures Sethe's own loss of bond with her mother and Sethe's delivery of Denver, and implies her connection with this young woman sitting outside her home. Sethe's body, long before her mind, recognizes something in Beloved as its own. This same connection with her children convinces Sethe to deliver her milk to the baby she sends on ahead and persuades her not to die on her way to Ohio. Though her death

didn't seem such a bad idea, all in all, in view of the step she would not have to take, . . . the thought of herself stretched out dead while the little antelope [i.e., the unborn Denver] lived on—an hour? a day? a day and a night?—in her lifeless body grieved her so she made the groan that made the person walking on a path not ten yards away halt and stand right still. (31)

We see that the link between mother and child can extend past death when José Arcadio's blood returns to Úrsula, for whom motherhood is such a magical connection with her children that, when he dies, "the blood of José Arcadio flows backwards, reattaching the umbilical cord, a kind of reverse menstrual flow" (Rabassa, "Beyond Magic Realism" 450). Erdrich associates this umbilical connection with the fate and future of the Native American heritage: "The red rope between the mother and her baby is the hope of our nation. It pulls, it sings, it feeds and holds. How it holds. The shock of throwing yourself to the end of that rope has brought many a wild young woman up short, slammed her down, left her dusting herself off, outraged and tender" (*Tracks* 6).

As Allende illustrates, sometimes mother and children connect even before the delivery. Both times Clara is pregnant, she knows the sex and names of the children. When Trueba jokes about naming their son after himself, he learns from Clara that "It's not one, it's two" and that these "twins will be called Jaime and Nicolás, respectively" (115). As P. Gabrielle Foreman notes, Clara "wrests Adamic power from her husband" in this scene (291), but she also proves that her bond with these sons has already begun. In other words, she already knows or recognizes them. As a clairvoyant, Clara might be expected to have such a talent, but her mother knows before Rosa's birth that "she was not of this world, because she had already seen her in dreams" (4). Of course, when she is a child, Clara's parents hope she will outgrow her disconcerting talents after she starts to "demonstrate," as Nana calls menstruation. Esquivel, though she denies such a bond to Mama Elena and Tita, tells us that Tita cries in the womb when onions are chopped because she is so sensitive to them. Tita, who is born in the kitchen and forms a bond with cooking because of it, might have been crying when she was born "because she knew then that it would be her lot in life to be denied marriage" (6) by her mother; in a sense, she does seem prenatally tuned in to the thoughts of her mother.

Of course, the womb is the site of both reproduction and sexuality. In *What the Crow Said*, Robert Kroetsch combines the two images, refiguring Vera Lang's womanhood as simultaneously a place of desire and conception or "nesting":

Scouting for a nest, a new place to hive, the first bees had found the scent of her sun-warmed body. What her terror must have been at the soft caress of those touching bees, at the trickle of gold along her bare thighs; what ultimate desperation caught in her throat at the ferocious and innocent need of those homeless bees, at the feverish high hum, she never told. . . . Vera, alone at the edge of the valley, lifted her body against the pressing bees. Her not daring to resist became the excuse, the cause of her slow yielding. . . . Her moving crushed the blue-purple petals of the crocus bed, broke the hairy stalks, the blossoms, into the dizzying sweetness of her own desire. . . . The bees found the swollen lips between her thighs; she felt their intrusive weight and spread farther her legs.

Then she gave her cry. (8–11)

While Kroetsch makes what is Vera's first experience—he describes "her world-old virgin body"(12)—highly pleasurable, it is equally significant that she has no choice. "Her not daring to resist" equates her impregnation with rape, even if the cry she gives convinces the listeners, without "knowing her name, or where she was, or what had touched her into that fierce and passionate and desperate undulation," that "no man would satisfy her. Not one. No mortal man would satisfy her" (12–13). Much like Úrsula and José Arcadio Buendía, who "wrestle" on the bed for one and a half years before the consummation of their marriage because of Úrsula's fears about the toll of their incestuous relationship on their offspring (12), Vera's first sexual encounter is contextualized both as a violence against her and as an act against nature.

Though more subtle in nature, Esquivel's account of Pedro and Tita's first sexual experience is just as paradoxical as Vera's. Esquivel describes Pedro "barring the door" and "throwing himself upon her," but she also says that Tita learns about "true love" in the process. Because Tita is born in the kitchen around food, her sexuality is also equated with cooking. She makes love to Pedro through the sense of taste long before she actually touches him. Her cooking absorbs her emotions and evokes them in those who taste her cooking. Thus, the wedding guests taste her longing for Pedro in Pedro and Rosaura's wedding cake; her sister Gertrude takes on Tita's lust after eating quail made with roses Pedro gives her and must act on it with a soldier; and, because her *mole* is made in Pedro's presence, it makes the guests at her engagement party euphoric. In *The House of the Spirits*, most of Esteban Trueba's encounters with "lower class" women are rapes, savagery that will literally breed the contemptible bastard grandson, Esteban García, who ravages Trueba's beloved Alba. In *The Bingo Palace*, Erdrich traces June's emotional problems back to her mother's boyfriend's attacks. "There was a way a man could get into her body and she never knew. Pain rang everywhere. June tried to climb out of it, but his chin held her shoulder. She tried to roll from underneath, but he was on every side[;] . . . she finally escaped into a part of her mind" (60).

Of course, wombs are not the only aspects of the female reproductive body at risk in these texts. In *So Far from God*, when Caridad is taken to the hospital after being attacked and left for dead, "Sofi was told that her daughter's nipples had been bitten off" (33). After her death and autopsy, Rosa's body is defiled by Dr. Cuevas's assistant in *The House of the Spirits* (39). Likewise, in *Beloved*, Sethe's milk is stolen from her by Schoolteacher's nephews, a violation that ranks, in her mind, above the beating she gets for telling on them. Ironically, they *protect* the womb that can multiply their slaveholdings when they beat her only after digging a hole for her distended, pregnant belly. In *Dreaming in Cuban*, Garcia recounts a strikingly similar scene. In Morningside Park, Pilar is accosted by three boys; one of them, she relates, "presses a blade to my throat. Its edge is a scar, another border to cross. . . . The boys push me under the elm, where it's somehow still dry. They pull off my sweater and carefully unbutton my blouse. With the knife still at my throat, they take turns suckling my breasts. They're children, I tell myself, trying to contain my fear" (202). And in an entry about a train ride into the "poverty of the countryside" that she had forgotten, her grandmother Celia reveals a pitiful scene of abuse:

At one station there was a little girl, about six, who wore only a dirty rag that didn't cover her private parts. She stretched out her hands as the passengers left the train, and in the bustle I saw a man stick his finger in her. I cried out and he hurried away. I called to the girl and lowered our basket of food through the window. She ran off like a limping mongrel, dragging it beside her. (55)

While Celia's reaction momentarily saves the girl, the injustices of poverty and childhood seem to conspire, suggesting that this "limping mongrel" will have little safety or protection from the abusers of the world. Although these vignettes rarely, if ever, compromise the reality of the text, they point to a prominent theme in the particular reality of magical realist texts that take on the marginalization of the female characters. In each case, the representation of female sexuality as an exploitable feature emphasizes the degree to which women will remain marginalized. The whips, fingers, and knives cut these women into unrecognizable parts and create yet "another border to cross."

In *Border Matters: Remapping American Cultural Studies*, Saldívar calls his "mapping of cultural theory within the discourse of the U.S.-Mexico borderlands . . . an invitation . . . to redraw the borders between folklore and the coun-ter-discourses of marginality, between 'everyday' culture and 'high' culture, and between 'people with culture' and 'people between culture' " (17). The authors represented above are similarly redrawing borders, working the fringe back into the central discourse. Magical realism provides a tool for such revision of margin-ality, perhaps especially for those authors who are themselves bound by geography, by race, by gender, or by other collective categorizations of identity. Magical real-ism permits the margins more than an entry into the main discourse; it offers the opportunity to reevaluate that central ideological constraint and to challenge the very features of the mainstream that allow for a margin in the first place. Moreover, as the marginalized female magical realists perhaps best illustrate, the revision of the center inevitably requires confronting the margins themselves. Their use of the mode allows magical realists, from the most mainstream authors like García Márquez to those authors who are rarely recognized at all by contemporary criti-cism, an additionally rich capacity for reinventing the margins.

NOTES

1. In fact, González Echevarría even makes the case for the marginalized *critics*, who, as "the 'colonized,' are cultural polyglots" ("Latin America and Comparative Literature" 48) and whose criticism of marginalized literatures is surely as marginalized as the works they discuss.

2. Kroetsch's quote is from his conversation with Linda Kenyon, cited below. Zamora agrees with Kroetsch in the importance of orality in Latin America, since "to select a general-izing metaphor for Latin American fiction that privileges written records over oral or visual modes of remembering . . . is to exclude portions of Latin America's usable past," a past that cannot merely be a negation of origins, Octavio Paz argues (*Usable Past* 125).

3. Third World status has also frequently been the delineating factor for considerations of geographic marginality as well, the very factor Delbaere disputes.

4. The juxtaposition of two such diverse systems can breed misinterpretation. Borges's "The Gospel According to St. Mark," where a "family in a rural region of Argentina reads the biblical account of the crucifixion and literally reenacts it . . . is a cautionary tale: in post-colonial contexts, readers must be cunning, creative, and critical, not merely literal" (Zamora, *Usable Past* 130).

5. For example, Juan Flores sees Puerto Rican writing as being more marginalized than any other literature available to the United States. He argues, "Among the 'ethnic' or 'mi-nority' literatures, it has probably drawn the least critical interest and the fewest readers" (53).

6. Harmannus Hoetink developed the theory of the "somatic norm image" and "somatic distance" (Jackson xii).

7. Slemon adds, "if not theoretical soundness" (407). Slemon's criticism of the theoreti-cal underpinnings of magical realism, which have already been discounted throughout this text, are further refuted in the conclusion.

8. As Charles M. Tatum (as quoted in Roland Walter's "Social and Magical Realism in Miguel Méndez's *El Sueño de Santa María*") defined "the pioneer novels of Chicano litera-ture" (103).

9. Later, Sanders adds,

Building on her own cross-cultural heritage as a German-American and a member of the Turtle Mountain Chippewa, Louise Erdrich creates families in her novels who arise from two traditions: the Chippewa culture of their ancestors and the Western traditions brought by Catholic missionaries who sought to "civilize" the tribe. These differing mythologies present contradictory messages of power and place for these men and women and thus illustrate the shifting nature of truth. (196)

10. Cortázar has a special bond with Europe, anyway, in that he was born in Brussels. His Argentinean parents returned to Argentina when he was still a child, but Cortázar later returned to Europe to live in France.

11. Though some would argue that his Canadian nationality does marginalize him, his situation as a mainstream author is perhaps not as complex a debate as that over García Márquez.

12. Discussing García Márquez as a mainstream writer is, of course, compromised by his position as an internationally acclaimed writer, perhaps especially after his receipt of the Nobel prize. As noted earlier, he and other Latin American writers such as Borges straddle the chasm between the marginal and the mainstream. However, earlier in his career, *as* García Márquez was writing such works as *One Hundred Years of Solitude* and *Leafstorm*, he was certainly writing from a position of marginalization. In addition, he addresses issues of marginality in his works, unlike the more European themes of Borges and Cortázar. Thus, he holds an ironic position as both mainstream and marginalized writer.

13. Some of these traditions are already overturning established discourses before the magical realists borrow them. Haitian voodoo, for example, has taken on the symbolism and terminology of the Catholic church in order to establish an uneasy compromise between the African-based and imperialist-imposed belief systems.

14 Though Tita feels relief when the pains in her breasts and belly subside and her period begins, she does not believe she was pregnant at all. The reactions of her dead mother and of their neighbor Paquita, who says she "can tell from a woman's eyes the minute she becomes pregnant," suggest that Tita *is* pregnant and not late as she concludes.

15. Slemon says "the dead Martin Lang . . . represents absence to Liebhaber but presence to Tiddy, throwing up an uncrossable barrier between them" (420), but Tiddy's periods of mourning seem more a matter of her balking at being tied to another potentially useless man than out of consideration for Martin's memory.

7

CONCLUSION:
MAGICAL SPACES IN REAL PLACES

Literature has long been subject to untimely assertions of its demise. Leslie Fiedler's now infamous pronouncement in the late 1960s that the novel was dead, for example, came at about the same time that *One Hundred Years of Solitude* was published in English. Then, "[s]carcely four years after its arrival on the U.S. scene, Latin American fiction, like the domestic fiction it was supposed to invigorate, becomes subject to identical rumors about its 'death' " (Payne 35). Even more recently, Raymond Williams seems to have sounded the death knell for magical realism when, in his 1995 work *The Postmodern Novel in Latin America: Politics, Culture, and the Crisis of Truth*, he dubs it "the now defunct magic realist enterprise" (5).[1] *Rediscovering Magical Realism* not only contends that Williams's proclamation is imprudent and that magical realism, like so many other modes and genres similarly (and prematurely) invalidated, has risen from the fiery ashes of such criticism; it also attempts to rescue a Pan-American legacy for the mode.

The fact that the tradition has been uprooted, carried along, and implanted elsewhere recalls John Barth's ironic "discovery" of the Latin American Jorge Luis Borges—ironic because the Argentinean was himself well-versed in North American literature. Thus, Barth's discovery of Borges was tantamount to a *rediscovery* of himself as an "American" writer: what he admired in Borges was in turn what Borges had admired, borrowed, and expanded on from the roots of Barth's own literary heritage—Hawthorne, Whitman, Thoreau. With magical realism the movement has been reversed to a certain extent, since it has been the Latin American tradition that has been transported northward, to be revised and "rediscovered" as a North American version of the mode.[2] Yet North American critics have been so intent on distinguishing the "otherness" of works largely from outside our boundaries that they have frequently neglected the vibrant magical realist traditions in the United States and Canada. In "both" Americas, magical realism has been flourishing and supplanting other modes.

Even critics of the magical realist mode who do *not* proclaim its death as an active narrative mode, who instead account for and describe its cultivation in the literatures of the Americas, may still seem to call for its *enforced* death, at least in its critical sense.[3] One scholar who contends that the term should be stricken from the literary critic's vocabulary is Emir Rodríguez Monegal, who advocates discarding the term because critics are engaged in "a dialogue among the deaf."[4] Another such critic, Tamás Bényei, implicates magical realism in its own death in literary criticism by revealing its faulty critical metadiscourse, but his argument falls short in its claim that magical realism has become the site of stagnant scholarship. Furthermore, as with other magical realist scholars, Bényei's own refusal to define magical realism in his article "Rereading 'Magic Realism' " culminates in the collapse of his textually based criticism. A detailed critique of his article illustrates the continued contention over the definition of the magical realist mode; more important, the following argument suggests the degree to which the mode remains a fertile topic for authors and critics alike.

Magical realism, as Bényei "rereads" it, is a phrase that deserves express critical attention. According to his article, "magical realism" is either an ubiquitous, commercial term or a critically suspicious, inadequate one. Bényei argues that, "as the 'name' for the *difference* (or the *essence*) of something that is proper to the subcontinent," both the mode and "*fiction* itself" have been compromised. "If the meaning of all textual strategies of a mode of writing . . . is always predetermined by a 'marvellously real' referent . . . , what we end up with is a critical short-circuiting, a forgetting of the very mode we are trying to describe" (149). Furthermore, he argues, the refined reappropriation of magical realism by postcolonial and even feminist critics—who put forth the premise that magical realism "responds to a particular cultural situation (marginalization, multiculturalism, displacement[)]" —has done little to correct such "critical short-circuiting" (149–50); some critics even suggest that this reappropriation commodifies "the colonial Other" (150).

Although Bényei believes "that geographical or cultural contextualizations of 'magic realism' " are neither unnecessary or "inevitably erroneous" (150), he finds purely contextual definitions limited and argues that his own criticism will "suggest ways of rereading the term 'magic realism' as well as the texts classified as 'magic realist' in order to be able to reread the relationship between the texts and the mode" (151). He adds, "Rereading the magic realist mode presupposes a rereading of its name," a practice that he says the few textually based explorations of magical realism generally neglect (151). Bényei also feels that "[m]ost definitions of magic realism that approach the mode in terms of its handling of the supernatural inherit . . . the ambiguities of Franz Roh's originary definition" (151).[5] But, he argues, our easy acceptance of the treatment of the supernatural in magical realist works is in itself insufficient to characterize magical realism. The critical distinctions drawn by literary critics between the fantastic and magical realism are similarly problematic because, he argues, magical realism seems to eliminate the antinomy between the supernatural and the real only to resurrect that conflict in the process of our reading the text.

As he considers the definitions of magical realism in terms of the reconciliation between codes like reality and supernatural, Bényei uncovers "the textual strategies that serve to express this alleged non-antinomy" (152). He mentions the "exposure of the real and the fantastic as rhetorical effects," as with García Márquez's "ingenu irony" and his questioning of "the verbal-rhetorical 'createdness' " of the existence of objects (153); the trope *zeugma*, "where events of two vastly different orders (e.g., the cosmic and the domestic) are ironically placed in the same syntactical and rhetorical position" (153)[6] ; and the multiple ontological boundaries that each require "a new (and different) act of adjustment from the reader" (154).

Bényei, rather than formulating "a general theory of the magic realist mode," is "more interested in a poetics of magic realism" (156). Instead of reading the term as an oxymoron that equates "realism" with the modern, the European, or the rational and that reads "magic" as "the opposite of rational and empirical thought" (157), Bényei explains that "[m]agic realist texts do not posit a qualitative difference between magical and rational world views" (158). He explains that his point of departure from typical readings of the mode is that he reads the mode

as if the catachrestical term had been created (summoned) by the mode itself as a properly impossible name for its own impossible modality ... of reconstructing the world in and through language and narrative. ... [He asks] questions on the one hand concerning the rhetorical, figurative, and narrative strategies that seem to be dominant in the texts, and, on the other, concerning the modality of reading/writing existence suggested or presented by the texts. (159)

Bényei uses what he calls "paradigmatic texts of the magic realist mode" (150)[7] to exemplify "the most conspicuous constituent of the 'magicalness' of magic realism: the inauguration, and perhaps domination, of *magical causality*" (159), where "causality appears as a magical activity that seeks to reveal secret connections between the objects of the world" (161). He argues, "magical realism—suspecting a supplementary relationship between [the magical and ordinary causality]—bases its figurativity on the Nietzschean insight that our conception of the world, our talk of the world, be it 'rational' or 'magical,' is always rhetorically constructed" (160). This figurativity saturates magical realist texts and blurs the distinctions between metaphor and metonym. Moreover, Bényei notes, "magical realist textual strategies are not based on a belief in the superiority of magical thought and the consequent valorisation of the transcendental" (165); indeed, "one of the most puzzling features of magic is that it is an interpretation of the world that appeals to the transcendental (the sacral) without becoming a religion or metaphysic" (166).

Bényei regards the paradoxical nature of magical realism as the means by which it surpasses our expectations of human existence. He explains, "The collapsing into each other of literal and figurative, event and figure leads to a mode that is 'magic realist' in the sense that it cannot be seen either as simply mimetic (magic as the description of the world) or as simply fictionalising or fabulating (magic as the projection of our desires into the world)" (167). Finally, Bényei describes magical realist texts in terms of their interest in narration and the act of story-telling. He notes that magical realist texts make use of recurring objects (talismanic words or objects) and themes (varieties of magical activities and stories), are self-reflexive, and that they borrow from or rewrite themselves as sacred texts. He acknowledges that it "would be pointless to define a limit or threshold beyond which a novel clearly embodies magic realism, or an exact number of particular features that define a text as magic realist," and he says that he "has been merely [rereading] the expression 'magic realism' in light of the fiction that is usually called magic realist, and [suggesting] ways of going back to the texts with the implications of this mobile and unstable term in mind" (174).

Criticism of magical realist texts has, as Bényei notes, been damaged most by the contradictions and misuse of magical realism in literary criticism. Unlike the smattering of critics who are interested in defining the term as distinct from other narrative styles, many scholars applying the term "magical realism" rely on their own vague and unsubstantiated notions of what the phrase means—and their criticism assumes that their readers' thoughts about the term are similarly vague. Unfortunately, relying on such vagaries is exactly what Bényei (despite his critical posturing to the contrary) would have critics do, for his "textual" approach does little more than beg the question of what defines the magical realist text. His decision to rely on a few works drawn from an accepted canon of magical realist literature, while extracting such rhetorical strategies as he finds important to the magical realism of those specific texts, does very little to suggest a means for identifying the mode in works outside that canon. Although Bényei describes in detail the limitations of criticism that attempts to define the mode, at the same time he trusts those very critics to enumerate his textual choices for him. Without his own working definition of magical realism, Bényei must presume that those scholars who have canonized magical realist texts could identify the mode.

In lieu of prescriptive criteria to mark the bounds of magical realism, Bényei relies on qualitative terminology—"most," "perhaps," "frequently"—in order to make claims about the texts he examines. He is forced to admit that not every magical realist text subscribes to the strategies he outlines based on his reading of these works, causing his reader to wonder what (if any) commonalities *do* exist in magical realism as Bényei rereads it. His argument that "[t]here is no need to impose any particular view about magical interpretations of the world upon magic realist texts in order to see that 'magic' supplies the grammar of the mode as a narrative and figurative blueprint" reveals that, in fact, there *is* such a need. He is unable to provide this blueprint because he lacks a constructed (constructive) definition of magical realism as a narrative mode, one that can subscribe to certain precepts and at the same time challenge our rational or realist or Western view of the world. By insisting that the "grammar" that magic supplies to magical realism is simultaneously obvious and indefinable, Bényei limits magical realism as much as the purely contextual definitions at which he scoffs.

The ontological boundaries Bényei describes in magically realists texts recreate the battlefields upon which non-Western (and those who are marginalized in other ways) fight their entire lives—yet we rarely discuss their "Otherness" as *readers* and expect (insist), instead, that they will train themselves as ideal readers for the Western canon. The work of the magical realist mode (perhaps of any mode)—and the literary devices Bényei says they fall back on—is to create the ideal reader for its text. Through figurative language and authorial reticence, these authors both invent the magically real world and provide the tools for navigating through that realm. Fredric Jameson's careful consideration of the dilemma inherent for first-world or Western readers of third-world texts informs Bényei's point about the conflicted readers of magically realist texts:

We sense, between ourselves and this alien text, the presence of another reader, of the Other reader, for whom a narrative, which strikes us as conventional or naïve, has a freshness of information and a social interest that we cannot share. The fear and the resistance I'm evoking has to do, then, with the sense of our own non-coincidence with that Other reader, so different from ourselves; our sense that to coincide in any adequate way with that Other "ideal reader"—that is to say, to read this text adequately—we would have to give up a great deal that is individually precious to us and acknowledge an existence and a situation unfamiliar and therefore frightening—one that we do now know and prefer *not* to know. ("On Magical Realism in Film" 66)

Yet Jameson argues that this fear should not limit our reading and, indeed, that we all "live at least a double life in the various compartments of our unavoidably fragmented society" (67).[8]

The paucity of inter-American scholarship seems at odds with the "fragmented," heterogeneous nature of the Americas. Indeed, the New World's postcolonial past and its geographic distance from and secondary status to Europe suggest that scholars should have produced an extensive array of comparativist criticism, yet the potential for such scholarship is perhaps hampered by the fact that the literary critical traditions of the two Americas are still in their infancy. As critics such as Lois Parkinson Zamora, Enrico Mario Santí, and Gustavo Pérez Firmat have begun to clamor for scholarship to fill this void, comparativists are beginning to appear (like many of the authors they discuss) on the margins of literary discourse. The work for these scholars has been to uncover useful ontological or "typological analyses" (Jameson, "On Magical Realism in Film" 87 n.5) for expanding this field of inquiry. As an encompassing and traditionally "New World"-oriented mode, magical realism functions as an ideal foundation for inter-American literary criticism.

Since Alejo Carpentier's appropriation of the term *lo real maravilloso americano* and his claim that it had exclusively Latin American traits, magical realism has been threatened by geographic constraints. Yet the mode continues to be explored in literature around the world. In particular, the marginalized status of many third-world countries encourages their turn to magical realism—the expectation being that only a mode juxtaposing the supernatural and the everyday can capture the dichotomies of third-world living. Its popularity, unfortunately, proves as potentially limiting as it does beneficial. The Latin American Boom and the increased interest in Latin America as a commodity have allowed the term, like currency, to be devalued. Magical realism's "easy" applicability as a marker of the supernatural for some critics has also allowed the mode to become increasingly misused in its critical context.

One reason that texts by indigenous authors so frequently get tagged as magical realism—with little more than the author's locale or ethnicity to recommend them to the mode—may also be that the supernatural is largely defined not simply by a Western culture, but by a Western culture that considers indigenous religions "myth" and that, therefore, ascribes a "supernatural" label to many of the features associated with their religions or cultures. Coyote being recognized as the storyteller, though, is not in and of itself a supernatural reality for many Native Americans, whereas Thomas King's revision of Coyote as dumbfounded listener to the tales and as intervener in the version of the story presented in the Westernized community can be considered supernatural (though verisimilar). What Bényei neglects to mention in his discussion of the sacred and the secular is the fact that, while many magical realist works juxtapose a spiritual magic with an everyday reality—texts that come to mind include *So Far from God*, *One Hundred Years of Solitude*, and *Green Grass, Running Water*—the authors of these works simply do not allow the religious or metaphysical elements to explain away the supernatural. Indeed, the use of religion or metaphysics in a magical realist work does more than simply borrow the language of the sacred text, it often refigures that spiritual aspect (which might otherwise be commonplace or real to its believers) in such a way as to revise the original work. They coexist—or, better yet, reference one another in such a way as to each make the other more authentic in the world the magical realist has created.

The critical (in both senses of the word) opinion held by Stephen Slemon suggests that, unless addressed and countered with text-based scholarship, the trend to misuse the phrase "magical realism" will only continue: "In none of its applications to literature has the concept of magic realism ever successfully differentiated between itself and neighboring genres such as fabulation, metafiction, the baroque, the fantastic, the uncanny, or the marvelous, and consequently it is not surprising that some critics have chosen to abandon the term altogether" (407). More astonishing than Slemon's hyperbolic declaration is his dogged determination to continue to use "magic realism" as a descriptor in his article even after this claim. Furthermore, if Slemon does not find it surprising that "critics have chosen to abandon the term" rather than resuscitate it, he is surely in the minority among contemporary critics of magically real texts.

The Americas, as they make use of magical realism, salvage the respectability, the importance, and the usefulness of the mode; they offer comparativists an opportunity to uncover new ideas about what both "Americanness" and "magical realism" signify. Magical realism and the Americas share a postcolonial history and a familial relationship with postmodernism, origins that are less frequently challenged than the terms' critical or denotative histories. The same desires that founded postmodernists' break with reality fuel magical realism and provide substance for otherwise unapproachable (unwritable) topics—political strife in Latin America, capitalism in North America, the continued subjugation of marginalized people, the neocolonial reverberations of popular culture.

The study of magical realism, at least for North American (or North Atlantic) critics, requires a return to Latin America; its roots provide the basis by which an American (in the all-encompassing form of the term) identity can be refigured and a Pan-American bridge of scholarship can be constructed. Magical realism reminds U.S. and Canadian critics and readers of their similarities—even in the face of drastically different texts. In this quest to redefine themselves historically, politically, and socially, authors have paved the way with new narratives and have begun to rectify the anomalies of contemporary life in the Americas.

If their commonalities ensure that the writers of the New World use magical realism, their differences equally guarantee that North and Latin America do so in significant ways. North American magical realism is distinguished by its intensive preoccupation with pop culture and capitalism, whereas Latin American literature assumes a more historically based, "anthropological perspective" (Jameson, "On Magical Realism in Film" 302) that "depends on . . . the coexistence of pre-capitalist with nascent capitalist or technological features" (311). Unlike the texts of North America, *One Hundred Years of Solitude* demonstrates a discomfort with the technological advances that popular culture so readily embraces. In its return to the more paradoxical alchemy, the novel describes a community for whom the advancement of modern science (and modernity in general) is a greater threat than the "unnatural" features of magic.

The comparativist juxtaposition of the North American version of magical realism with its Latin American counterpart may show North American magical realism to be a product of a "first world" consciousness, but authors like Morrison, King, and Erdrich remind us that the failure of the American dream for certain margins more clearly reflects North America's sisterhood with Latin America than its collegiality with the North Atlantic. It is on these fringes, too, that most similarities between Latin American and North American magical realism reside. Here, the "consumed" (Morrison's slave community, King's Native Americans) supply the magic not because of their marginalized status but rather in direct proportion to the consumers' appetites. The margins are often too illiterate to survive a hyphenated American existence without the supernatural. As texts like *Beloved* illustrate, the definition of the American marginalized self borrows from history and memory. Without these elements, realism would subsume the text. Beloved's multiplicity both threatens and mediates between the margins and a present that only pushes the marginalized closer to the fringe.

As Slemon suggests, *most* problematic is the mode's misappropriation due to this lack of a clear-cut definition; the term "magical realism" has become synonymous with and mistaken for other modes and movements, including some that

Slemon's disheartening pronouncement neglects. To combat this confusion, *Rediscovering Magical Realism* draws from Amaryll Chanady's prescriptive criteria. Chanady posits that magical realism juxtaposes the real and the supernatural as "conflicting, but autonomously coherent, perspectives" (*Magical Realism and The Fantastic* 21), that the antinomy between these perspectives is resolved, and that authorial reticence is responsible for this resolution. Chanady's criteria not only inform this text but also manage to incorporate the beliefs of many critics into a single, cohesive definition that scholars can apply to magical realist literature around the world; her concrete approach to finding the means by which to alleviate the critical maelstrom plaguing magical realism as a critical term answers the charge of those critics who will it dead.

The work of magical realist scholarship should not be to "savage" the mode but rather to salvage it, yet contemporary critics tend to add to the discussion of "magical realism" in one of two ways—either disparaging the mode entirely, as does Williams when he pronounces magical realism "defunct," or by adding to the frenzy of confusion over the term, as do Slemon and Bényei. Magical realism is an active mode, very much alive and expanding its influence upon a wide range of contemporary writers. To suggest, like Rodríguez Monegal, that writers continue to employ the magical realist mode but that critics should discount it is ludicrous. When Jean-Pierre Durix ponders "whether it is not preferable to abandon the term 'magical realism' altogether," he quickly amends that the alternative to this severe plan is rather "to restrict it severely in order to differenciate it from other narrative styles" (146). Durix is specifically thinking of the fantastic here—the narrative style against which, according to Bényei, magical realism is most frequently measured—but scholars of magical realist criticism can quickly add to the list of terms against which magical realism must also be distinguished: surrealism, *lo real maravilloso*, the science fiction, horror, fairy tales, fables, folktales. Each has in some way been presumed to be a part of, or more aptly, to have been subsumed into the magical realist tradition. Bényei's supercilious attitude toward definitions that distinguish magical realism from the fantastic neglects the fact that such terms are used interchangeably (and will continue to be, barring critical agreement on a definition of magical realism). In addition, when Bényei quibbles about critics describing the relationship between the supernatural and the real as a means of defining magical realism, he seems to forget that our evaluation and definition of narrative styles and modes *must* be couched in such rhetoric. He would do well to consider the fundamental definitions of realism or naturalism, where we relate the terms to their uses of "reality" and "nature," respectively, in order to describe and apply them.

The arguments of critics Bényei, Slemon, and Williams prove most constructive for magical realist scholarship in that they reveal the single most troubling aspect of magical realism as a critical term—its vague and unpredictable application in literary criticism to an overwhelming number of works. As Bényei rightly notes, to "define magic realism in very general terms as 'the amalgamation of the ordinary and the supernatural' " is to be "left with a definition encompassing a large number of narratives that are clearly not magic realist ([such as the works of] Borges, Wells, Gogol, etc.)" (155). Nor is it enough "to reserve the label [magical realism for] those texts that share strong similarities with García Márquez's *One Hundred Years of Solitude* and [Salman] Rushdie's *Midnight's Children* or *Shame*" (Durix 146), since such a proviso would ultimately restrict the growth of magical realism as a mode and resign magical realist scholarship solely to the comparativists. Durix says, "I have advocated a narrowing of the definition if this term is to have any generic validity instead of merely serving temporary marketing strategies. But perhaps the merit of the phrase 'magic realism' is to suggest a field of possibilities in which the term will no longer be an oxymoron" (190). Despite Bényei's criticism of attempts to provide a definition of magical realism, he too sees the term as "appropriate precisely because of its blatant inappropriateness—it is an adequate name because it is so obviously a misnomer, an impossible name" (151). Yet magical realism as a narrative style lends legitimacy, *possibility*, to what might otherwise be oxymoronic. Moreover, the magical realism of the Americas, once the appropriate prescriptive criteria are delineated, is perfectly capable of standing on its own feet—perhaps even literally, in the magical realist worlds it creates.

NOTES

1. Williams makes this pronouncement in relation to García Márquez and the author's own sense that he has been falsely categorized as a magical realist. "Gabriel García Márquez makes numerous statements about being a 'realist' who attempts to describe the reality of Colombia as truthfully as possible, despite the insistence of many foreign readers on classifying him as a fantasy writer or an imaginative fabricator of the chimeras associated with the now defunct magic realist enterprise" (5).

2. And works such as Ron Arias's *The Road to Tamazunchale* suggest that magical realism offers Latino/a Americans a chance to *revisit* their Latin American roots through their texts.

3. Oddly enough, while Slemon might appear to claim that critics have dropped "magical realism" as a critical term, he undermines the threat by using it himself, seemingly without concern for its denotative ambiguity.

4. Rodríguez Monegal made this statement in his keynote address at the 1973 convention of the Institute Internacional de Literature Iberoamericana (Menton, "Magic Realism" 125)

5. Roh's definition is covered by many critics of magical realism, and his own essay on magical realism in art is included in *Magical Realism: Theory, History, Community*. Bényei chooses to define magical realism as a mode "precisely because of [the word mode's] vagueness" (150).

6. In fact, Bényei suggests, "zeugma should be seen as the condensed form of the general narrative parataxis of the magic realist mode" (153).

7. His examples include García Márquez's *One Hundred Years of Solitude*, Salman Rushdie's *Midnight's Children*, Jack Hodgins's *The Invention of the World*, Kroetsch's *What the Crow Said*, Allende's *The House of the Spirits*, Peter Carey's *Illywhacker*, and Jeanette Winterson's *Sexing the Cherry*.

8. Jameson's work, though a close reading of magical realism as it applies to the medium of film, begins with more general claims about the mode's literary, Latin American heritage.

SELECTED BIBLIOGRAPHY

Abel, Elizabeth, Barbara Christian, and Helene Moglen, eds. *Female Subjects in Black and White: Race, Psychoanalysis, Feminism.* Los Angeles: U of California P, 1997.

Aínsa, Fernando. "The Antinomies of Latin American Discourses of Identity and their Fictional Representations." Trans. Amaryll Chanady. *Latin American Identity and Constructions of Difference.* Chanady 1–25.

Allen, Woody. "The Kugelmass Episode." *The Complete Prose of Woody Allen.* New York: Wing, 1991. 345–60.

Allende, Isabel. *The House of the Spirits.* Trans. Magda Bogin. New York: Bantam, 1986. Trans. of *La casa de los espíritus,* 1982.

Amado, Jorge. *Dona Flor and Her Two Husbands.* Trans. Harriet de Onís. New York: Avon, 1988. Trans. of *Dona Flor e seus dois maridos,* 1967.

Anaya, Rudolfo A. *Bless Me, Ultima.* Berkeley, CA: Tonatiuh-Quinto Sol International, 1972.

Angelo, Bonnie. "The Pain of Being Black." Interview with Toni Morrison. *Time* 22 May 1989: 120–22.

Angula, María-Elena. *Magic Realism: Social Context and Discourse.* New York: Garland, 1995.

Appiah, K. Anthony. "Identity, Authenticity, Survival: Multicultural Societies and Social Reproduction." *Multiculturalism: Examining the Politics of Recognition.* Ed. Amy Gutman. Princeton, NJ: Princeton UP, 1994. 149–63.

Arias, Ron. *The Road to Tamazunchale.* Chicano Classics 3. Tempe, AZ: Bilingual P, 1987.

Baker, Suzanne. "Magic Realism as a Postcolonial Strategy: *The Kadaitcha Sung.*" *Span* 32 (1991): 55–63.

Bartlett, Catherine. "Magical Realism: The Latin American Influence on Modern Chicano Writers." *Confluencia: Revista Hispanica de Cultura Y Literatura* 1:2 (1986): 27–36.

Bayles, Martha. "Special Effects, Special Pleading." *The New Criterion* (Jan. 1988): 34–40.

Bell-Villada, Gene H. "García Márquez and the Novel." *Critical Essays on Gabriel García Márquez.* McMurray 209–18.

Benevento, Joseph. "An Introduction to the Realities of Fiction: Teaching Magic Realism in
    Three Stories by Borges, Fuentes, and Márquez." *Kansas Quarterly* 16.3 (1984): 125–31.
Benítez-Rojo, Antonio. "The Repeating Island." Trans. James Maraniss. *Do the Americas
    Have a Common Literature?* Pérez Firmat 85–106.
Bényei, Tamás. "Rereading 'Magic Realism.'" *Hungarian Journal of English and American
    Studies* 3.1 (1997): 149–79.
Biagiotti, Luca. "Bees, Bodies, and Magical Miscegenations." *Coterminous Worlds: Magical
    Realism and Contemporary Post-colonial Literature in English*. Linguanti, Casotti, and
    Concilio 103–14.
Birat, Kathie. "Stories to Pass On: Closure and Community in Toni Morrison's *Beloved.*"
    The Insular Dream: Obsession and Resistance. Ed. Kristiaan Versluys. Amsterdam: VU
    UP, 1995. 324–34.
Boccia, Michael. "Magical Realism: The Multicultural Literature." *Popular Culture Review*
    5.2 (1994): 21–31.
Boland, Roy C., and Sally Harvey. "Magical Realism and Beyond: The Contemporary Span-
    ish and Latin American Novel." Introduction. *Antipodas* 3 (1991): 7–12.
Broad, Robert L. "Giving Blood to the Scraps: Haints, History, and Hosea in *Beloved.*" *Afri-
    can American Review* 28.2 (1994): 189–96.
Buitrago, Fanny. *Señora Honeycomb*. Trans. Margaret Sayers Peden. New York: Harper-
    Collins, 1996. Trans. of *Señora de la miel*, 1993.
Burckhardt, Titus. *Alchemy: Science of the Cosmos, Science of the Soul*. Trans. William
    Stoddart. Baltimore, MD: Penguin, 1972.
Camurati, Mireya. "Introduction to Writers." *Philosophy and Literature in Latin America*.
    Gracia and Camurati 87–90.
Cândido, António. "Literature and Underdevelopment." *Latin America in its Literature*.
    Moreno 263–82.
Carpenter, Lynette, and Wendy K. Kolmar, eds. *Haunting the House of Fiction: Feminist Per-
    spectives on Ghost Stories by American Women*. Knoxville: U of Tennessee P, 1991.
Carpentier, Alejo. *The Kingdom of This World*. Trans. Harriet de Onis. New York: Noonday,
    1989. Trans. of *El reino de este mundo*, 1949.
Castillo, Ana. *So Far From God*. New York: Penguin, 1994.
Castillo, Debra A. "Latin American Fiction." *The Columbia History of the American Novel*.
    Elliot et al. 607–48.
Chanady, Amaryll. "Latin American Discourses of Identity and the Appropriation of the
    Amerindian Other." *Sociocriticism* 6.1–2 (1990): 33–48.
———. "Latin American Imagined Communities and the Postmodern Challenge." Intro-
    duction. *Latin American Identity and Constructions of Difference*. Chanady ix–xlvi.
———. *Magical Realism and the Fantastic: Resolved versus Unresolved Antinomy*. New York:
    Garland, 1985.
———. "The Territorialization of the Imaginary in Latin America: Self-Affirmation and
    Resistance to Metropolitan Paradigms." *Magical Realism: Theory, History, Commu-
    nity*. Zamora and Faris 125–44.
———, ed. *Latin American Identity and Constructions of Difference*. Hispanic Issues 10. Min-
    neapolis: U of Minnesota P, 1994. ix–xlvi.
Christian, Barbara. "Fixing Methodologies: *Beloved.*" *Female Subjects in Black and White:
    Race, Psychoanalysis, Feminism*. Abel, Christian, and Moglen 363–70.
Colchie, Thomas, ed. *A Hammock Beneath the Mangoes: Stories from Latin America*. New
    York: Plume, 1992.

Comfort, Susan. "Counter-Memory, Mourning, and History in Toni Morrison's *Beloved.*" *Lit* 6 (1995): 121–32.

Conniff, Brian. "The Dark Side of Magical Realism: Science, Oppression, and Apocalypse in *One Hundred Years of Solitude.*" *Modern Fiction Studies* 36.2 (1990): 167–79.

Cooper, James Fenimore. *The Last of the Mohicans: A Narrative of 1757.* Albany: State U of New York P, 1982.

Coutinho, Afrânio. *An Introduction to Literature in Brazil.* Trans. Gregory Rabassa. New York: Columbia UP, 1969.

Cowan, Bainard. Introduction. *Poetics of the Americas.* Cowan and Humphries 1–13.

Cowan, Bainard, and Jefferson Humphries, eds. *Poetics of the Americas: Race, Founding, and Textuality.* Horizons in Theory and American Culture Ser. Baton Rouge: Louisiana State UP, 1997.

Daily, Gary W. "Toni Morrison's *Beloved*: Rememory, History, and the Fantastic." *The Celebration of the Fantastic: Selected Papers from the Tenth Anniversary International Conference on the Fantastic in the Arts.* Eds. Donald E. Morse, Marshall B. Tymn, and Csilla Bertha. Contributions to the Study of Science Fiction and Fantasy Ser. 49. Westport, CT: Greenwood, 1992. 141–47.

Daniel, Lee A. "Realismo Mágico—True Realism with a Pinch of Magic." *The South Central Bulletin* 42.2 (1982): 129–30.

Danow, David. *The Spirit of Carnival: Magical Realism and the Grotesque.* Lexington, KY: UP of Kentucky, 1995.

Davidson, Arnold E. "Canada in Fiction." *The Columbia History of the American Novel.* Elliot et al. 558–85.

Delbaere, Jeanne. "Magic Realism: The Energy of the Margins." *Postmodern Fiction in Canada.* D'haen and Bertens 75–104.

Delbaere-Garant, Jeanne. "Psychic Realism, Mythic Realism, Grotesque Realism: Variations on Magic Realism in Contemporary Literature in English." *Magical Realism: Theory, History, Community.* Zamora and Faris 249–63.

Denard, Carolyn C. "Beyond the Bitterness of History: Teaching *Beloved.*" *Approaches to Teaching the Novels of Toni Morrison.* McKay and Earle 40–47.

D'haen, Theo L. "Magical Realism and Postmodernism: Decentering Privileged Centers." *Magical Realism: Theory, History, Community.* Zamora and Faris 191–208.

D'haen, Theo, and Hans Bertens, eds. *Postmodern Fiction in Canada.* Postmodern Studies 6. Amsterdam: Rodopi, 1992.

Duff, David, ed. *Modern Genre Theory.* New York: Longman, 2000.

Durix, Jean-Pierre. *Mimesis, Genres and Post-Colonial Discourse: Deconstructing Magic Realism.* New York: St. Martin's, 1998.

Edwards, Thomas. R. "Ghost Story." Rev. of *Beloved,* by Toni Morrison. *Critical Essays on Toni Morrison's Beloved.* Solomon 78–83.

Elliot, Emory, et al., eds. *The Columbia History of the American Novel.* New York: Columbia UP, 1991.

Erdrich, Louise. *The Bingo Palace.* New York: HarperCollins, 1994.

———. *Love Medicine.* New York: Holt, Rinehart, and Winston, 1984.

———. *Tracks.* New York: Harper & Row, 1988.

Erickson, John. "Metoikoi and Magical Realism in the Maghrebian Narratives of Tahar ben Jelloun and Abdelkebir Khatibi." *Magical Realism: Theory, History, Community.* Zamora and Faris 427–50.

Esquivel, Laura. *Like Water for Chocolate: A Novel in Monthly Installments with Recipes, Romances, and Home Remedies.* Trans. Carol Christensen and Thomas Christensen. New York: Doubleday, 1992. Trans. of *Como agua para chocolate,* 1989.

Faris, Wendy B. "Marking Space, Charting Time: Text and Territory in Faulkner's 'The Bear' and Carpentier's *Los pasos perdidos.*" *Do the Americas Have a Common Literature?* Pérez Firmat 243–66.

———. "Scheherazade's Children: Magical Realism and Postmodern Fiction." *Magical Realism: Theory, History, Community.* Zamora and Faris 162–90.

Feal, Rosemary Geisdorfer. "Women Writers into the Mainstream: Contemporary Latin American Narrative." *Philosophy and Literature in Latin America.* Gracia and Camurati 114–24.

Ferguson, Rebecca. "History, Memory, and Language in Toni Morrison's *Beloved.*" *Feminist Criticism: Theory and Practice.* Ed. Susan Sellers. Buffalo: U of Toronto P, 1991. 109–27.

Fields, Karen E. "To Embrace Dead Strangers: Toni Morrison's *Beloved.*" *Mother Puzzles: Daughters and Mothers in Contemporary American Literature.* Ed. Mickey Pearlman. Contributions in Women's Studies 110. New York: Greenwood, 1989. 159–69.

Finney, Brian. "Temporal Defamiliarization in Toni Morrison's *Beloved.*" *Critical Essays on Toni Morrison's* Beloved. Solomon 104–16.

Flores, Angel. "Magical Realism in Spanish American Fiction." *Magical Realism: Theory, History, Community.* Zamora and Faris 109–17.

Flores, Juan. "Puerto Rican Literature in the United States: Stages and Perspectives." *Recovering the U.S. Hispanic Literary Heritage.* Eds. Ramón Gutiérrez and Genaro Padilla. Houston, Arte Público Press, 1993. 53–68.

Foos, Laurie. *Ex Utero.* New York: Harcourt Brace, 1996.

Foreman, P. Gabrielle. "Past-On Stories: History and the Magically Real, Morrison and Allende on Call." *Magical Realism: Theory, History, Community.* Zamora and Faris 285–303.

Foster, David William. *Cultural Diversity in Latin American Literature.* Albuquerque: U of New Mexico P, 1994.

———. "Popular Culture: The Roots of Literary Tradition." *Imagination, Emblems and Expressions: Essays on Latin America, Caribbean, and Continental Culture and Identity.* Ed. Helen Ryan-Ranson. Bowling Green, OH: Bowling Green State U Popular P, 1993. 3–27.

Foster, John Burt, Jr. "Magical Realism, Compensatory Vision, and Felt History: Classical Realism Transformed in *The White Hotel.*" *Magical Realism: Theory, History, Community.* Zamora and Faris 267–83.

Fox-Genovese, Elizabeth. *Unspeakable Things Unspoken: Ghosts and Memories in the Narratives of African-American Women.* The 1992 Elsa Goveia Memorial Lecture. Mona, Jamaica: Department of History, University of the West Indies, 1993.

Franco, Jean. *Introduction to Spanish-American Literature.* 3rd ed. New York: Cambridge UP, 1994.

Fuentes, Carlos. "Central and Eccentric Writing." *Lives on the Line.* Meyer 112–24.

Ganguly, S. P. "Reality as Second Creation in the Latin American Novels: Marquez and His Cosmovision." *Garcia Marquez and Latin America.* Ed. Alok Bhalla. London: Oriental UP, 1987. 169–81.

Garcia, Cristina. *Dreaming in Cuban.* New York: Ballantine, 1992.

García Márquez, Gabriel. *One Hundred Years of Solitude.* Trans. Gregory Rabassa. New York: HarperCollins, 1970. Trans. of *Cien años de soledad,* 1967.
———. "The Solitude of Latin America: Nobel Address 1982." *Gabriel García Márquez: New Readings.* McGuirk and Cardwell 207–11.
———. "A Very Old Man with Enormous Wings: A Tale for Children." 1968. *Leafstorm and Other Stories.* Trans. Gregory Rabassa. New York: Harper, 1972. 105–12.
García-Moreno, Laura. "Situating Knowledges: Latin American Readings of Postmodernism." *Diacritics* 25.1 (1995): 63–80.
Glidewell, M. E. "Alchemy and Symbols." *The Hexagon of Alpha Chi Sigma* (Summer 1993): 28–29, 38.
González, Aníbal. "Translation and Genealogy: *One Hundred Years of Solitude.*" *Gabriel García Márquez: New Readings.* McGuirk and Cardwell 65–79.
González Echevarría, Roberto. "Latin America and Comparative Literature." *Poetics of the Americas.* Cowan and Humphries 47–62.
———. *The Voices of the Masters: Writing and Authority in Modern Latin American Literature.* Latin American Monographs 64. Austin, TX: U of Texas P, 1985.
Gracia, Jorge T. E., and Mireya Camurati, eds. *Philosophy and Literature in Latin America: A Critical Assessment of the Current Situation.* Albany: State U of New York P, 1989.
Griffin, Clive. "The Humor of *One Hundred Years of Solitude.*" *Gabriel García Márquez: New Readings.* McGuirk and Cardwell 81–94.
Hancock, Geoff. "Magic or Realism: The Marvellous in Canadian Fiction." *Magic Realism and Canadian Literature.* Hinchcliffe and Jewinski 30–48.
Harris, Trudier. "Woman, Thy Name Is Demon." *Critical Essays on Toni Morrison's* Beloved. Solomon 127–37.
Hart, Stephen. "Magical Realism in Gabriel García Márquez's *Cien años de Soledad.*" *Inti* 16–17 (1982–83): 37–52.
Hawthorne, Nathaniel. "Rappaccini's Daughter." *Nathaniel Hawthorne's Tales.* Ed. James McIntosh. New York: Norton, 1987. 186–209.
Heinze, Denise. "Beloved and the Tyranny of the Double." *Critical Essays on Toni Morrison's* Beloved. Solomon 205–10.
Heller, Dana. "Reconstructing Kin: Family, History, and Narrative in Toni Morrison's *Beloved.*" *College Literature* 21.2 (1994): 105–17.
Hicks, D. Emily. *Border Writing.* Minneapolis: U of Minnesota P, 1991.
Hill-Rigney, Barbara. " 'A Story to Pass On': Ghosts and the Significance of History in Toni Morrison's *Beloved.*" *Haunting the House of Fiction.* Carpenter and Kolmar 229–35.
Hinchcliffe, Peter, and Ed Jewinski, eds. *Magic Realism and Canadian Literature: Essays and Stories.* Ontario, Canada: U of Waterloo P, 1986.
Holland, Sharon P., and Michael Awkward. "Marginality and Community in *Beloved.*" *Approaches to Teaching the Novels of Toni Morrison.* McKay and Earle 48–55.
Holmes, Kristine. " 'This Is Flesh I'm Talking about Here': Embodiment in Toni Morrison's *Beloved* and Sherley Anne Williams' *Dessa Rose.*" *Lit* 6 (1995): 133–48.
Horvitz, Deborah. "Nameless Ghosts: Possession and Dispossession in *Beloved.*" *Critical Essays on Toni Morrison's* Beloved. Solomon 93–103.
House, Elizabeth. "Toni Morrison's Ghost: The Beloved Who Is Not Beloved." *Critical Essays on Toni Morrison's* Beloved. Solomon 117–26.
Interpreter's Dictionary of the Bible, The. New York: Abingdon, 1962.
Jackson, Richard L. *The Black Image in Latin American Literature.* Albuquerque: U of New Mexico P, 1976.

Jameson, Fredric. "On Magic Realism in Film." *Critical Inquiry* 12.2 (Winter 1986): 301–25.

———. "Third-World Literature in the Era of Multinational Capitalism." *Social Text* 15 (Fall 1986): 65–88.

Jessee, Sharon. " 'Tell Me Your Earrings': Time and the Marvelous in Toni Morrison's *Beloved*." *Memory, Narrative, and Identity*. Singh, Skerritt, and Hogan 198–211.

Jung, C. G. *Alchemical Studies*. New York: Princeton UP, 1967.

———. *Psychology and Alchemy*. 2nd ed. New York: Princeton UP, 1968.

Katrak, Ketu H. "Colonialism, Imperialism, and Imagined Homes." *The Columbia History of the American Novel*. Elliot et al. 649–78.

Keenan, Sally. " 'Four Hundred Years of Silence': Myth, History, and Motherhood in Toni Morrison's *Beloved*. *Recasting the World: Writing after Colonialism*. Ed. Jonathan White. Baltimore: John Hopkins UP, 1993. 45–81.

Kenyon, Linda. "A Conversation with Robert Kroetsch." *The New Quarterly* 5.1 (1985): 9–19.

King, Thomas. *Green Grass, Running Water*. New York: Bantam, 1994.

Kolmar, Wendy K. " 'Dialectics of Connectedness': Supernatural Elements in Novels by Bambara, Cisneros, Grahn, and Erdrich." *Haunting the House of Fiction*. Carpenter and Kolmar 236–49.

Kroetsch, Robert. *What the Crow Said*. Don Mills, Ontario: General Publishing, 1978.

Kuester, Martin. "Kroetsch's Fragments: Approaching the Narrative Structure of His Novels." *Postmodern Fiction in Canada*. D'haen and Bertens 137–60.

Lattin, Vernon E. "The Quest for Mythic Vision in Contemporary Native American and Chicano Fiction." *American Literature* 50:4 (Jan 1979): 625–40.

Lawrence, David. "Fleshly Ghost and Ghostly Flesh: The Word and the Body in *Beloved*." *Toni Morrison's Fiction: Contemporary Criticism*. Ed. David L. Middleton. New York: Garland, 1997. 231–46.

Leach, William. *Land of Desire: Merchants, Power, and the Rise of a New American Culture*. NY: Pantheon, 1993.

Leal, Luis. "Magical Realism in Spanish American Literature." *Magical Realism: Theory, History, Community*. Zamora and Faris 119–24.

Linguanit, Elsa, Francesco Casotti, and Carmen Concilio, eds. *Coterminous Worlds: Magical Realism and Contemporary Post-Colonial Literature in English*. Cross/Cultures: Readings in the Post/Colonial Literatures in English 39. Atlanta: Amsterdam, 1999.

Livingston, James. "Modern Subjectivity and Consumer Culture." *Getting and Spending*. Strasser, McGovern, and Judt 413–29.

Lock, Helen. " 'Building Up from Fragments': The Oral Memory Process in Some Recent African-American Written Narratives." *Race-ing Representation: Voice, History, and Sexuality*. Eds. Kostas Myrsiades and Linda Myrsiades. New York: Rowman & Littlefield, 1998. 200–12.

Maguire, James H. "Fictions of the West." *The Columbia History of the American Novel*. Elliot et al. 437–64.

Malamud, Bernard. "The Jewbird." 1963. *The Complete Stories*. Ed. Robert Giroux. New York: Ferrar, 1997. 322–330.

Martin, Gerald. *Journeys Through the Labyrinth: Latin American Fiction in the Twentieth Century*. London: Verso, 1989.

———. "On 'Magical' and Social Realism in García Márquez." *Gabriel García Márquez: New Readings*. McGuirk and Cardwell 95–116.

Martinac, Paula. *Out of Time*. Seattle: Seal P, 1990.

Martínez, Eliud. "Ron Arias' 'The Road to Tamazunchale': Cultural Inheritance and Literary Expression." Introduction. *The Road to Tamazunchale*. Arias 9–24.

Martínez, José Luis. "Unity and Diversity." *Latin America in its Literature*. Moreno 63–83.

Mathieson, Barbara Offutt. "Memory and Mother Love: Toni Morrison's Dyad." *Memory, Narrative, and Identity*. Singh, Skerritt, and Hogan 212–32.

McCluskey, Phil. "The Handsomest Drowned Man in the Outback: Contextualizing a Structural Magic Realism." *Span* 36 (1993): 88–94.

McGuirk, Bernard, and Richard Cardwell, ed. *Gabriel García Márquez: New Readings*. Cambridge: Cambridge UP, 1987.

McKay, Nellie Y., and Kathryn Earle, eds. *Approaches to Teaching the Novels of Toni Morrison*. New York: MLA, 1997.

McMurray, George R., ed. *Critical Essays on Gabriel García Márquez*. Critical Essays on World Literature Ser. Boston: G. K. Hall, 1987.

———. *Gabriel García Márquez: Life, Work, and Criticism*. Authoritative Studies in World Literature. Fredericton, N.B., Canada: York, 1987.

———. Introduction. *Critical Essays on Gabriel García Márquez*. McMurray 1–23.

McNerney, Kathleen, and John Martin. "Alchemy in *Cien años de soledad*." *West Virginia University Philological Papers* 27 (1981): 106–12.

Mendoza, Plinio Apulayo, and Gabriel García Márquez. *The Fragrance of Guava*. Trans. Ann Wright. London: Verso, 1983.

Menton, Seymour. "Jorge Luis Borges, Magic Realist." *Hispanic Review* 50 (1982): 411–26.

———. "Magic Realism: An Annotated International Chronology of the Term." *Essays in Honor of Frank Dauster*. Hispanic Monographs 9. Eds. Kirsten F. Nigro and Sandra M. Cypess. Newark, DE: Juan de la Cuestra, 1995. 125–53.

Merrell, Floyd. "José Arcadio Buendía's Scientific Paradigms: Man in Search of Himself." *Latin American Literary Review* 2.4 (1974): 59–70.

Meyer, Doris. Introduction. *Lives on the Line*. Meyer 1–11.

———, ed. *Lives on the Line: The Testimony of Contemporary Latin American Authors*. Los Angeles: U of California P, 1988.

Moglen, Helene. "Redeeming History: Toni Morrison's *Beloved*." *Female Subjects in Black and White*. Abel, Christian, and Moglen 201–20.

Monegal, Emir Rodríguez. "Tradition and Renewal." *Latin America in its Literature*. Moreno 87–114.

Moreno, César Fernández. Introduction. *Latin America in Its Literature*. Moreno 7–26.

———, gen. ed. *Latin America in Its Literature*. Trans. Mary G. Berg. English edition. Ed. Ivan Schulman. New York: Holmes & Meier, 1980.

Morrison, R. W. "Literature in an Age of Specialization." *Brave New Universe: Testing the Values of Science in Society*. Ed. Tom Henighan. Ottawa: Techumseh, 1980. 112–124.

Morrison, Toni. *Beloved*. 1987. New York: Plume, 1998.

———. "The Opening Sentences of *Beloved*." *Critical Essays on Toni Morrison's* Beloved. Solomon 91–92.

Mosher, Mark. "Humanistic Science in Macondo: The Missing Link." *Confluencia* 11.1 (1995): 89–93.

Naylor, Gloria, and Toni Morrison. "A Conversation." *Southern Review* 21.3 (1985): 567–93.

Neubauer, Paul. "The Demon of Loss and Longing: The Function of the Ghost in Toni Morrison's *Beloved*." *Demons: Mediators Between This World and the Other. Essays on Demonic Beings from the Middle Ages to the Present*. Ed. Ruth Petzoldt and Paul Neubauer.

Beiträge zur eropäischen Ethnologie und Folklore. Reihe B: Tagungsberichte und Materialien 8. New York: Peter Lany, 1988. 165–74.

O'Donnell, Patrick. "Introduction: The Late Twentieth Century." *The Columbia History of the American Novel*. Elliot et al. 513–14.

Ormerod, Beverley. "Magical Realism in Contemporary French Caribbean Literature: Ideology or Literary Diversion?" *Australian Journal of French Studies* 34.2 (1997): 216–26.

Ortega, Julio. *Poetics of Change: The New Spanish-American Narrative*. Trans. Galen D. Greaser. The Texas Pan Am Ser. Austin, TX: U of Texas P, 1984.

Pachter, Henry M. *Paracelsus: Magic into Science*. New York: Collier, 1961.

Payne, Johnny. *Conquest of the New Word: Experimental Fiction and Translation in the Americas*. The Texas Pan Am Ser. Austin: U of Texas P, 1993.

Paz, Octavio. "Translation: Literature and Letters." *Theories of Translation: An Anthology of Essays from Dryden to Derrida*. Eds. Rainer Schultze and John Biguenet. Chicago: U of Chicago P, 1992. 152–62.

Pérez Firmat, Gustavo. "Cheek to Cheek." Introduction. *Do the Americas Have a Common Literature?* Pérez Firmat 1–6.

———. *Life on the Hyphen: The Cuban-American Way*. Austin: U of Texas P, 1994.

———, ed. *Do the Americas Have a Common Literature?* Durham, NC: Duke UP, 1990.

Powell, Neil. *Alchemy, the Ancient Science*. London: Aldus Books, 1976.

Preble-Niemi, Oralia. "Magical Realism and the Great Goddess in Two Novels by Alejo Carpentier and Alice Walker." *The Comparatist* 16 (1992): 101–14.

Prieto, René. "In-Fringe: The Role of French Criticism in the Fiction of Nicole Brassard and Severe Sarday." *Do the Americas Have a Common Literature?* Pérez Firmat 266–81.

Rabassa, Gregory. "Beyond Magical Realism: Thoughts on the Art of Gabriel García Márquez." *Books Abroad* 47 (1973): 444–50.

———. "No Two Snowflakes Are Alike: Translation as Metaphor." *The Craft of Translation*. Eds. John Biguenet and Rainer Schulte. Chicago: U of Chicago P, 1989. 1–12.

Reed, Ishmael. *Mumbo Jumbo*. New York: Avon, 1978.

Retamar, Roberto Fernández. "Intercommunication and New Literature." *Latin America in Its Literature*. Moreno 245–59.

Reyes, Alfonso. "Major Aranda's Hand." *The Eye of the Heart*. Ed. Barbara Howes. New York: Avon, 1973. 135–42.

Reyes, Angelita. "Using History as Artifact to Situate *Beloved*'s Unknown Woman: Margaret Garner." *Approaches to Teaching the Novels of Toni Morrison*. McKay and Earle 77–85.

Rivera, Tomás. . . . *Y no se lo tragó la tierra*. [. . . *And the Earth Did Not Devour Him*.] Trans. Evangelina Vigil-PiZón. Houston: Arte Publico, 1992.

Rochel, Juan Antonio Pereles. "Social Change in Ana Castillo's Narrative." *Women, Creators of Culture*. Eds. Ekaterini Georgoudaki and Domna Pastourmatzi. American Studies in Greece 3. Thessaloniki, Greece: Hellenic Association of American Studies, 1997. 127–32.

Roh, Franz. "Magic Realism: Post-Expressionism." *Magical Realism: Theory, History, Community*. Zamora and Faris 15–31.

Rosa, João Guimarães. *The Third Bank of the River and Other Stories*. Trans. Barbara Shelby. New York: Knopf, 1968. Trans. of *Primeiras Estórias*, 1962.

Rowe, John Carlos. "Postmodern Studies." *Redrawing the Boundaries: The Transformation of English and American Literary Studies*. Eds. Stephen Greenblatt and Giles Gunn. New York: MLA, 1992. 179–208.

Ruffins, Fath Davis. "Reflecting on Ethnic Imagery in the Landscape of Commerce, 1945–1975." *Getting and Spending.* Strasser, McGovern, and Judt 379–405.

Rushdy, Ashraf H.A. "Daughters Signifyin(g) History: The Example of Toni Morrison's *Beloved.*" *American Literature* 64.3 (1992): 567–97.

Saine, Ute M. "Einstein and Musil in Macondo: *One Hundred Years of Solitude* and the Theory of Relativity." *Essays on Gabriel García Márquez.* Eds. Kemy Oyarzúnard and William W. Megenney. U of California at Riverside: Latin American Studies Program, 1984. 36–50.

Saldívar, José David. *Border Matters: Remapping American Cultural Studies.* Berkeley, CA: U of California P, 1997.

———. "The Dialectics of Our Americas." *Do the Americas Have a Common Literature?* Pérez Firmat 62–84.

———. "Postmodern Realism." *The Columbia History of the American Novel.* Elliot et al. 521–41.

Sanders, Karla J. "Healing Narratives: Negotiating Cultural Subjectivities in Louise Erdrich's Magical Realism." Ph.D. Diss. Penn State University, 1996.

Sands, Scott. "Relationship Between Western European Alchemy and Other Philosophies." *The Hexagon of Alpha Chi Sigma* (Summer 1993): 25–27, 35.

Santí, Enrico Mario. "The Accidental Tourist: Walt Whitman in Latin America." *Do the Americas Have a Common Literature?* Pérez Firmat 156–76.

Schaack, Francis Joseph. "Magical Realism in the Narratives of Maxine Hong Kingston, Toni Morrison, and William Kennedy: The Replenishment and Validation for the Liminal Experience in America." Ph.D. Diss. U of Texas, Arlington, 1992.

Scheel, Charles Werner. "Magical Versus Marvelous Realism as Narrative Modes in French Fiction." Ph.D. Diss. U of Texas at Austin, 1991.

Schulman, Ivan. "Introduction: English Edition." *Latin America in Its Literature.* Moreno 27–35.

Shannon, Edward A. "Outlaw Knot-Makers: Context, Culture, and Magic Realism." Ph.D. Diss. U of NC-Greensboro, 1995.

Shaw, Donald L. *The Post-Boom in Spanish American Fiction.* Albany: State U of New York P, 1998.

Sichel, Berta. "Jorge Amado." *Américas* 36.3 (1984): 16–19.

Silko, Leslie Marmon. *Ceremony.* New York: Penguin, 1977.

Simmons, Philip E. *Deep Surfaces: Mass Culture and History in Postmodern American Fiction.* Athens, GA: U of Georgia P, 1997.

Simpkins, Scott. "Sources of Magic Realism/Supplements to Realism in Contemporary Latin American Literature." *Magical Realism: Theory, History, Community.* Zamora and Faris 145–59.

Singh, Amrijit, Joseph T. Skerritt, Jr., and Robert E. Hogan, eds. *Memory, Narrative, and Identity: New Essays in Ethnic American Literature.* Boston: Northeastern UP, 1994.

Slemon, Stephen. "Magic Realism as Postcolonial Discourse." *Magical Realism: Theory, History, Community.* Zamora and Faris 407–26.

Solomon, Barbara H., ed. *Critical Essays on Toni Morrison's Beloved.* Critical Essays on American Literature. New York: G. K. Hall, 1998.

Spark, Debra. "Curious Attractions: Magical Realism's Fate in the States." *AWP Chronicle* 29:1 (1996): 15–20.

Spears, Keith. "A Genetic Model of Duality in Latin American Magical Realism." Thesis. Eastern Illinois U, 1995.

Stevens, L. Robert, and G. Roland Vela. "Jungle Gothic: Science, Myth, and Reality in *One Hundred Years of Solitude.*" *Modern Fiction Studies* 26 (1980): 262–66.

Stewart, Melissa. "Roads of 'Exquisite Mysterious Muck': The Magical Journey through the City in William Kennedy's *Ironweed,* John Cheever's 'The Enormous Radio,' and Donald Barthelme's 'City Life.'" *Magical Realism: Theory, History, Community.* Zamora and Faris 477–95.

Strasser, Susan, Charles McGovern, and Mattias Judt, ed. *Getting and Spending: European and American Consumer Societies in the Twentieth Century.* Publications of the German Historical Institute. Cambridge: Cambridge UP, 1998.

Swanson, Philip. *The New Novel in Latin America: Politics and Popular Culture after the Boom.* Manchester: Manchester UP, 1995.

Todorov, Tzvetan. *The Conquest of America.* Trans. Richard Howard. New York: Harper and Row, 1984.

Ude, Wayne. "Forging an American Style: The Romance-Novel and Magical Realism as Response to the Frontier and Wilderness Experience." *The Frontier Experience and the American Dream: Essays on American Literature.* Ed. David Mogen, Mark Busby, and Paul Bryant. College Station, TX: Texas A & M UP, 1989. 50–64.

———. "North American Magical Realism." *Colorado State Review* 8:2 (1981): 21–30.

Vincent, Jon S. *Jono Guimarnes Rosa.* Boston: Twayne, 1978.

Walker, Steven F. "Magical Archetypes: Midlife Miracles in *The Satanic Verses.*" *Magical Realism: Theory, History, Community.* Zamora and Faris 347–69.

Walter, Roland. "Social and Magical Realism in Miguel Méndez's *El Sueño de Santa María.*" *The Americas Review* 18.1 (1990): 103–12.

Williams, Raymond. *Keywords: A Vocabulary of Culture and Society.* Rev. ed. New York: Oxford UP, 1983.

———. *The Postmodern Novel in Latin America: Politics, Culture, and the Crisis of Truth.* New York: St. Martin's, 1995.

Williamson, Edwin. "Magical Realism and the Theme of Incest in *One Hundred Years of Solitude.*" *Gabriel García Márquez: New Readings.* McGuirk and Cardwell 45–63.

Willis, Susan. *Specifying: Black Women Writing the American Experience.* Madison: U of Wisconsin P, 1987.

Wilson, Rawdon. "The Metamorphoses of Fiction: Magic Realism." *Magical Realism: Theory, History, Community.* Zamora and Faris 209–33.

Winn, Peter. *Americas: The Changing Face of Latin America and the Caribbean.* New York: Pantheon Books, 1993.

Wishnia, Kenneth. "Science Fiction and Magic Realism: Two Openings, Same Space." *Foundation* 59 (1993): 29–41.

Wyrwa, Ulrich. "Consumption and Consumer Society: A Contribution to the History of Ideas." *Getting and Spending.* Strasser, McGovern, and Judt 431–47.

Young, David, and Keith Hollaman, ed. Introduction. *Magical Realist Fiction: An Anthology.* New York: Longman, 1984. 1–8.

Zamora, Lois Parkinson. "Magical Romance/Magical Realism: Ghosts in U.S. and Latin American Fiction." *Magical Realism: Theory, History, Community.* Zamora and Faris 497–550.

———. "The Usable Past: The Idea of History in Modern U.S. and Latin American Fiction." *Do the Americas Have a Common Literature?* Pérez Firmat 7–41.

———. *The Usable Past: The Imagination of History in Recent Fiction of the Americas.* Cambridge: Cambridge UP, 1997.

Zamora, Lois Parkinson, and Wendy B. Faris. "Daiquiri Birds and Flaubertian Parrot(ie)s."
    Introduction. *Magical Realism: Theory, History, Community*. Zamora and Faris 1–11.
———, eds. *Magical Realism: Theory, History, Community*. Durham, NC: Duke UP, 1995.

INDEX

ABOUT THE AUTHOR

SHANNIN SCHROEDER is Assistant Professor in the Department of English and Foreign Languages at Southern Arkansas University. She also serves on the editorial board of *The Philological Review*.